illustrated guide to basketball's swing-and-cut offense

Illustrated Guide to Basketball's Swing-and-Cut Offense

JIM GUDGER

Parker Publishing Company, Inc.

West Nyack, New York

© 1981, by

PARKER PUBLISHING COMPANY, INC.

West Nyack, N.Y.

All rights reserved. No part of this
book may be reproduced in any form or
by any means, with permission in
writing from the publisher.

Library of Congress Cataloging in Publication Data

Gudger, Jim.
    Illustrated guide to basketball's
swing-and-cut offense.

    Includes index.
    1. Basketball—Offense. 2. Basketball
coaching. I. Title.
GV889.G82   796.32′32   81-9492
ISBN 0-13-450767-3   AACR2

Printed in the United States of America

how this offense will prove valuable to you

Have you wished that your athletes could cut quicker, set better screens, pass more intelligently, get better percentage shots, and keep all five men moving, while keeping the defense completely occupied? How many times have you admired or envied an opponent, perhaps a victorious opponent, who did these things smoothly and effectively? How many times have you said to yourself, "I wish I could get my players to execute with such perfection."? If so, this book is for you. It explains in simple, easy-to-follow terms, how a coach may develop through an all-purpose offense, the confidence, poise, and techniques necessary to create a winning tradition.

As a coach you probably already feel as if you have too little time to prepare for the many eventualities you might encounter. Let this book relieve you of an unnecessary burden. Spend your time on an offense that attacks all defenses and provides for the rehearsing of offensive techniques and fundamentals at the same time.

I believe that the coach should teach the proper alignments and the basic techniques and fundamentals of basketball and allow the players to do the rest.

The material in this book may be used effectively on any level, whether it be junior high school, senior high school, junior college, or senior college. It will most certainly simplify your offensive practice plans. The offense itself employs practically every offensive technique. Thus, you rehearse as you work to polish your offensive patterns. As a result, your offensive practice plans are greatly simplified.

This book offers diagrams and detailed specifics of the entire swing-and-cut concept, plus supplementary tactics that complement the swing-and-cut. It describes in detail the swing-and-cut's effectiveness against all defenses. It clearly describes in detail how the offense may be initiated from various sets (two-man front, one-man front, high-low post, etc.). A special effort has been made to describe relief moves to meet any eventuality, such as unexpected defensive changes or changes in offensive personnel.

The offensive theory and techniques presented here provide the coach with an offensive background capable of enhancing the win column and stabilizing the loss column considerably, and turning a defeat into a victory by presenting an equalizer against formidable odds.

In basketball, the winner scores the most points. Regardless of what else takes place on the court, only the score is recorded on the scoreboard. The finest shooters may be available, but fine shooters are effective only if their teammates and the offensive pattern help them reach a position for the high percentage shot, the shot that wins. Consequently, an effective offensive plan is a must.

Granted, the passing game is the current rage. Some feel the passing game is replacing the pattern offense but, in reality what can be more patterned than a passing game? Especially when it is effectively defended, when it attempts to exploit certain defensive weaknesses, or when a team becomes conservative. All offenses, whether patterned, passing game or otherwise, are truly effective only when the offense is truly adept at reading, adjusting, and reacting to defensive mistakes. Patterned basketball may suggest strict regimentation to some, but this is not necessarily true. In fact, with multiple sets, multiple entries, relief moves, counteraction and clearouts, patterned basketball permits the flexibility to capitalize on defensive miscues just as effectively as those offenses that claim to have more freedom in their movement. Patterned basketball is far from obsolete.

This book presents in detail a diversified offense capable of exploiting the individual abilities of certain players and of camouflaging weaknesses of others. The offense gives a diversified attack employing basic offensive fundamentals that will completely occupy a defense; yet, the structure is very simple. The ideas presented will help you establish a definite philosophy, concerning your offense, early in your coaching career — a philosophy of coaching that will serve to guide: (1) the teaching of offensive skills, (2) the planning and conduct of practice sessions, (3) use of personnel, and (4) game strategy. It is essential to believe in and have faith in an idea, and to channel all of your efforts toward becoming more knowledgeable and improving on it. It is not necessary to run identical patterns year after year. The core and basics of an offense should be retained and new ideas added if you expect to cope with varying situations and changing personnel.

The swing-and-cut is an all-purpose offense. As such, it is an offense that: (1) can be utilized with any personnel, (2) contains all the offensive ingredients, (3) allows the presentation of teaching situations as drills, (4) will be effective against any defense, and (5) will keep all five players involved in its execution.

Since we elected to go with the swing-and-cut as our basic offense, many of our perennial problems have been eliminated. No longer must we start from scratch in the teaching of techniques since we always have enough returnees who can demonstrate our patterns to the new people and show them what we expect. The swing-and-cut by its very nature teaches passing, cutting, faking, and many other offensive maneuvers. As we turn our offense over during the learning stage in early season games, or throughout the season if we unexpectedly face a zone defense or a variation thereof, we confidently continue with our swing-and-cut pattern, thereby eliminating the possibility of panic or confusion. The swing-and-cut is simply continued as a zone attack.

There are six essential phases to a good basketball offense: (1) an inside phase, (2) an outside phase, (3) movement, (4) a quick swing, (5) penetration possibilities, and (6) floor balance.

The swing-and-cut has all of these ingredients. The fact that these elements are present, along with the fact it is an exceptional offense at keeping the defense occupied and making them work and move, contributes to its versatility.

One of the most difficult decisions a coach has to make is deciding when to begin a control game. When carrying a lead of a few points into the waning moments of a game, this problem is eliminated with the swing-and-cut. Only a very slight change in shot selection is necessary to change from the normal tempo to moderate control or the freeze. Total pattern change is unnecessary. This is a tremendous factor in maintaining poise and confidence in pressure situations.

We all borrow from other coaches. There are very few staggering developments arising. The swing-and-cut is the hub around which my entire philosophy is blended. I have borrowed from the best to build a simple and effective offensive attack. I am confident your offensive outlook will be challenged by the time you finish this book. Select the part you like and fit it to your personnel. The swing-and-cut is designed for all personnel and to challenge all defenses. It has been used successfully with all types of personnel and in all types of situations, from preseason practice games to national tournament play. I think you will like its effectiveness and versatility.

JIM GUDGER

TABLE OF CONTENTS

HOW THIS BOOK WILL PROVE VALUABLE TO YOU.... 5

1. ADVANTAGES OF THE SWING-AND-CUT OFFENSE... 15

   Philosophy...Six Offensive Ingredients...Inside Phase...Outside Phase...Movement...Swing Action...Penetration...Floor Balance...Benefits of the Swing-and-Cut...Fits Any Personnel...Places Personnel to Offensive Advantage...Keeps All Players Involved...Enhances Individual Initiative...Keeps Defense Occupied...Tempo Control...Returnees as Teachers...Provides Teaching Drills...

2. THE BASIC SWING-AND-CUT ALIGNMENT
   OR WORKING POSITION...................... 23

   Freeing Yourself to Receive a Pass...Crouched or Flexed Body Position...Forward Alignment...Guard Alignment...Post or Center Alignment...Spacing...Passing Lanes...Alignment After First Cut...Alignment After Swing...

3. CUTTING, SCREENING, AND ROLLOUTS
   IN THE SWING-AND-CUT 29

   Post Screens...Forward and Guard Screens..

Teaching Screening...Basic Cuts...Initial Cut—Setting Up Cuts...Evading Contact...Backdoor Cuts...Interchanging...

4. THE FIVE BASIC CUTS 39

Guard Cuts...Forward Cuts...Center Cuts...The One Cut...The Two Cut...The Three Cut...The Four Cut...The Five Cut...The Turnover or Swing...Alternate Moves...One-J...Screen to the Same Side...Swing and Choke...Swing and Pinch...

5. RELIEF MOVES FROM EACH FLOOR POSITION 51

Clear...Split...Backdoor...Overthrows...Penetrating Dribble...Dribble Over...

6. RELIEVING PRESSURE........................ 61

The Drive Through...Split...Backdoor...One-Man Front...Three-Man Front...Changing the Point of Attack...Full-Court Attack Against Pressure...

7. OFFENSIVE ENTRIES—MULTIPLE SETS 77

Screening the Same Side...Strongside Set...One-Man Front...Three-Man Front...High Stack...Low Stack...Low Stack and Cross...Low Double Stack...Guard-Forward Interchange...

8. COUNTERACTION............................ 91

Guard Counter...Three-Cut Counter...Swing-Pass Counter...Post Counter...Lob Counter...

9. POST SERIES 99

Post Action Off the Pattern...Single Post...Pass to the Post...Single Split...Cutaway...Double

Split...Backdoor...Pinch Post...Penetrating Dribble...Choke Post...Post Counter...Combination Post...Double Flash Post...Sneak Post...

10. SWING-AND-CUT INTO OTHER PATTERNS........ 117

    Swing-and-Cut into the Single Post...Swing-and-Cut into the Double Flash Post...Swing-and-Cut into the Combination Post...

11. OTHER PATTERNS INTO THE SWING-AND-CUT SERIES 123

    Single Post into the Swing-and-Cut...Double Flash Post into the Swing-and-Cut Offense...Flash Post...Pass to the Wing...1-3-1 into the Swing-and-Cut...Pass to High Post...Pass to the Wing... High Post Screen Low...

12. THE SWING-AND-CUT OFFENSE VERSUS THE ZONE 143

    Normal Swing-and-Cut Versus Zone...Movement and Swing...Bringing in the Back-side...Attacking the Seams...Movement and Continuity...Penetrating the Seam...Screening the Zone...Swing-and-Cut into the Combination Post Versus the Zone...

13. OFFENSIVE REBOUNDING FROM THE SWING-AND-CUT ALIGNMENTS 155

    Position and Form...Blocking Out...Judging the Flight of the Ball...Going Up to Meet the Ball... Snatch and Control...Offensive Rebounding... Offensive Rebounding Techniques...Basic Rebounding Fundamentals...Tipping...The Power Move...Reverse Power Move...Turn and Jump... Rebound Areas from the Swing-and-Cut...Shot from the Strongside Wing...Shot from the Weakside Wing...Shot from the Point...

14. CONTROL AND TEMPO CHANGE 169

Situations to Be Considered...Offensive Philosophy...Normal Phase...Control Phase...Delay Phase...High and Wide Adjustment...High Stationary Post Adjustment...

15. TEACHING DRILLS AROUND THE SWING-AND-CUT PATTERN 179

Four-Man Swing-and-Cut...Three-Cut Shooting Drill...Four-Cut Shooting Drill...Cutting Drill ...Basic Shooting Drill...Screen and Roll Drill...

16. THE FAST BREAK 191

Fast-Break Philosophy and Principle...Fast-Break Opportunities...Fast-Break Situations...Teaching Phases...Primary Ignition Points...Secondary Ignition Points...Rebound Positions...First Move After Capturing Rebound...Fast-Break Post Rebound...Forward Rebounding...Complete Fast-Break Pattern...3-on-2 or 3-on-1...Fast Break After Made Field Goal...Fast Break After Made Free Throw...

17. SUPPLEMENTARY DRILLS FOR IMPROVING OFFENSIVE TECHNIQUE 205

Mastery of the Little Things...Knowledge of the Fundamentals...A Valuable Learning Experience ...Daily Dozen...Situation Drills...

INDEX **231**

illustrated guide to basketball's swing-and-cut offense

1
advantages of the swing-and-cut offense

PHILOSOPHY

Webster calls philosophy the "love of wisdom." In actual usage, it is the science that investigates the facts and principles of reality and of human nature and conduct, the science that comprises logic. I suppose to be the successful individual that society expects you to be, or that you expect yourself to be, you should have several written pages outlining your philosophical approach to the job at hand. This is all well and good, providing you do not let yourself become too involved in the word game and forget that in most instances you must get your hands dirty to be effective.

Basketball coaches are involved in a business that takes as much preparation, organization, research, wisdom, logic, good judgment, and maturity as any business I know. Basketball requires long hours, much sweat, and hard work, if you are to be successful. I know you can outwork a lot of people. Your players can outwork a lot of teams. Combine this labor with a well-organized offensive approach, and your task is made considerably less difficult.

My philosophy would probably fall considerably short if measured for its worded approval, but it is simply this: work hard and keep it simple. There is no substitute for hard work and perfection of the simple fundamentals. These two ingredients added to the right offense approach will provide the winning edge.

SIX OFFENSIVE INGREDIENTS

An offense needs six basic ingredients or phases in order to successfully apply constant pressure to the defense: (1) it must have an inside phase, (2) it must have an outside phase, (3) it must have movement, (4) it must have a good swing or reverse action, (5) it must provide penetration possibilities, and (6) it must have floor balance. The swing-and-cut contains all of these ingredients.

inside phase

The swing-and-cut offers two quick cuts to the inside off of screens, plus a possible overthrow to the swing man as he moves to the basket to provide the necessary inside game. An *overthrow* is a simple lob pass over the defensive personnel to the receiver cutting to the basket. Three perimeter cutters coming to the basket area, plus the center rolling back, create a movement and confusion defensively that eventually will force defensive breakdowns in the inside area. It will force switches and mismatches to an offensive advantage. A team that is not blessed with an ideal center is not necessarily handicapped. A center of any size can be used effectively as a screener and feeder, as he constantly looks for a defensive breakdown and a high percentage shot close to the basket or a short, quick jump shot. The constant movement enables a smaller, less talented center to compete successfully. He can be an invaluable screener, an effective scorer, and a much needed feeder, by applying simple basics and reading the defense properly.

outside phase

The outside phase is greatly enhanced by the movement and swing actions of the swing-and-cut. The three cut and four cut, as described and diagrammed in Chapter 4, Diagrams 4-3 and 4-4, provide excellent 15- to 18-foot perimeter shots on just the turnovers or continuity movement alone. Add a couple of screens, interchanges, and counterplays and the outside game becomes even more effective. Many teams, in order to stop the screening and cutting inside game, slough so deep toward the basket that the perimeter shots become easily accessible. Several countermoves that are described in detail later in the book also enhance the outside phase to a most positive degree.

movement

The swing-and-cut has an abundance of movement, a must factor if you are to keep the defense vulnerable. Five offensive players are totally involved. One of the most difficult coaching assignments is to teach players to play productively without the ball. The swing-and-cut makes this an easy task, because with each pass all five players are fully involved. Every time you swing the ball there is one cut to the inside off a double screen, a quick rollback to the ball or to daylight (an opening), one cut away for a possible overthrow or interchange, one cut to the swing position, and a pop cut to the weak side. I challenge any other offense to offer this type of effective movement.

swing action

The swing or reverse is the consistent factor in the offense. The quick swing from the strong side to the weak side completely changes the defensive set. Two quick passes or a long overthrow, plus the offensive movement that goes with it, gives the defense a difficult task just to keep position. It is impossible to prevent the swing if the offense will correctly analyze the defense. The swing through the point, the backdoor area, the post man, or the long overthrow is always available.

penetration

A good offense must attack. It must keep constant pressure on the defense and look constantly for defensive breakdowns. Intelligent penetration presents an attack technique that takes advantage of defensive lapses. The swing-and-cut presents two effective penetration opportunities: (1) when the ball is passed back to the point, and (2) when it is swung quickly to the weak side. Unless the defense adjusts quickly and with sound defensive techniques, penetration could be most effective. Even with the ball in the strongside forward's hand, a penetrating dribble can set up a rollback, backdoor cut, or fan to the open spot. All of these will be thoroughly explained and illustrated later on.

floor balance

The very nature of the swing-and-cut continuity or turnover, as described in Chapter 4, Diagram 4-6, will keep a team in excellent floor balance. One man is always moving to the top of the key, which places him in excellent position to get back on defense. Extra defensive floor balance is provided because there are always two wings in position to get back. This is adequate coverage against most opponents. We feel our defensive floor balance should provide one-plus protection. This we have. If personnel is such that we might have a strong rebounder on the point and an ineffective rebounder inside, we may assign one man or two men to sprint back on the shot and drive our rebounders toward the boards. Floor balance, as related to offensive rebounding, is presented in detail in a later chapter.

BENEFITS OF THE SWING-AND-CUT

fits any personnel

One of the most important aspects of the swing-and-cut is the fact that it fits any personnel, or *you* can fit it to any personnel. If you have a big, mobile, effective center, emphasize this phase of the game. If you have good outside shooters, use your cutting and screening to keep the defense honest inside and set up the outside game. If your personnel is below average, emphasize the basics and control the game tempo until you get what you want. This movement will provide strong forwards or guards with low post, choke post, and pinch post possibilities that will prove most reliable.

place personnel to offensive advantage

Personnel can be placed so they will be brought into position to exploit their individual abilities with only a minimum amount of ball handling. Through the constant movement provided by the swing-and-cut continuity, personnel may be brought to their positions as a result of the movement, therefore presenting a different problem for the defense each time.

keeps all players involved

This offense and all of its supplements keep all personnel totally involved. Most coaches agree that playing effectively without the ball is difficult to teach. The swing-and-cut by its very nature solves this problem.

enhances individual initiative

The swing-and-cut in no way inhibits individual initiative through strict ball control. In fact, the movement, cutting, and screening involved greatly enhances individual abilities. It enables the less talented player to gain offensive edges he probably would find difficult obtaining in an offense with less movement. It enables the highly talented individual to be even more effective, as he can challenge the defense in so many more ways and with so much more help. The swing-and-cut is especially adept at disguising an individual's attack points, which makes it extremely difficult for the defense to set in a position to consistently help out.

keeps defense occupied

The defense is always totally occupied and must stay so on every pass or else you have shooters open for high percentage shots. Every pass presents a defensive problem, because every pass in the swing-and-cut is a definite change of floor position. This alone causes enormous defensive adjustments. Add the screen, the low cuts, the high cuts, the unusual movement, and your defense has quite a task. The more effective the offensive execution, the more difficult the defense task.

tempo control

The swing-and-cut is most proficient in controlling the pace and tempo of the game. It provides quick, high percentage shots to complement the fast-pace type of game. It can be a most productive control game with patience and good judgment. It presents the opportunity to build your offense around one man or one-scoring threat while disguising the approach. It affords the opportunity to cool off the hot shooting opponent by controlling the ball and slowing down his effort with patience, movement, and good-shot selection. It affords the opportunity to come from behind and get back in the game wisely by working the defense into defensive mistakes that provide the high percentage shot. The end of the game opportunities, ranging from lay-ups only to the complete stall, are most advantageous. A slight adjustment of moving the wings higher and wider and the point higher while continuing to cut and screen inside provides a devastating stall with the effectiveness of the basic swing-and-cut continuity.

Probably one of the most outstanding features of the swing-and-cut is that it consistently works against all defenses. Some slight adjustments are usually necessary, but the basic continuity remains constant and the same offensive rules apply. The swing-and-cut is our first method of attack against any zone, bearing in mind that we must read the defenses thoroughly and must not let the defense take the swing on reverse tactic away. It is especially effective against combination defenses such as the box-and-one, and triangle-and-two, as the man-for-man tactic clears areas that the defense will find it nearly impossible to adjust to. The basic continuity will place people in open shooting areas or force the defense into man-for-man tactics.

returnees as teachers

Players love the swing-and-cut. The movement is exciting, and the shot possibilities are challenging, because they know each player will be afforded opportunities to score. There will always be enough returnees each year to run the basic continuity, whether they be starters or substitutes. These people perform for the new players and teach them the offense. When new players first witness the complete swing-and-cut continuity without a defense opposing it, they become most intrigued and are anxious to get involved. When they first play defense against it, they immediately realize how effective it is and become even more intrigued and challenged. When they begin to compensate in an attempt to cope with it they are sold on it. The swing-and-cut sells itself. Players will accept it with open arms.

provides teaching drills

The best drill we have is our swing-and cut continuity. We place the centers in the four-man continuity and teach footwork, position, quick cutting, screening, rollouts, ball handling, interchanging, backdooring, and conditioning. All of this takes place while rehearsing the timing and movement of our basic pattern. Shooting drills and rebounding drills, to complement the basic structure, will be explained later. One of our basic team defensive drills is involved around defensing our swing-and-cut offense. We feel if we can adequately do a defensive job on our offense that we will be prepared for all defensive eventualities. The potential of the swing-and-cut is unlimited. The advantages have been pointed out. Now they will be explained and illustrated.

2 the basic swing-and-cut alignment or working position

FREEING YOURSELF TO RECEIVE A PASS

Bear in mind as we discuss basic alignment or working position that we are relating to the ideal spots from which we believe our swing-and-cut offense most effectively operates. Also, we are explaining these alignments with no defense involved. It is imperative that our offensive tactics be sharp enough to place our players in the positions from which we believe our timing, cutting, and passing to be most proficient when being confronted by defensive tactics. This, of course, involves the basic fundamentals concerned with freeing players or getting players open at the most opportune time and in the floor position to execute the offense involved.

It is very important to teach several ways to assure your players that they will be able to respond with poise and expediency. Perhaps a simple pop out or V-in-V-out will suffice. If not, use stacks, drive throughs, and clear outs.

Freeing yourself to receive a pass is not to be explained and then taken for granted. As in any basic fundamental, the details must be perfected by constant repetition both with and without the defense. This takes only a few minutes each day; constant reminders are extremely important.

CROUCHED OR FLEXED BODY POSITION

The fact that a player has freed himself from the defense and has received the exact floor position you desire may not necessarily be enough. He should receive the ball in an attack position from which he can shoot, pass, or drive immediately. It is extremely important to make your players aware that basketball is a game that is played in a *crouched* or a *flexed* position. There is never an instance, offensively or defensively, while the ball is in play, that a player should be in a perfectly upright body position. The degree of the crouch or flex depends on how close the player is to the ball. This will vary from a slight crouch away from the ball to a more pronounced crouch or flex as the player prepares himself to meet the ball, receive a pass, or set a screen. Being in a crouch or flex is similar to turning a switch on or starting a motor. It puts the muscles in motion and enables the player to move quicker and more alertly.

When the player receives the ball in all perimeter positions it is imperative that he does so with feet spread to about the width of his shoulders, applying the crouch or flex rule, and facing the basket. This will enable him to take advantage of poor defensive alignment, see all cutters in the basket area, and drive and shoot. In other words, pressure the defense, and never lose sight of the basket area.

So many times we see the ball received with the player's back to the basket, thereby losing sight of the cutter or open man in the basket area and giving the defense the opportunity to relax.

Freeing yourself to receive the ball and the crouched or flexed body position will be dwelt on more in the chapter on teaching drills.

FORWARD ALIGNMENT

The best spot at which the forward or wing can receive the ball to initiate the basic swing-and-cut pattern is two and one-half to three steps in from the sideline and one step below the foul line extended. (Diagram 2-1) He should receive the ball as he frees himself and face the basket immediately, looking for the cutters, ready to pass, shoot, or drive.

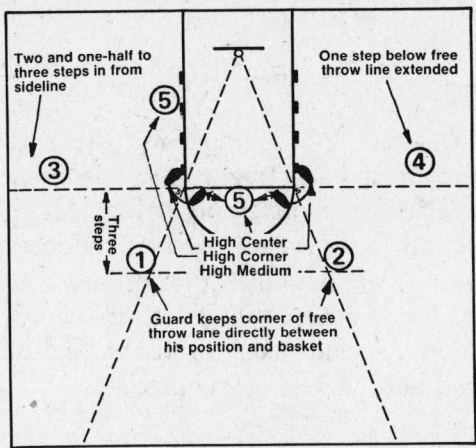

Diagram 2-1
Basic Working Conditions

GUARD ALIGNMENT

The guards should attempt to place the corner of the free throw line directly between themselves and the basket and as close on a line with the top of the free throw circle as the defense will let them, preferably about two and one-half steps above the key. This places them in a position to pass and cut effectively with perfect timing. We ask the guards to keep the corner of the foul line in line between themselves and the basket, as this is exactly where the screen will be set on the initial cut. (Diagram 2-1) Again, the guards should always be in the crouch or flex position, ready to react to all eventualities.

POST OR CENTER ALIGNMENT

The center may line up on the high center post, high corner, or medium. We usually place him at high center because we believe our attack is more versatile with the center in this spot.

26 the basic swing-and-cut alignment or working position

(Diagram 2-1) He is in a position to screen quickly either way and handle pressure defenses by being the hub around which splits and backdoors occur; this also brings the defensive center away from the basket. Emphasize repeatedly the value of the crouch or flex body position.

SPACING

Notice in Diagram 2-1 the spacing of the basic alignment. All personnel are in an effective attack alignment. Much effort and detailed practice is involved in being able to obtain these positions when confronted with various defenses. The defense will make every effort to push the offense away from their alignment. The offense must recognize this and be prepared to adjust to the defense and execute to perfection the counteraction that will obtain the desired alignment.

PASSING LANES

Keep your passing lanes to a maximum of 15 to 18 feet. (Diagram 2-2) This assures crisp, sharp, two-hand passes that carry high percentage of ball-handling accuracy. Maintaining these desirable passing lanes is the responsibility of the men without the ball.

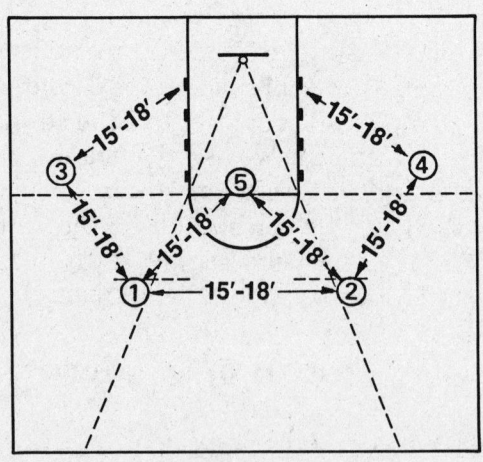

Diagram 2-2
Spacing

ALIGNMENT AFTER FIRST CUT—ALIGNMENT AFTER SWING

The first pass changes the initial alignment to the swing alignment. (Diagrams 2-3 and 2-3A) The forward or wing with the ball maintains his initial alignment. The offside guard is now on the low post with his baseline foot on the wide-lane marker and with his high foot spread well up the lane. The center cuts back to the ball after the initial screen, placing his baseline foot right

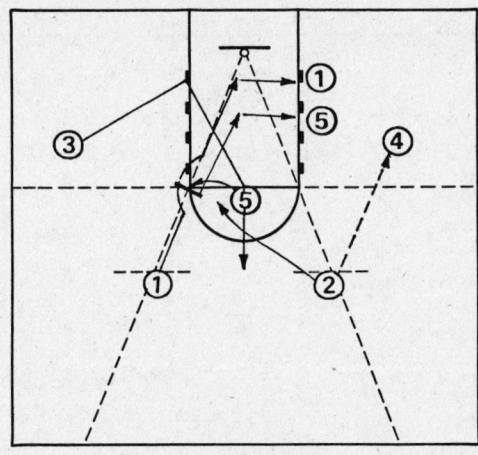

Diagram 2-3
Alignment Following First Pass

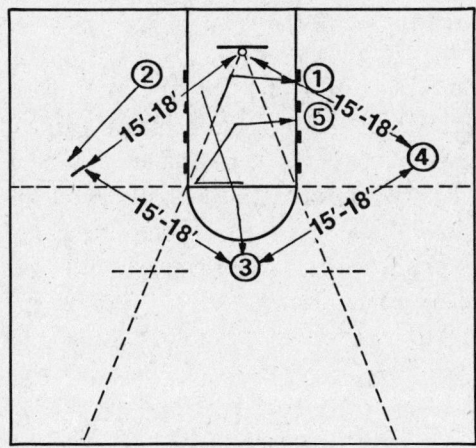

Diagram 2-3A
Swing Alignment and Spacing

the basic swing-and-cut alignment or working position

beside the foot of the low man. He also spreads as wide as possible. The offside wing fakes to the basket and is now at the top of the key, facing the basket and in position to receive a pass from the strongside wing. The strongside guard, after the first pass, moves away and low, in the vicinity of the wide-lane marker. There he has become the back-side rebounder and moves in position to pop out and receive a pass from the point or swing man. This completes the turnover. (Diagram 2-4) A continuation of this provides the movement and continuity of the pattern.

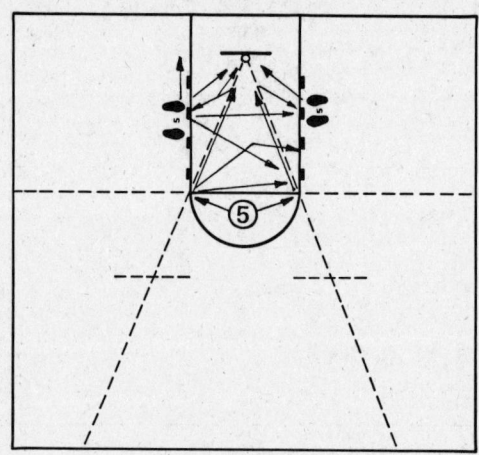

Diagram 2-4
*Post Cuts from High
and Medium Positions*

It is extremely important for the center to always cut to daylight or to the ball. An effective inside game demoralizes the defense. The center may step forward, cut to basket, cut to high corner, cut to low post, cut to the ball when the ball is on the point, or delay for an overthrow. (Diagram 2-4) This calls for a lot of work and patience with the center while you teach him to adjust to the defensive tactics and how to keep the continuity effective if the shot does not present itself.

3 / cutting, screening, and rollouts in the swing-and-cut

The previous chapter discussed the basic alignment from which the swing-and-cut offense is most forcefully executed. This chapter discusses the cutting, screening, and rollout techniques from the post, wing, and point positions. The basics are the core of the offense. These are the fundamentals that make the offense effective or ineffective. These are the techniques that any basketball player can efficiently perform. It is true that quickness and speed with proper execution will make the super team; however, where overall quickness and speed may not be available, it may be replaced to a degree with intelligence, persistence, and daily exposure to these basic elements. These are the fundamentals that, when properly used, make the swing-and-cut an all-purpose offense. Game temp, slow downs, game control, and zone offense will only be as effective as the attention given to, and the execution of, these elements.

POST SCREENS

The center or post man has three basic screens he must perfect. The first is when he screens away from the ball for the weakside guard on the initial move. When the guard with the ball passes to the strongside forward, the post moves to the opposite corner of the free throw line. We ask him to place his top foot inside the circle and above the free throw lane, and the bottom foot on the outside of the free throw lane and below the free throw line. (Diagram 3-1) This insures a wide spread and a low body balance that will withstand the force of the defensive man. It is the cutter's responsibility to place the defensive man on the screen. This prevents a moving screen and cheap offensive fouls. We ask our screeners to carry their hands and arms high or folded into their chests so that no illegal hand tactics will be called against them.

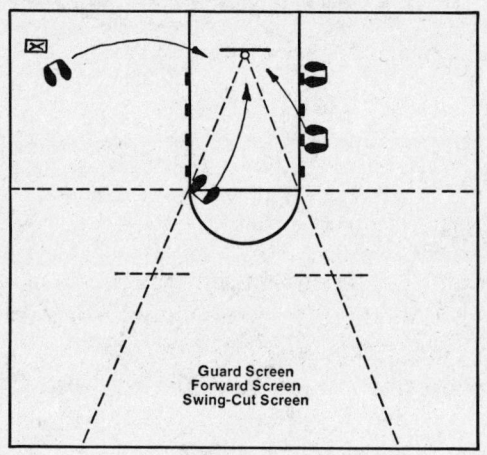

Diagram 3-1
Post Screens

The second post screen and the screen the post man uses most often is the high part of the double screen. He helps the guard or forward set a screen for the wing as the ball is reversed. His low foot should be placed outside of the lane and should touch the high foot of the low man. The high foot should be spread up the lane slightly wider than the shoulders. (Diagram 3-1) This places a double screen six or seven feet wide in a position the wing may use to the best advantage as he cuts over or under the wall. Remember, the screeners do not move to the defensive man. They hold their position and expect the cutter to place the defense into the wall to the advantage of the cutter.

The third screen is our basic screen and roll action, which

we use on all but specified spots. We call these *perimeter screens*. In the event of effective denial tactics, the wing may call the low man in the double screen to the corner, pass to him, and cut through. The center or post man moves out and screens the corner defense. This enables the ball handler to drive, jump shoot, or check back to him on the rollout. As on all perimeter screens, we ask that their screen be set at a 45-degree angle, feet spread, with hands up or folded to chest. (Diagram 3-1) We do not want the screen set behind the defense because it is easy to slide over. Nor do we want it set to his side as it is easy to slide under. Setting the screen at a 45-degree angle insures a legal vision screen, makes it more difficult for the defense to slide over or under, and places the screener in a position for a quick rollout.

FORWARD AND GUARD SCREENS

The guards and forwards are involved in two basic screens in the swing-and-cut continuity, plus an occasional perimeter screen where relief moves or counteraction is involved.

The basic forward and guard screen is the low screen along the baseline in the double screen. The low or baseline foot is placed on the wide-lane marker; the high foot is spread up the lane slightly more than the width of the shoulders, with hands high or folded into the chest. (Diagram 3-1) This places the screener in a strong position that the cutter may use while in a stationary position.

The second guard forward screen is the screen down after the ball has been reversed through the point or wing position. The point man moves down to screen for the low man in the double screen. The screen should become stationary as the low man fakes low to the ball. This again insures against a moving screen. The screener must be aware that he is in the lane and must move out quickly after the cutter clears the screen. The technique again is the same as that for any stationary spot screen as previously described. In the event an overzealous official counts too fast, the screen should be moved slightly outside the lane and defensive adjustments will be controlled with the counteraction.

TEACHING SCREENING

In teaching screening in the perimeter area, we adhere to the following rules: (1) set the screen at a 45-degree angle; (2) the ball handler never moves until the screener has come to complete stop (This prevents an unnecessary moving screen.); (3) the ball handler crosses over with the foot farthest from the direction he is driving and attempts to step on the screener's inside foot (This enhances a tight move.); (4) the screener rolls out slightly before the ball handler's foot descends on his. In actuality, this is a fake screen because no contact may be made. This counteracts switching defenses and hedging or helping out on the part of the man defensing the screener. In the event a defensive adjustment renders this ineffective, we merely hold the screen and roll out on the contact. It is essential every perimeter screen is terminated with a rollout to prevent double-teaming and jump switching.

BASIC CUTS

Cutting to the basket and cutting to the ball is a precise technique that, when properly executed, completely defeats defensive mistakes. There are four very important cuts in the continuity of the swing-and-cut offense. These not only place the cutters in high percentage scoring opportunities, but they also enhance the swing of the ball. When these cuts are performed properly, they so completely control the defense that defensive denials are virtually impossible.

These four cuts that make up the swing-and-cut continuity are (1) the initial cut, (2) the wing cut, (3) the post cut, and (4) the cut to the top. Auxiliary or countercuts such as backdoors, interchanges, and clear outs must be perfected for the offense to perform as effectively as possible.

The basic techniques of the guard cuts and forward cuts are essentially the same. In fact, quick, sharp movement and timing are absolute musts in all cuts. It is also a must to be able to recognize the defensive alignment and quickly interpret the proper way to place the defensive man on the screen or beat him to the basket.

When a cutter is using a screen, many times the defensive

man will place himself in a poor defensive position, and a quick, simple, tight cut will tie him up on the screen. The term *tight cut* means cutting so close to the screener that you actually brush his shoulders. Don't loop or cut wide and invite the defense through with you. Pinch him off.

This chapter deals primarily with the basics of screening, cutting, and rollouts, the basic elements we expect our cutters and screeners to master. The following section deals more specifically with a particular cut or screen in the offense.

INITIAL CUT—SETTING UP CUTS

There are many ways, all very simple, to set up a cut. However, a little intelligence and ingenuity must come into play. A cutter can place his defensive man in any position he wants by using intelligence and good judgment. For example: in our initial cut, the post is setting a stationary screen at the corner of the free throw line for the weakside guard. First, the cutter must be in a position to exhibit quickness and not over four steps (five at the most) from the screen. In this position many times the quick move completely defeats the defensive man before he has time to react to the cut and screen. (Diagram 3-2) Second, it is possible to make the cut over or under, whichever you wish to do, simply by moving to the inside or outside a step or two, thereby moving the defense and cutting opposite. (Diagram 3-2)

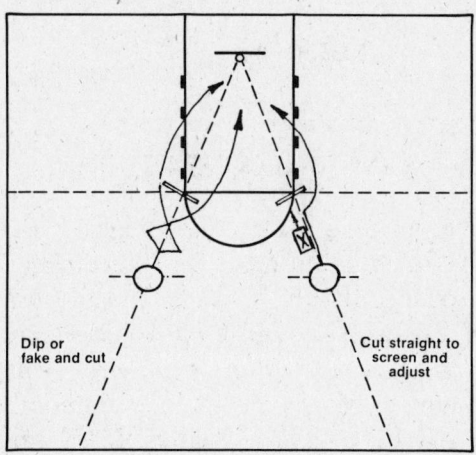

Diagram 3-2

34   cutting, screening, and rollouts in the swing-and-cut

A third way is to fake or dip one way and cut the other way. A quick, sharp dip or fake to the middle and cutting under the screen, or a quick, sharp dip or fake of one or two steps to the baseline and cutting over the screen are the most reliable choices. (Diagram 3-2) A fourth possibility is to move the defensive man to his strength and quickly evade him. Most defensive men will take the position they believe will make your move the most difficult. In this event, don't overcompensate. Simply take a quick one- or two-step jab definitely into his strength (Diagram 3-2A) thereby forcing him to hold, and at the last fraction of a second, cut opposite, over, or under, as the case may be.

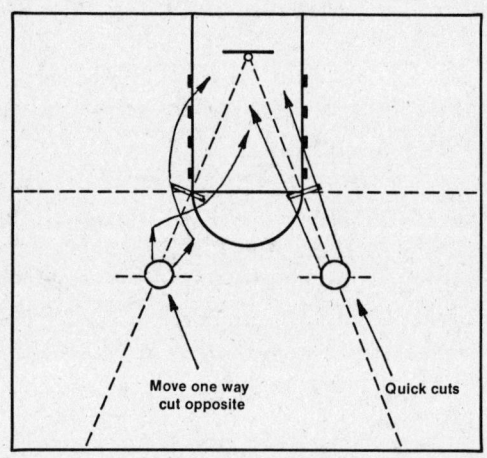

Diagram 3-2A

EVADING CONTACT

The most fatal mistake a cutter can make is that of fighting contact physically. It not only destroys the offensive timing that is so important to the effectiveness of the offense, but it also picks up a lot of unnecessary offensive fouls. Chucking or body checking the cutters is a very popular defensive play. If the offense does not counter this, it completely demoralizes your offensive strategy. All of our inside cuts off of screens provide over and under possibilities. Use these effectively. If on your cut you are checked or body checked, as infuriating as it might be, don't fight it. Immediately, as the body check is made, stop. Do a complete back pivot on the inside foot and roll over the screen on the opposite side. If this chucking and body checking takes place behind the screen, use the cutter to occupy or screen down on the defense and counter with a short comeback jump shot, as will be illustrated and explained in alternate moves and counteractions.

BACKDOOR CUTS

Backdoor cuts are important to any offensive strategy. They fall into two categories: the influence cut and the quick-score cut. The influence cut is used basically when we find ourselves completely denied as we come down the floor and run a wing through to take the defense out of the area. The quick action comes when our passing lanes are approximately 15 feet, and the defense is denying, lunging for passes, or turning heads. The backdoor cut is a result of perfect coordination between the ball handler and cutter. Total cooperation makes this a most effective offensive maneuver. When the defense is overplaying the wings or top, the ball handler should fake the pass as the receiver steps for it, with hands toward the ball. The exact moment the ball handler withdraws the pass, the receiver quickly cuts to the basket. The ball handler, of course, hits him immediately with a crisp two-hand pass or quick bounce pass. We have a rule specifying that any time the ball handler fakes a pass and does not release it, the intended receiver must quickly cut backdoor. This rule simplifies backdoor action. We also advise our players without the ball never to move higher than the desired spots we want them to receive the ball. We advise them to backdoor or to clear the area in unison with the ball handler any time denial type of defense action occurs.

INTERCHANGING

Interchanging is another simple basic, simply started and simply executed. The most difficult part is working out the timing between the cutter and the ball handlers. The cut or interchange must be precise, quick, and sharp to be effective, either as a scoring or a relief move.

The swing-and-cut uses two basic interchanges. The first is a simple guard forward interchange on one side or on both sides simultaneously. This interchange is used for two basic reasons. The first is to exchange positions between the guard and forward, placing the forward outside and the guard inside. Many times this tactic places the defense in an unfamiliar position and they do not respond defensively. The big forward is now making the initial cut as previously described. It is reasonable to assume the defensive forward would not react to this as well as the defensive guard, who has been prepared to cope with the cut and the screener. This also enables us to cut a big man low off the post screen rather than the smaller guard. (Diagram 3-2)

The interchange also enables us, against switching defenses, to place the smaller defensive guard on the big forward and take him inside. (Diagram 3-4) By the same token, we can easily take advantage of the big guard by taking his man inside.

When using the interchange to place the big forward in position for the initial cut, it is important that the guard pass to the forward and loop inside wide enough so that a switch will not occur. (Diagram 3-3) If the defense is not switching, the guard may simply dribble to and inside the forward, and give him a simple handoff as he comes out. (Diagram 3-4)

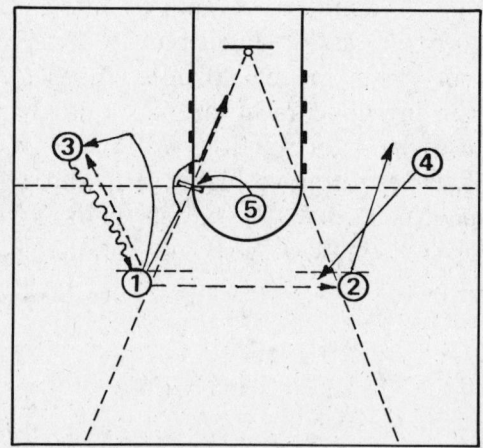

Diagram 3-3
Interchange—No Switch

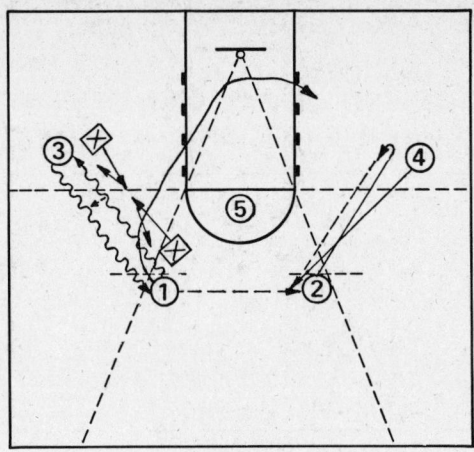

Diagram 3-4
*Interchange for Mismatch
if Defense Is Switching*

The most important interchange in the swing-and-cut occurs when the point or wing man is being overplayed. At the very instant he realizes he cannot receive the ball, he quickly and sharply cuts directly to the basket. If the defense does not react properly, the cutter should receive a quick pass on his second or third step or an overthrow at the basket. If the defense does react properly, he will follow the cutter. The low man, faking to the inside, will cut to the point or swing position to complete the interchange. (Diagram 3-5) In the event zoning or switching takes place, the cutter must take two or three quick steps toward the basket and quickly turn and step to the ball, becoming the backdoor agent. The cutter, interchanging to the top, quickly reverses and cuts to the basket as the backdoor agent receives the ball. This action splits or counteracts the zoning or switching defensive techniques. (Diagram 3-6)

It is very important that the swing man being overplayed does not hesitate or drift higher. He should immediately plant his high or outside foot and push off in direct line for the basket, never turning his back on the ball.

38 cutting, screening, and rollouts in the swing-and-cut

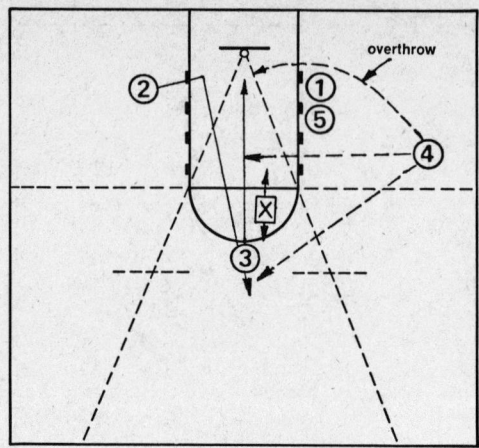

Diagram 3-5
Interchange Point or Low Man

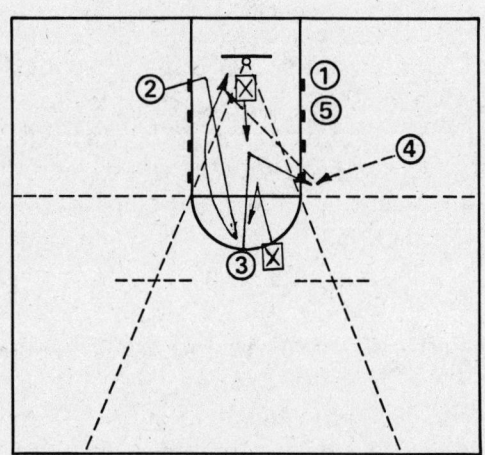

Diagram 3-6
*Interchange and Split Switching
or Zone Tactics*

4

the five basic cuts

The previous chapter described cutting, screening, rollouts, and interchanging in detail. You will notice that some of the material in this book appears more than once. This is intentional. Our entire philosophy, when a set pattern is called for, is closely centered around the swing-and-cut concept, or the five basic cuts. Consequently, it is necessary to remention a lot of material in order to help you maintain your line of thought.

Quick, sharp cuts, either to the basket or to free yourself to receive the ball, are absolutely essential. Blinding speed is not necessary. Intelligence, quickness, and timing are important. Blending all of these opportunistic executions is most essential. If a player is slow cutting into position, the swing-and-cut will be ineffective. You cannot dwell on these basics too much, because the simple basics properly taught and properly rehearsed are the core of this offense. Settle for nothing less than perfection. In fact, ask for more than you can possibly expect.

GUARD CUTS

The guard cuts, with the exception of the initial cut, are practically identical to the forward cuts. The initial cut is most effective and should be good for two to four baskets a game, possibly more. It is very important that each cut is executed to perfection. If the defense is reacting properly to the cut being executed and the cut is executed to perfection, even though that particular cut may not be successful, the perfect execution will involve the defense to the point that the following cut may be successful. A slow, poorly timed, lazy movement enables the defense to hedge and to think several moves ahead.

FORWARD CUTS

Forward cuts, as a rule, all come off the double screen while cutting from the wing position. If this cut is unsuccessful, the forward cut to the top or the point as the ball is swung follows.

CENTER CUTS

Center cuts are more flexible. Basically, the center or post man cuts to daylight or to the position the defense leaves open. Emphasis should be placed on training the center not to cut to the same spot every time.

THE ONE CUT

The one cut is the most important cut in the offense. It initiates the action. It must be executed properly to get the offense in action. Many times we begin our offense to our best cutter rather than our best scorer or best offensive guard. This cut has to challenge the defense. All of the basic elements described in Chapter 3 must be considered.

As explained in Chapter 2, the guard, on the initial cut, must keep the corner of the free throw line as nearly as possible between himself and the basket, as this is the exact spot the center will set the screen for him. He must also move as close on a line with the top of the circle as possible or as close as the defense will permit. The closer he is to the screen, the more effective the cut will be, as it will not give the defense time to adjust. Distance between the cutter and the screener is most important. It is not impossible to cut effectively when the cut is initiated at a great distance from the screen, but this does allow the defense time to compensate. The initial cut or the one cut must be quick and sharp, and must not get delayed by the defense. The cut is aimed under or over the screen directly at the basket, using all techniques described in the previous chapter. It is essential that the cutter get his hands up and start looking for the ball the moment he clears the screen. A common error cutters are prone to commit is that of cutting to the next spot and not to the basket. This causes errors and missed scoring opportunities as they are not looking for or expecting the ball. It also makes the defensive task much easier.

As guard 2 passes to forward 3, guard 1 makes his cut. Forward 3, as a first responsibility, immediately looks for guard 1 to clear the center screen. If he cuts open, he immediately passes to him. Center 5, on the initial pass to forward 1, screens away from the ball at the corner of the free throw line. Guard 2, after completing the initial pass, starts his move away toward the wide-lane marker on the opposite side. We advise him to pick up the top of the circle as he goes away and follow the circle and the lane lines down the inside as he is learning. Forward 3 moves directly toward the basket, following the cut. He becomes a back-side rebounder first. Second, he places himself in a position to cut to the top off the screen of guard 2, who is coming down. (Diagram 4-1)

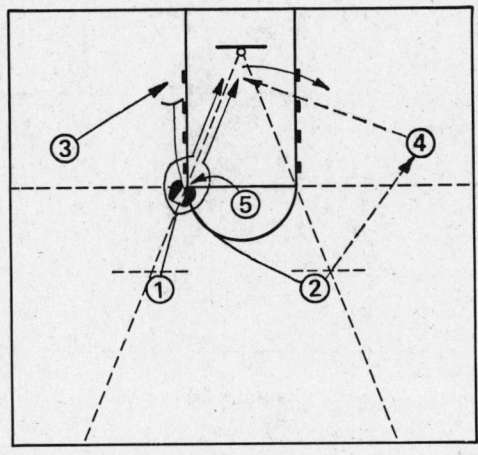

Diagram 4-1
One Cut

THE TWO CUT

The two cut is the center or post cut. It depends entirely on the adjustment of the defense. This cut also comes off the initial pass. Forward 4, after looking at the one cut to no avail, immediately looks for the two cut. If guard 1 correctly places his defensive man on the center screen, a switch is most likely. In the event of the switch, the center takes a deep drop step with his inside foot and cuts directly to the basket. In this case, it is impossible for the center to cut to the basket, since he has the confusion of the defensive center hedging and covering plus the defensive guard who he has screened in his lap. This creates a rather tight area. Under these circumstances, the center should cut to an opening (cut to daylight) for a short jump or hook shot. Cutting to daylight can vary from directly to the basket, to the area around the wide-lane marker all the way up to the corner of the free throw line. The center's ability to shoot the facing jump shot from six to fifteen feet will add a positive dimension to the overall offense. Occasionally, the center may adjust his two cut by delaying and rolling opposite behind the defensive jam for a quick overthrow from forward 4. (Diagram 4-2)

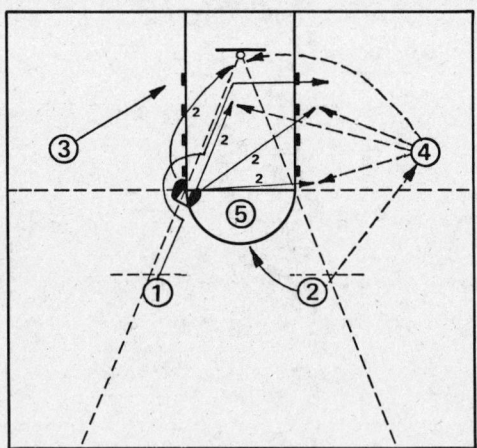

Diagram 4-2
Two Cut

THE THREE CUT

The three cut is probably as important in the execution of the swing-and-cut as the one cut. Where the one cut initiates the action, the three cut insures the swing. It is also an excellent scoring opportunity for a good 15- to 20-foot jump shooter. (Diagram 4-3) The ball is passed to forward 3, the one cut and two cut are performed, and guard 2 moves away and down. Forward 3 moves directly to the basket, positioning himself as a back-side rebounder, ready to begin the three cut. If forward 3 is not used as a rebounder, he immediately looks for guard 2 coming low, fakes his man to the inside, and cuts off guard 2's screen to the top. It is important that the three cut is made to the center of the free throw line to pinch off the defense and then pop out to the top of the key, freeing himself to receive the pass. In the execution of the three cut, three important points must be kept in mind. First, you must fake your defensive man to the inside before beginning your cut. Second, you must cut quickly and sharply. Third, you must cut to the foul line to pinch off the defense and pop out. (Diagram 4-3) This precise execution should insure the cutter of a 15- 18-foot jump shot, or place him in excellent position to swing the ball.

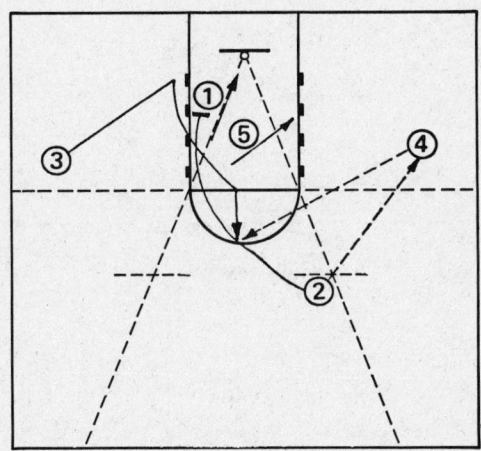

Diagram 4-3
Three Cut

THE FOUR CUT

This cut is a simple pop out. After guard 1 moves away and down to screen for forward 3, he replaces him momentarily as the back-side rebounder. As the ball is passed from forward 4 to forward 3 at the point, guard 2 cuts out to an initial forward working position, one step below the foul line extended and about two-and-one-half to three steps in from the sideline. (Diagram 4-4) He should receive the pass just as he reaches this position, therefore eluding the defense. He should immediately face the basket and look for the five cut rather than the possible shot, because the five cut is coming off a double screen. Many defenses will have guard 2's defensive man drop off to jam this area. If this happens, it is easily recognized and the shot or the one-on-one move is still available.

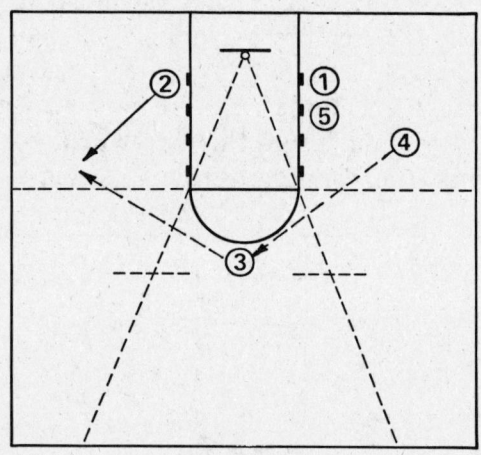

Diagram 4-4
Four Cut

We sometimes use the four cut as a one-on-one situation. When the ball is swung to the four cut, in this case, guard 2, we clear the area by holding forward 4, which will be the five cut, and center 5, which will be a second two cut. This will clear the entire side and enable the four cut to go one-on-one for a drive or jump shot. It is quite simple to place the player you so desire in this position by having him initiate the pass. You may interchange him into the proper position or wait until the continuity the five basic cuts   45

brings him to this position. This is a most effective way of camouflaging the one-on-one situation.

THE FIVE CUT

The five cut is the terminating move in the basic attack. The five cut is the most challenging move in the offense because it is executed off a double screen, directly involving three offensive and three defensive players in close proximity. As the ball is passed from the point to the four cut on the wing, and after the ball leaves the point man's hands, forward 4 cuts over or under off the double screen set by guard 1 and center 5. (Diagram 4-5) He should employ the same techniques described for the wing cut in Chapter 3. It is most important that, immediately upon clearing the screen, the cut should be to the basket and in position immediately to receive the ball and shoot. Expect the ball immediately upon clearing the screen. Cut to score. Do not cut mechanically.

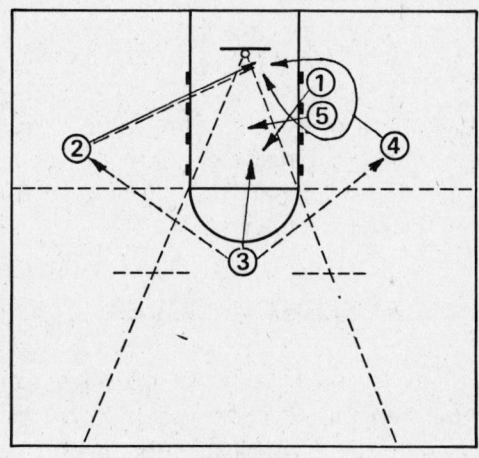

Diagram 4-5
Five Cut

THE TURNOVER OR SWING

The five basic cuts carry us through a strongside set and the first swing-and-cut to the weak side, thereby reestablishing a strong side. (Diagrams 4-3 and 4-5) You will notice the one cut

46   the five basic cuts

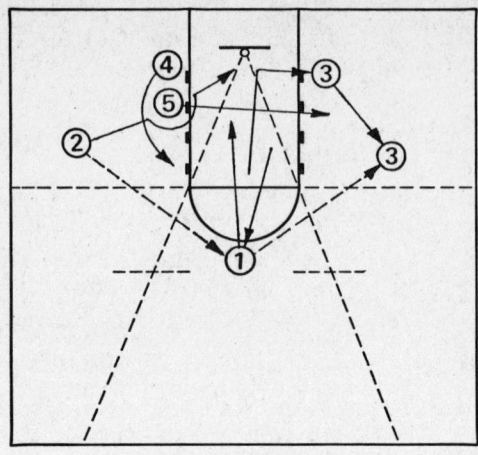

Diagram 4-6
Complete Turnover

is evidenced only on the initial move; however, the two, three, four and five cuts are involved with each swing of the ball from the strong side to the weak side. You will also notice all personnel are involved in all cuts except the two cut as the continuity progresses. The two cut is relegated to the center or post man alone.

I will swing the ball one more time for the sake of explanation, pointing out the fact that after five passes and two turnovers or swings, both guards and both forwards have cut to all offensive positions. (Diagram 4-6)

ALTERNATE MOVES

We use four alternate moves that we have found the most effective in complementing the five basic cuts. When properly used, they greatly aid the five basic cuts in challenging the defense and limiting their defensive possibilities. The first alternate we call the One-J. The *J* denotes a jump shot on the comeback. (Diagram 4-7) One-J is used when the guard finds his defensive man sloughing deep or waiting for the cut behind the screen. We see this a lot, even to the extent of finding the defensive guard looking all the way to the wide-lane marker on the initial pass. This is easily discouraged or countered. It may be an instinctive move by guard 1 or it may be used as a called play.

the five basic cuts   47

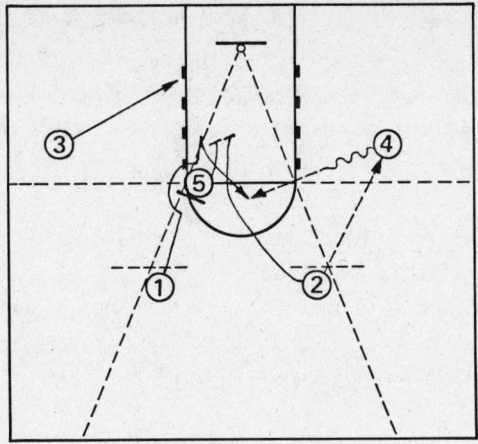

Diagram 4-7
Alternate One-J

In reality, no change is necessary from the normal one-cut technique. In fact, it is entirely possible that only the guard cutting to the basket may be aware this adjustment is being made. It is the cutting guard's prerogative to make this adjustment. If the play is a called play, guard 2 should make a slight adjustment in his cutting lane. The center, seeing or knowing this action is taking place, would roll *slowly* and directly toward the basket. I emphasize *slowly* so he will not move too fast into the crowded area and be called for an offensive foul rather than offering a passive effective screen.

One-J

As guard 1 begins his cut, and upon finding the defense sloughing behind the center screen, he should drive at least two steps below the screen on the outside of the center. He should plant his outside foot and come back to the free throw line behind the center as he rolls down. The center should, upon recognition of the change, or by the fact that the play was called, perform a front pivot on the inside foot and slowly move toward the basket, therefore giving the cutter a screen to work back over. Guard 2, or the guard who initiated the pass, adjusts his cut away to the ball side of the center, moving slowly forward below the free throw line, or coming to a complete standstill if the defense so permits. This enables the cutter to come back be-

48   the five basic cuts

hind the double screen and receive a pass from the ball-handling forward for a 15- to 18-foot jump shot. (Diagram 4-7)

One-J is necessary only perhaps two times in a game, to inform the defense they cannot afford to completely ignore the perimeter in order to stop the inside cut.

In the event the defense does sift through, the continuity of the offense may be maintained by having forward 3, who has now closed in to the wide-lane marker, cut back to his initial position. Guard 2 and center 5 move through to the screen position on the lane. The ball is now passed to guard 1 at the top. He swings the pass to forward 3, and forward 4 cuts off the double screen.

screen to the same side

The second alternate we call screener to the same side. This again is a very simple adjustment that may be most efficient against defenses that are waiting for our basic moves. On the initial move, the center, instead of screening away from the ball on the initial pass, moves to the ball using the same basic techniques and screens for the guard who makes the initial pass. (Diagram 4-8) Guard 1 or the weakside guard moves down the lane and screens for forward 3, cutting to the top, thereby maintaining the swing-and-cut continuity.

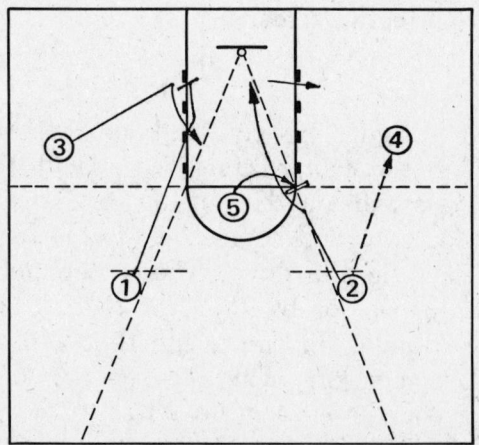

Diagram 4-8
Alternate—Screen the Same Side

swing and choke

The third alternate amplifies our inside game and takes advantage of a strong inside forward or big guard posting from a constantly moving offense. Let us assume the first swing has been made. The ball is in the hands of guard 2 at the wing position on the left side looking in. Forward 3 has just passed him the ball. Forward 4 has cut off the double screen and is now low on the free throw line. Center 5 has rolled to daylight, setting a double screen beside forward 4. Forward 3, who was the swing man, now cuts down the lane toward the basket. Guard 1, who was low man in the double screen, fakes to the inside and cuts to the top off forward 3's screen. The choke post action begins here. Forward 3, never turning his back on the ball, steps outside the lane at the wide-lane marker. As the ball is passed back to guard 1 at the top, forward 3 quickly and forcefully *crabs* to the inside and to the ball. He now has a low post position, with the defense behind him and the entire side of the court cleared. This places him in excellent position for a quick feed from guard 1 at the point, for a short hook shot, power move, or quick turn and jump shot off the board.

Perhaps at this point, I should explain the term crab or crabbing. (Diagram 4-9) The player on the low post, looking for the ball, is asked to step across his defensive man with his inside foot

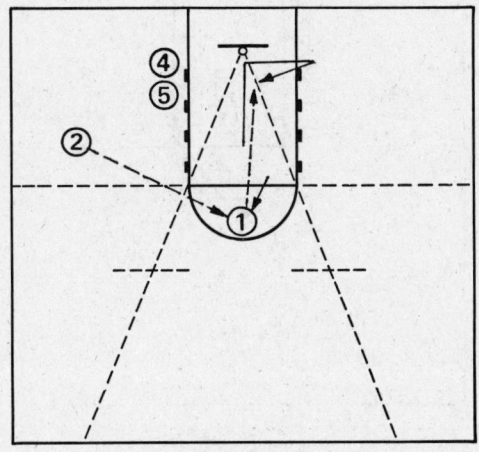

Diagram 4-9
Alternate—Choke Post

spread wide, hips low and solid, back straight, and hands out toward the ball. The player maintains this strong, solid position and moves toward the ball in short, choppy steps — hence, the term crab or crabbing. The crabbing movement, as a rule, should not be flat or vertical; we find the defense will be held in check more adequately when we crab in at a 45-degree angle.

In the event the point or swing man does not get the pass low to the choke post, the choke man cuts to the outside to a wing position, receives the pass from the point, and the offense is maintained.

Each player in the continuity may choke if his talent so dictates. This may slow the movement slightly, but it will also greatly enhance inside possibilities.

swing and pinch

The fourth alternate is used as a change of pace. The technique is exactly the same as the choke post except that the low man, instead of choking, cuts to the corner of the free throw line, (Diagram 4-10) receives a pass from the swing man, guard 1, and plays two-on-two with him. This creates a jump shot or drive for guard 1, as his defense is pinched off by forward 3, or a rollout to the basket by forward 3, who is looking for a check pass from guard 1.

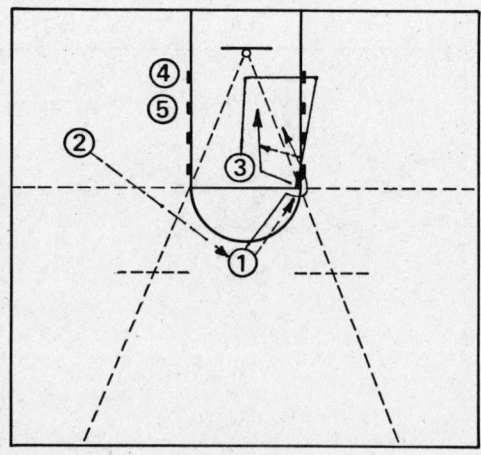

Diagram 4-10
Alternate—Pinch Post

5

relief moves from each floor position

It is essential that from every position in the offense the ball handler be aware of and have his reflexes conditioned to immediate offensive adjustments, should the defense take away its normal routine. Properly rehearsed in the techniques of relief action, the offense will maintain the offensive continuity without panic and with poise and confidence. This is not only a confidence builder from an offensive point of view, but it is a demoralizing factor for the defense to find that special defensive strategy is destroyed by alert offensive awareness.

It is common knowledge that when on defense you must keep pressure on the offense. If you allow the offense to operate freely, it will eventually score. It is also essential that when the offense is involved, pressure must be placed on the defense or you will be forced into areas where the offense is ineffective. *Relief moves* are essential in maintaining this constant pressure.

Relief moves and relieving pressure are essentially the same. We do, however, refer to our relief moves from the point and wing positions in our basic offensive sets. Relieving pressure will be discussed as a separate entity, with emphasis on initiating or getting into the offensive pattern. Two thirds of the assist possibilities in the swing-and-cut come from the wing positions. With this in mind, we will proceed with relief moves from the wing.

CLEAR

Forward 4 has the ball on the right wing. Guard 1 cuts low and is now the low part of the double screen. Center 5 rolls across to become the high position in the double screen. Guard 2, who made the initial pass, moves away to the low position on the backside. Forward 3 moves to the basket, fakes inside and cuts off guard 2's screen to the top. (Diagram 5-1)

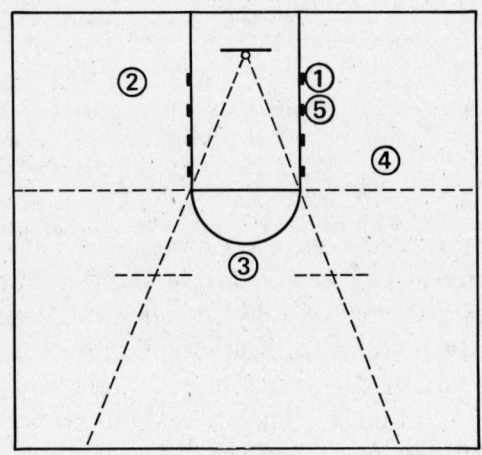

Diagram 5-1
Strong Set—Ball on Wing

Relief moves are designed primarily to insure the continuity of the offense when facing defensive denials. However, all offensive maneuvers should be designed with the ultimate goal in mind—to score baskets. With this in mind, the ball handler should always have the relief move in mind that offers, considering the personnel involved, the greatest percentage toward scoring baskets. Also, bear in mind that relief moves may be used as an effective change of pace or, for that matter, as a set play.

The ball is in forward 4's hands, as illustrated in Diagram 5-1. Center 5, who is the high man in the double screen, is being split defensively on the high side, with the defensive man's right hand extending over the center's chest into the passing lane, denying him the ball. The defensive man guarding guard 1, the low man in the double screen, is playing him the same way with his left hand across the passing lane. Forward 3 is being overplayed at the top. Guard 2, who has cut to the backdoor area, is being totally denied. Forward 4, observing this defensive action and finding himself being closely guarded, immediately calls "clear." From his position as low man in the double screen, guard 1 cuts quickly to the corner, and forward 4 passes him the ball at a point about six feet from the sideline.

Guard 1 immediately turns and faces the basket, challenging the defense. Forward 4, upon releasing the pass to guard 1, cuts quickly to the basket on the baseline side of the center, looking for a quick return and give-and-go action. If guard 1 does not return the pass to forward 4 cutting to the basket, center 5, after forward 4 has cut by him, quickly steps out and sets a 45-degree angle screen for guard 1 as previously described in Chapter 3. Guard 1, using a head and step fake to the baseline, crosses over and drives off the center's screen to the inside. (Diagram 5-2) As guard 1 clears the center screen, the center rolls back, pivoting on the baseline foot and swinging the high foot wide and deep, never turning his back on the ball. As the high foot is planted, he immediately cuts to the basket expecting a check pass. Executed cor-

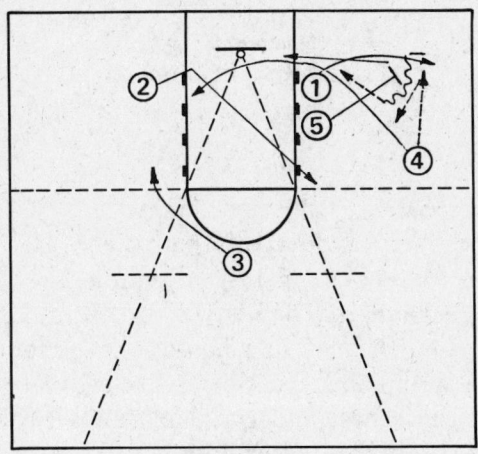

Diagram 5-2
Clear

rectly and considering any possible defensive action, the results should be a high percentage drive, jump shot, or check pass to the center.

In the event this move is defended adequately, and a shot does not materialize, guard 1 will pass to forward 4, who cut through and moved to the top. Forward 3, who is being overplayed at the top, interchanges low and then cuts out to the wing position as the center rolls back. Guard 2, who is being overplayed in the backdoor area, sets the double screen for guard 1. The ball is swung to the weak side and the continuity continues. (Diagram 5-3)

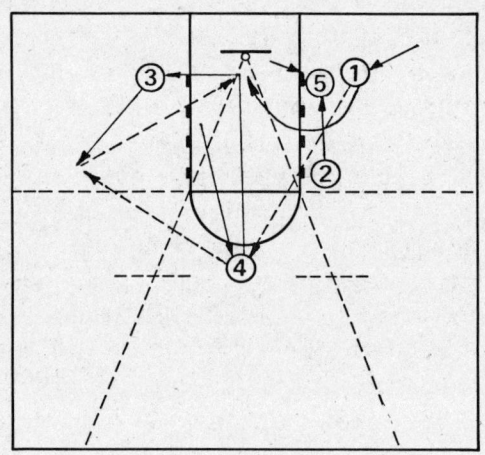

Diagram 5-3
Move Back into Continuity

SPLIT

With a good jump shooter at the point, or if the clear has been successfully defended against, a simple split action could prove beneficial. Again, the ball is with forward 4 as in Diagram 5-1. Forward 4 calls the center's name; the center quickly steps forward one step with hands up. Forward 4 passes to him and cuts straight between the center and guard 1. Guard 1 rolls behind forward 4's cut and across the center, looking to screen for forward 3 at the top. Forward 3 fakes a direct cut to the basket, plants his left foot on the second step and cuts over guard 1's screen about

relief moves from each floor position   55

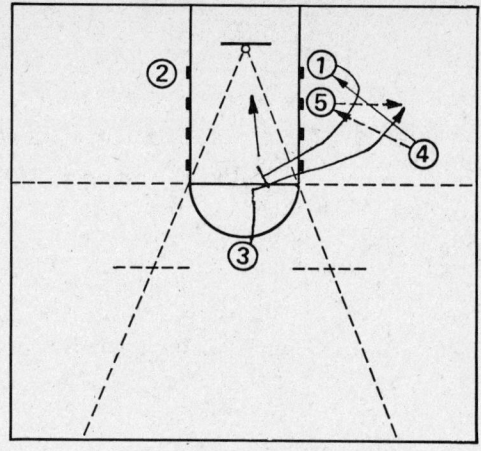

Diagram 5-4
Double Split

two steps in front of the center for a jump shot. (Diagram 5-4) As forward 3 finds his jump shot did not materialize, he will quickly pass to guard 2 coming to the top. Guard 2 will swing the ball to guard 1 cutting to the wing position, and forward 3 will cut off the double screen by center 5 and forward 4 as the offense continues. (Diagram 5-4A)

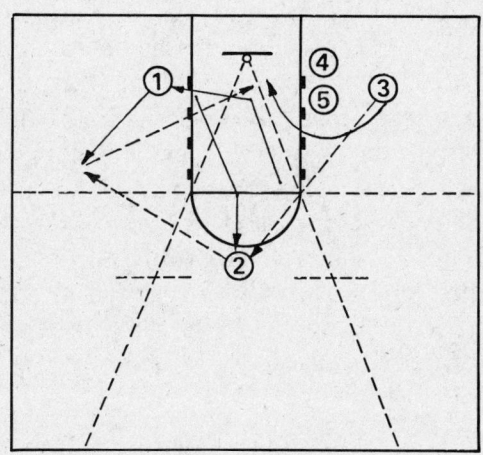

Diagram 5-4A
Move Back into Continuity

BACKDOOR

There are many versions of the backdoor move. In fact, any reverse action to counter a denial can be considered backdoor action. The backdoor action I am describing here, and the backdoor action that is an important part of our offense, is keyed to the way the defense plays the center or post man. We have a rule that directs our weakside forward or, for that matter, anyone in that position to always be aware of how the defense is playing the center or post. If the post is being fronted, the rule advises the offside forward to cut to what we term the *backdoor area*. This is an area in the vicinity of one step below the corner of the free throw line on the strong side. This move does not allow the defensive man defending the offside or weakside forward to slough off and cover the overthrow. If the defense fails to follow his man, he presents him with a 15-foot jump shot.

Let us look again at Diagram 5-1. The strong forward 4 is handling the ball. He immediately recognizes that both men in the double screen are being fronted. Forward 3 at the point is being denied. The defensive man guarding guard 2 on the back-side is sloughing deep behind the double screen to protect against the overthrow. Upon reading this defensive strategy, the weakside man, guard 2, fakes two steps toward the basket and quickly cuts to the backdoor area. (Diagram 5-4) Forward 4 passes to guard 2 as he cuts to the ball. This presents guard 2 with four options. If his defensive man does not close up, he faces the basket for a 15-foot jump shot. If he does close up, guard 2 quickly checks to the center, who already has inside position, as he spreads out, checks the defensive man fronting him, and cuts to the basket. The third option lies with forward 3, who is being overplayed at the top. Upon seeing the pass to the backdoor area, he makes a backdoor cut to the basket (Diagram 5-5) for a quick pass from guard 2. The fourth option lies with forward 4. After passing to guard 2, he will fake two steps to the baseline and cut over guard 2 for a jump shot or possible drive.

OVERTHROWS

The overthrow is a natural relief move from any court position. This is an especially effective relief move if you are fortunate

relief moves from each floor position   57

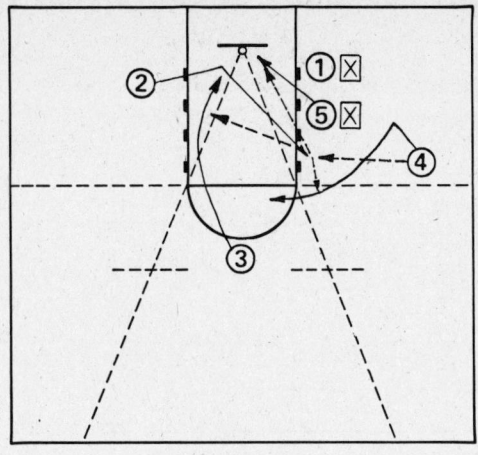

Diagram 5-5
Backdoor

enough to have an exceptionally tall, agile, mobile center with outstanding leaping ability. These dimensions make the overthrow more than a relief move because it is nearly always a possibility, even though the defense is aware that the threat exists. Even if the ideal personnel is not available, the overthrow still offers a valuable relief opportunity.

Forward 4 again is in possession of the ball in the wing position. Center 5 and guard 1 in the double screen along the lane are being fronted. Forward 3 at the swing position is being overplayed. Guard 2 on the back-side reads the defensive fronting of center 5 and guard 1, and immediately cuts to the backdoor area. Guard 1's defensive man follows him closely, disregarding his back-side responsibility. This clears the entire back-side and sets a perfect stage for the overthrow. (Diagram 5-6)

There are three important steps in executing an effective overthrow. First, the defense must be read properly and the possibility of success must be 100 percent probable. Second, the center, or the player being overthrown to, must turn his hips into his defensive man, feet well spread, and completely seal him off from the basket area. He should raise his hands and arms high in order to prevent an instinctive push off that results in a cheap foul. He should hold his position on the defensive man he is screening off and time the flight of the ball so that he and the ball will arrive at

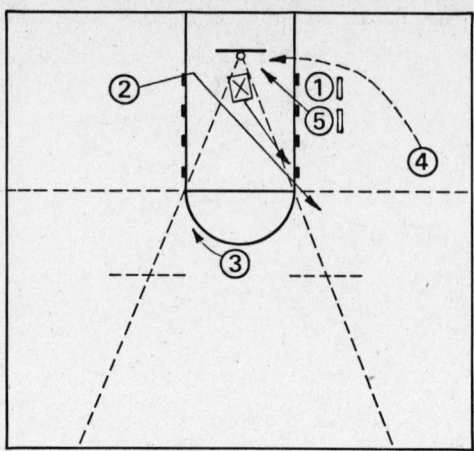

Diagram 5-6
Overthrow

the contact spot at the same time. Third, the ball handler must deliver a perfect pass. The pass must be just high enough to clear the outstretched hands of the defensive man. Unnecessary height is detrimental to the success of the play, as the ball is in the air longer and allows defensive men more time to adjust.

PENETRATING DRIBBLE

If the center is being played behind, the defensive man guarding the ball is sloughed back to prevent a pass to the center, and all other players are being aggressively denied, the stage is set for a penetrating dribble. The slough to prevent a pass to the center allows forward 4 an 18- to 20-foot shot. It would be reasonable to believe the defense will slough off only from a questionable shooter. To counteract this move, forward 4 should take one dribble toward the baseline, thus indicating his intention. He then crosses over without taking up his dribble and dribbles over the screen by center 5, who has moved up the lane and placed his high foot slightly below the foul line. Forward 3, now on the point, finding his defensive man watching the penetration, cuts to the opposite end of the foul line. Guard 2, on the back-side, finding his man involved with the penetration, cuts backdoor to the basket. As forward 4 clears the center screen, the center drop-steps with his high foot always facing the ball, and cuts to the basket. The penetrating forward 4 has five options. He can check to the center rolling to the basket, pass to forward 3 for a 15-foot jump shot, pass backdoor to guard 2 cutting to the basket, take a jump shot himself coming off the center screen, or drive toward the basket. (Diagram 5-7)

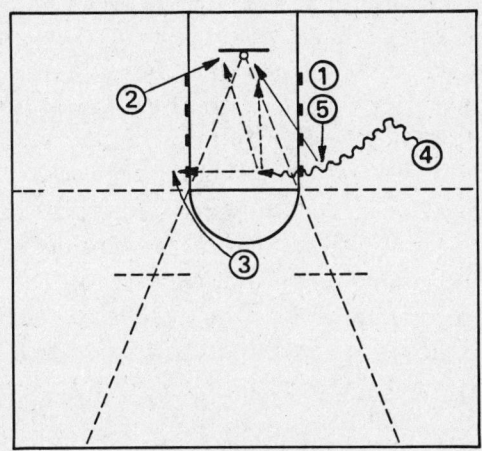

Diagram 5-7
Penetrating Dribble

The five relief moves I have just described are designed to provide relief from the wing positions. The clear, the backdoor, and the overthrow are probably the most often used and most effective to provide relief facing most defensive plays. Seventy percent of our assist opportunities occur from the wing positions. A scout report or previous game will in most cases apprise you of possible defensive alignments and how certain individuals and certain situations will be defended against. Choose and rehearse the relief moves you think will be the most effective for the next game. Rehearse these moves against the defensive alignments you feel will present a problem. Preparation will enable your personnel to execute these relief moves to perfection.

DRIBBLE OVER

The point or swing position, even though one of the most important points of execution relating to the continuity of the offense, does not require as many relief opportunities because it is not subjected to as many possible defensive alignments. The dribble over is our basic relief move from the swing position. The ball is now in possession of forward 3 in the swing position or on the point with all personnel positioned as in Diagram 5-1. If a shot does not present itself, forward 3 swings the ball to guard 2 who has cut out to the wing position on the weak side. In the event guard 2 is being denied in order to prevent the swing, forward 3 dribbles straight at guard 2. Guard 2, recognizing the action, immediately cuts backdoor straight to the basket. If he eludes his defensive man, forward 3 will give him a quick bounce pass for a lay-up or short jump shot off the board. If the defense does not allow this backdoor action, guard 2 continues his cut to the spot occupied by guard 1, the low man in the double screen. Guard 1 cuts to the top to replace forward 3, who has dribbled to the wing. As forward 3 replaces guard 2 on the dribble over, forward 4 waits for forward 3 to pick up his dribble and cuts off the double screen to the basket. Forward 4 looks for a pass from forward 3 (Diagram 5-8) in maintaining offensive continuity.

Relief moves are important. Prepare for the game at hand. Rehearse diligently your offensive attack. Do not, however, clutter the player's mind with too many options. Keep it as simple as possible. Bear in mind that the swing-and-cut offense, the options, counteractions, and relief moves can be as simple or as complicated as you choose.

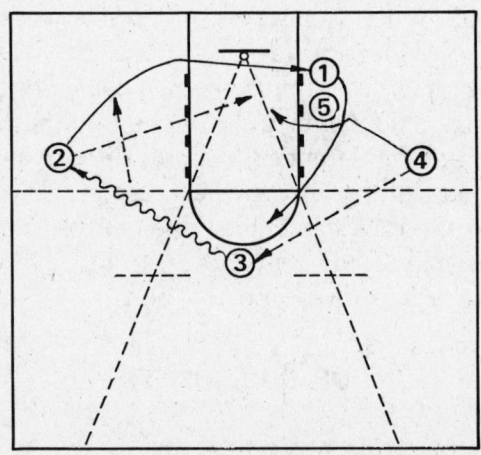

Diagram 5-8
Dribble Over and Return to Continuity

6

relieving pressure

Relief moves and relieving pressure are essentially the same. We think of relieving pressure as successfully defeating defensive tactics designed to prevent the opponent's offense from initiating its basic offensive patterns, or the phase of the offense in which it has the most confidence.

Pressure defense has been used effectively by some of the outstanding teams in high school and collegiate circles for the past 25 or 30 years. In 1952-53, the University of Kansas, coached by Phog Allen, lost a very close decision to Indiana University for the National Championship as a result of a devastating half-court pressing defense employed by Indiana. This is but one example of what pressure can do to even a top-flight team. Pressure tactics can have a demoralizing effect on the opposition if they are not prepared to adjust to it. A team must be well-prepared in the fundamentals of the basic skills such as ball handling, passing, cutting, body balance, etc. Even with these skills properly mastered, the team concept is the ingredient that insures poise and confidence and results in turning pressure tactics into an advantage for the team being pressed. The team that can move, has mastered the basics, and has been properly rehearsed as a team will have little trouble against pressure.

Pressing tactics fall into several categories:
1. Man-to-man or zone pressure in front court (30 feet)
2. Man-to-man or zone pressure at half court (47 feet)
3. Man-to-man or zone pressure at the three quarters point (70 feet)
4. Man-to-man or zone pressure at full court (94 feet)

Zone pressure is probably used more because it is easier to teach. Man-to-man pressure, properly taught in its most aggressive form, is probably the most difficult to defeat. The team concept for attacking either tactic is virtually the same.

Pressure tactics are used to force a team out of its normal pattern by taking away its normal floor positions and upsetting the timing. It will change the tempo of the game so that the team with the better speed and quickness will usually excel. It creates confusion and forces fundamental mistakes that create easy baskets, and it is a must when a team is behind during the final moments of the game.

It is absolutely essential to be prepared for pressure, since every team playing the game today will have some sort of pressure tactics. The better teams will not let the offense move the ball to within 25 feet of the basket unchallenged. They are aware that this leads to high percentage scoring opportunities.

Occasionally a team may be blessed with a player or two with such exceptional ability that it is virtually impossible to confuse them with pressure tactics. It is a common mistake, however, to rely so much on this individual's ability that very little time is spent rehearsing an attack against pressure, thus leaving the team susceptible in the event of injury or excessive fouls.

Confidence and poise are probably the two most important ingredients in facing any difficult task. We gain confidence and poise only through exposure to the situation at hand. We learn the basics and techniques flawlessly and rehearse the difficult situation tirelessly. The pressure situation that we most commonly face is man-to-man pressure in the front court. This is usually a result of the ball handler being played strong and hard and all lead passes being strongly denied. There are several effective ways to face this pressure. The one we rely on the most is the drive through.

Any time man-to-man pressure is exerted, if we will clear the area or position we want the ball, our ball handler can take it there one-on-one. (Diagram 6-1) We also believe if this pressure is applied with zone tactics that we can always overthrow. These are simple moves, but they will get us into our pattern and give our personnel a feeling of confidence by knowing the percentage of effectiveness that is involved.

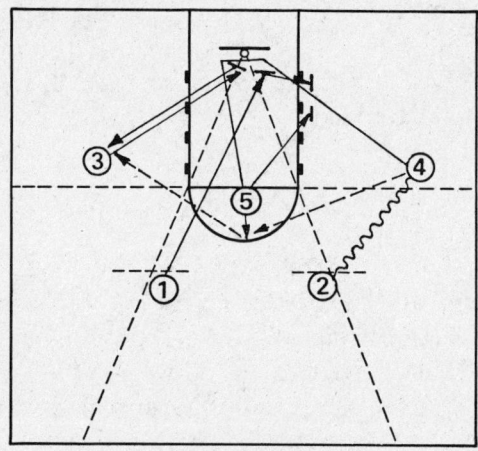

Diagram 6-1
Drive Through

THE DRIVE THROUGH

The drive through is a very important part of our offensive plan because it offers us a flexible entry into the offense. Not only is the one-on-one move effective, but the drive through affords a quick opportunity to get into the offense on the move as we move down the floor quickly.

When we face pressure tactics in the front court while attempting to get the ball in the initial operating position ready for the initial pass, the ball handler will dribble one-on-one directly at forward 4. (Diagram 6-1) Forward 4, recognizing this action or depending on guard 2's verbal directions, will cut backdoor to the basket, being aware that a backdoor pass is possible. Guard 1 and forward 3 make their normal cuts low, but instead of completing cuts, both will screen low for forward 4 coming low and cutting to

64 relieving pressure

the top. (Diagram 6-1) Center 5 will roll to his normal position as the top man in the double screen. When guard 2 reaches the spot that forward 4 has vacated, he will pull up and look for forward 4 cutting back to the free throw line. Not only is this an excellent way to relieve pressure, but it is also an exceptional scoring move for a good shooting forward or wing coming to the top. We use it many times as a set play. If forward 4 does not have the shot, guard 1 steps out into his normal position as low man in the double screen. Forward 3 cuts back out to the original forward position. Forward 4 swings the ball to forward 3, and we are in the swing-and-cut. (Diagram 6-1)

SPLIT

Another effective method toward relieving pressure is the center split. This is one of the oldest methods and is effective against either a man-for-man or a zone, providing the execution is perfect and the cuts are carried all the way to the basket.

Normally, the center cannot be completely fronted at the high post when overall pressure is exerted. Complete denial makes the defense vulnerable to the overthrow. When pressure tactics are exerted, we ask the center to take two quick steps forward to the top of the key. Guard 2 passes the ball to center 5 and cuts over

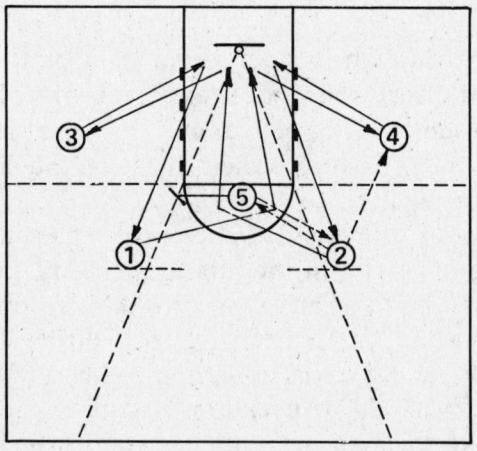

Diagram 6-2
Split

him directly to the basket, always watching for a return pass. Guard 1 fakes to his left on the outside foot, cuts back over guard 2's hip, and cuts directly to the basket, always watching for the ball. (Diagram 6-2) As the ball is received by the center, both forwards cut backdoor all the way to the basket. Both are alert for a backdoor pass from the center. If a scoring opportunity does not present itself, both forwards, on reaching the wide-lane marker, plant the baseline foot and cut quickly to the initial guard position. This is a long cut but extremely effective, as it is most difficult for the defense to pursue. The guards who have split low now cut to the original wing positions. Center 5 will screen away for forward 3, thus having defeated the pressure, and we are in the swing-and-cut. (Diagram 6-3)

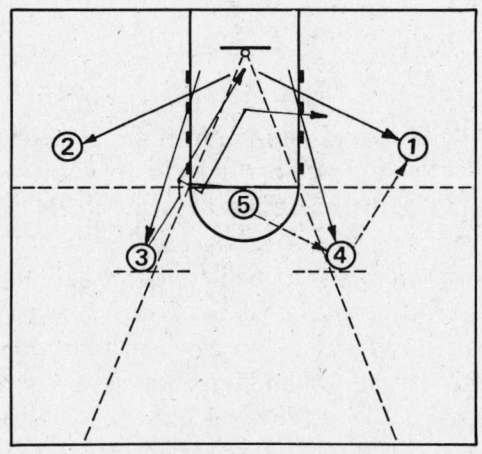

Diagram 6-3
Return to Swing-and-Cut

BACKDOOR

A backdoor cut is always effective in relieving pressure. Essentially, all backdoor action is quite similar. Floor position involves different personnel. When pressured in the front court or at half court, offside forward 3 will take two or three quick steps directly toward the basket, taking his defensive man with him. On his second or third step he will plant his baseline foot, change di-

relieving pressure

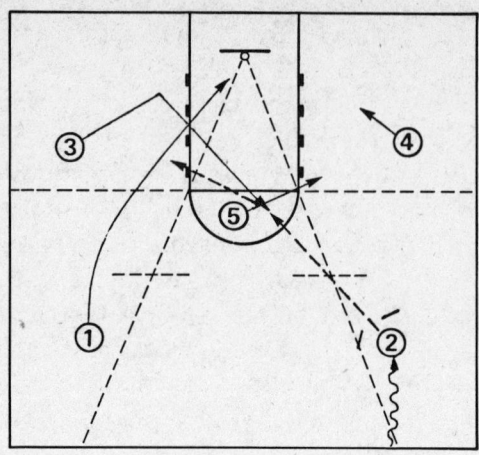

Diagram 6-4
Backdoor

rection, and cut quickly to the ball in the vicinity of the top of the key. (Diagram 6-4) Guard 2 passes him the ball as he is cutting the ball and eluding the defense. Strongside forward 4 at the same time is faking a cut to the baseline to occupy his defensive man. Center 5 has moved over to the strongside corner of the free throw line to open up the area. As the ball touches the hands of forward 3, guard 1 cuts back-side to the basket. Guard 2, who made the initial pass and has moved his defensive man two steps toward the baseline, changes his direction and cuts across forward 3. (Diagram 6-4) Forward 3 first looks at guard 1 cutting backdoor. If he isn't open, he gives a short flip pass to guard 2 cutting across for a drive, jump shot, or he may dribble to the wing position. We are now in the swing-and-cut with forward 4 ready to cut off the double screen by guard 1 and center 5.

The split and the backdoor action are equally effective against zone pressure, utilizing the pass to the middle, cutting to the baseline, and passing to the perimeter concept. Zone pressure nearly always traps or double-teams the ball. Consequently, if the center on the backdoor pass is denied the long overthrow is always available. (Diagram 6-5) This will immediately relieve pressure and place us in the swing-and-cut pattern. The swing-and-cut versus the zone defense will be explained in a later chapter.

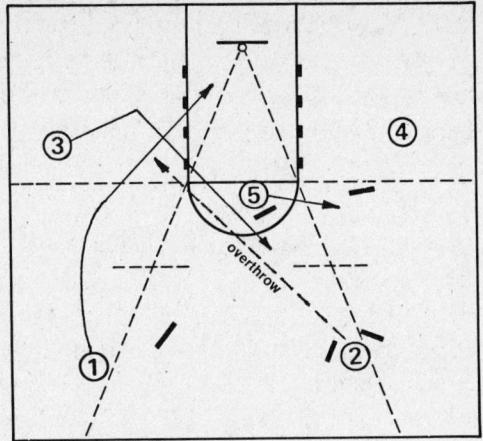

Diagram 6-5
Backdoor—Long Overthrow

If previous reports tell us the opponent we are preparing to play will use pressure at midcourt, we will attempt through offensive deployment to make their task a more difficult one while enabling the offense to advance the ball to the desired position to initiate the pattern.

ONE-MAN FRONT

When facing a team that uses a lot of double-team tactics at midcourt, it is sometimes wise to attack with a one-man front. This enables a good ball handler and dribbler to operate more freely, since distances between players do not permit the defense the position required to make double-team or trap pressure effective. One of the advantages of the swing-and-cut is that several offensive entries can successfully initiate the offense. This will be explained further in Chapter 7.

It is nearly impossible for one defensive man to satisfactorily pressure a good ball handler and dribbler in a one-man front. The distances between the wings or the stack, as the case might be, provides the point man with a wide area of the court in which to maneuver in his effort to defeat the pressure and get the offense into motion or provide a free-lance drive

68   relieving pressure

The one-man front against zone pressure is proficient because the deployment has a tendency to spread the defense to the point where the pressure is diminished by the balance and deployment of the offense. This will be covered in the chapter relating to the swing-and-cut against zones.

THREE-MAN FRONT

A successful maneuver toward relieving pressure may be found in the three-man front with two post men against either a man-for-man or zone (Diagram 6-6) in either the front court or at midcourt. The middle or point man, guard 1, will initiate the attack exactly halfway between the two sidelines or as near to this point as possible. Guard 2 and forward 4 will position themselves 15 to 18 feet from guard 1 and on a line approximately two steps in front. The two post men, forward 3 and center 5, line up with their inside feet on the wide-lane marker. With recognition and timing, the two post men, using straight cuts, crosses, or fake crosses (Diagram 6-7), cut quickly to their respective corners of the free throw lane. The middle or point man will determine the best possibility and pass him the ball. (Diagram 6-6)

The two outside players, at the exact moment the ball reaches the post man, will cut backdoor. Guard 1 fakes a cut dir-

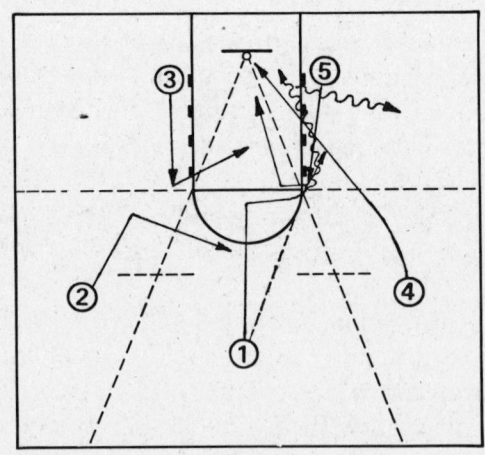

Diagram 6-6
Three-Man Front—Two Posts

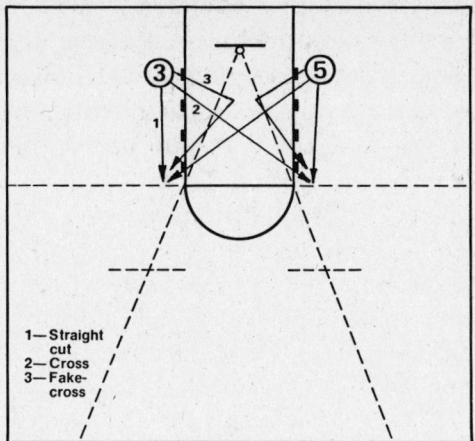

Diagram 6-7

ectly toward the basket, moving his defensive man with him. On reaching the desired position and seeing the post man still has the ball, guard 1 will plant his away foot and cut over the post with the ball. The post man, upon receiving the ball, looks for the outside man on his side, cutting backdoor or with the middle man cutting over him. If the backdoor cut is not open, the ball is flipped to guard 1, cutting over him.

Guard 1 can jump shoot, drive, pass to post rolling to basket, or dribble wide. If he dribbles wide, forward 3 crosses to become the low man in the double screen. Center 5 slides down. Guard 2 fakes to the basket and cuts to the top. Forward 4 continues his backdoor cut to the opposite wing. Guard 1 passes to guard 2 coming to the top. Guard 2 swings the ball to forward 4 and guard 1 cuts off the double screen. The pressure is defeated and the swing-and-cut is in motion.

CHANGING THE POINT OF ATTACK

A very simple maneuver in combating midcourt or frontcourt pressure is changing the point of attack, or more simply stated, changing the side of the floor just before the defense attacks. This is a very easy move, providing that the ball handlers are alert and do not get a lateral pass picked off. When the defensive team is using midcourt or frontcourt pressure, the attack usually begins just as the ball crosses center line or is keyed on a certain offensive move or signal of some sort. As soon as the defense moves, quickly move the ball to another point of attack. This makes it more difficult for the defense to attack with full team support, since much of pressure defense is anticipation. By taking away this element of team anticipation with one quick lateral pass, the defense could find it difficult to regroup before the offense is in motion. If the defensive adjustment is quick enough on the first pass, it is easily countered by a quick return pass. (Diagram 6-8)

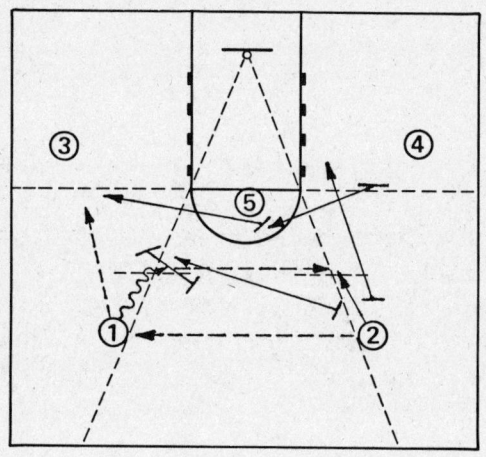

Diagram 6-8
Changing Point of Attack

If a defense elects to do so, it is quite easy to cut off the lateral pass and channel the offense into the area the defense is prepared to attack. This, of course, makes them vulnerable to one of the aforementioned tactics concerning relieving pressure.

FULL-COURT ATTACK AGAINST PRESSURE

A team that is pressure-defense oriented will apply pressure anywhere in the court. It is important to spend a few minutes each day rehearsing tactics and exposing your personnel to pressure situations. We try to keep the full-court, midcourt, and frontcourt attack against pressure as closely related as possible. We try to keep in mind the concept of passing to the middle, cutting to the baseline, and passing to the back-side or strongside perimeters.

Normally, a team activates full-court pressure after a successful free throw, basket, out-of-bounds, or any type of a lull in the action that will permit the defense time to set. Even in those situations our first attempt is to defeat the pressure quickly with our fast-break tactics before it has time to set. This prevents the defense from taking the fast break away. If this does not prove effective, we will set and attack.

After a successful basket or successful free throw, we have our center 5 take the ball out-of-bounds directly under the basket. He must be aware of the fact that the backboard will prohibit a long pass, and he must take one step to the side if he is to attempt such. The best ball handlers, usually guard 1 and guard 2, will line up quickly on the free throw line extended and about two steps in from the sideline. Forwards 3 and 4 will position themselves at center line about one step in from the sideline. (Diagram 6-9)

We do not like to set against pressure. It slows our attack down. It takes our fast break away, and this may be an accomplishment in itself for the defense. It makes us play their game. We are, however, realistic enough to understand that when encountering well-planned pressure, we must have an attack that we feel any of our personnel will have confidence in.

We ask the center not to grab the ball too quickly when using a set attack against pressure. This gives the other four players an opportunity to position themselves before the five second count starts. When the center picks up the ball, he immediately slaps it to initiate the action. On the signal, guard 1 and guard 2 cut directly to the wide-lane marker. I should add here that the defense may take the straight cut away. The guards will then find it necessary to fake two to three steps to the middle or to the baseline in order to set up the straight cut to the wide-lane marker. Upon reaching the wide-lane marker and receiving the ball, guard 1 will now become the middle man. Guard 2 will cut back to the corner parallel to the baseline. Upon reaching a point approximately two steps from the sideline, he will, facing the ball, move slowly up the sideline until needed in the attack. Center 5, upon passing in bounds, will loop behind guard 1, to whom he has passed, and as-

72   relieving pressure

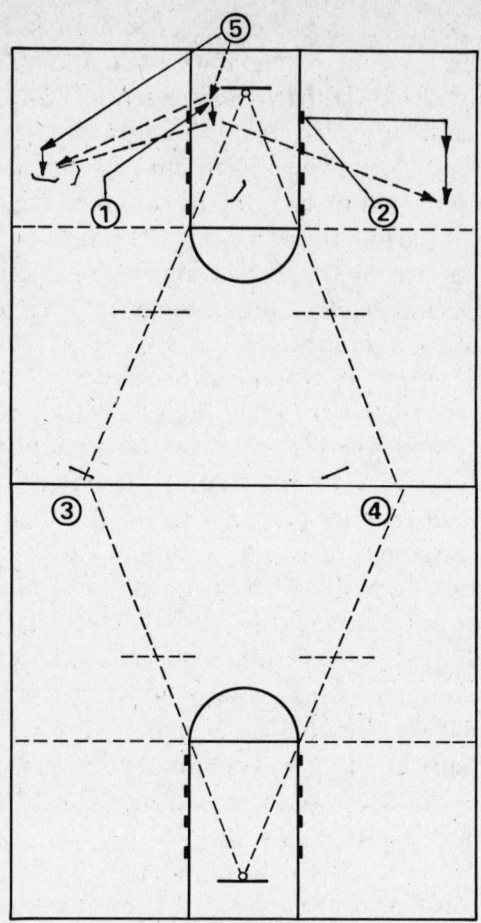

Diagram 6-9
*Full-Court Attack
Versus Pressure*

sume the same position of guard 2 on the opposite side. With the spread and the ball in bounds, you can tell immediately if you are facing a man-for-man or zone press. If it is a man-for-man press, we simply clear the area and have guard 1 bring the ball up the court one-on-one. If it is a zone press, it will probably attempt to force the ball to the side and then trap. If this takes place, guard 1 holds his position and looks for a quick return pass before the side man has been trapped. He will then, since the defense has overplayed to the trap, pass to the opposite side to guard 2, who will move the ball up the side by passing or dribbling to initiate the offense. (Diagram 6-10) If by chance guard 2 is denied, forwards 3

relieving pressure   73

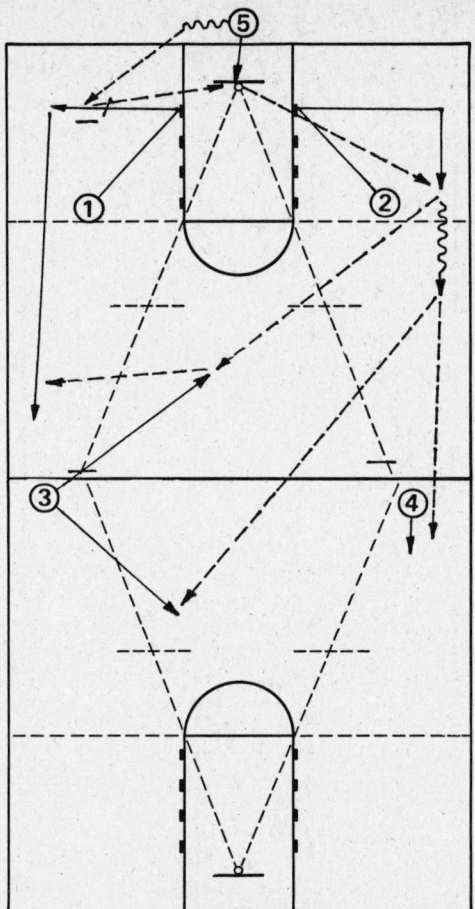

Diagram 6-10
*Full-Court Attack
Versus Pressure*

and 4 cut straight to the ball. Guard 1 will pass to the one that is open, in this case, forward 3. Both side men, guard 2 and center 5, go backdoor.

If the pass to the side is immediately trapped and guard 1 is denied, forward 3 cuts straight to the ball, receives the pass, and looks for guard 2 going backdoor. As forward 3 cuts to the ball, forward 4 cuts to the basket to draw the defense. (Diagram 6-11)

Again, the center has just picked up the ball. Both guards cut to the wide-lane marker on the signal. They are not free, but they have jammed their defensive men. It is important that they move all the way to the lane marker, plant their inside foot, and cut

74 relieving pressure

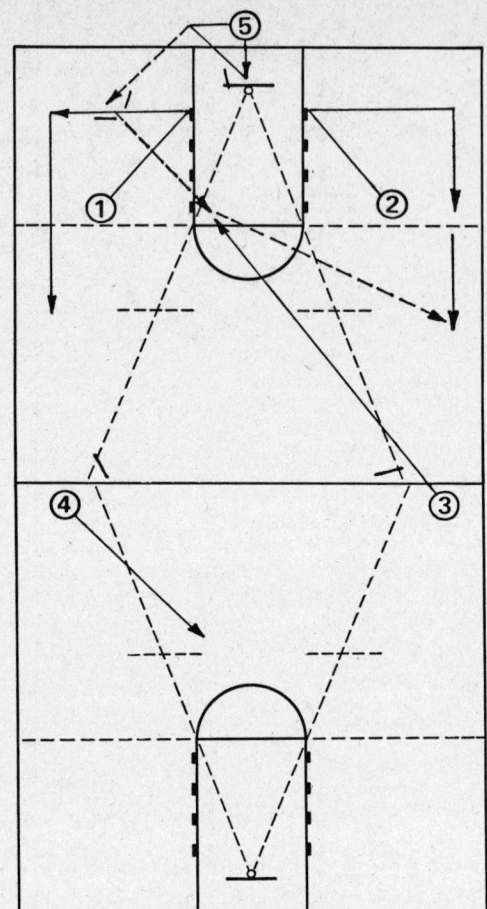

Diagram 6-11
Full-Court Attack
Versus Pressure

straight to the sideline. (Diagram 6-11) Center 5 determines the open man. It should be pointed out that he may in this instance run with him, pass him the ball, and step quickly inside. If the center is not denied, he may receive a quick return pass and pass the ball to guard 2, as illustrated in Diagram 6-10. If the center is denied, forward 3 cuts straight to the ball. Forward 4 cuts to the basket. Guard 2 moves up the sideline. Guard 1 passes to forward 3, who looks for guard 2 going backdoor, forward 4 cutting to the basket, or guard 1 cutting out of the double-team. This will enable

relieving pressure 75

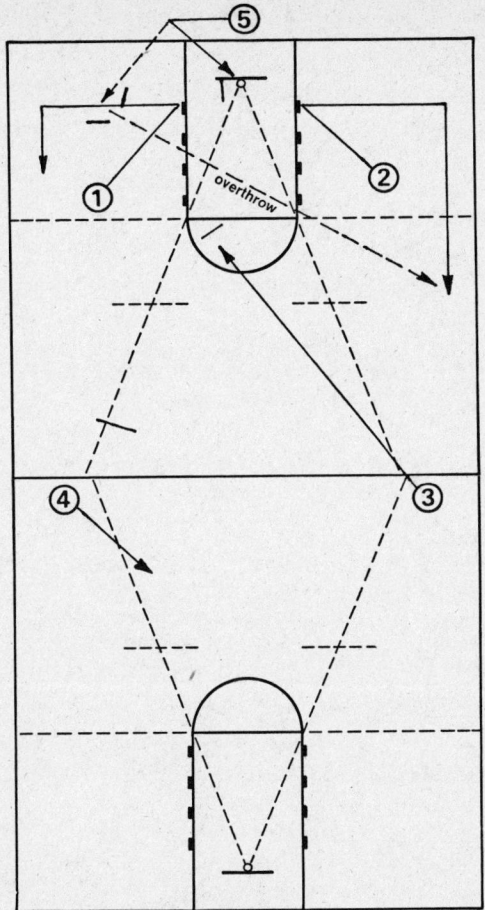

Diagram 6-12
*Full-Court Attack
Versus Pressure*

us to penetrate with a delayed fast-break type action or run into our swing-and-cut pattern. If center 5 and forward 3 coming to the ball are denied, guard 2 moves up to the sideline and looks for an overthrow. (Diagram 6-12) This is a safe pass since the entire side of the floor is open as a result of the double-team and denials.

A team must work against pressure daily. The success of pressure relief is almost entirely on the element of surprise, the lack of preparation, and the immaturity of the opposing team.

7
offensive entries—
multiple sets

Offensive entries or multiple sets are virtually the same thing. Different offensive entries have long been a part of the overall offensive scheme. Football coaches have used multiple sets successfully to spread defenses and to force specific coverage by the defense. Basketball coaches, as a rule, attempt to stick fairly close to their basic sets. However, a few employ these tactics very effectively.

A team that can use these tactics without detracting from its basic offensive philosophy will add another dimension to its offensive attack. Most teams, through scouting reports, films, and previous games, are well-prepared for their opponents' normal sets. Facing a team with a different look forces the defense to adjust in a manner it has not prepared for. A different look or different entry may be very simple offensively. By the same token, it could in reality present problems for the defense. Multiple sets offer the chance to place certain individuals in advantageous positions for quick, individual moves and scoring opportunities. This philosophy also serves to make pressing teams play a little more conservatively as it is virtually impossible to prepare for all possibilities.

78   offensive entries — multiple sets

Many offenses, by their design, are not flexible enough to carry out these methods capably. The flexibility of the swing-and-cut offers excellent opportunities to add this efficient dimension.

I discussed the basic alignment or normal set in Chapter 2. However, let me make one addition at this point. In the normal approach, center 5 always screens opposite the initial pass. It is effective to screen the same side occasionally.

SCREENING THE SAME SIDE

From the normal or basic set, guard 2 makes the initial pass to forward 4. Center 5, instead of moving to the opposite corner of the free throw line, steps to the ball side and sets the identical screen previously described in the basic cut for guard 2, who made the initial pass. Guard 2 makes his initial move as though he was going away and low (as in our basic pattern). On his second or third step, as he moves away he will plant his left foot and cut quickly and sharply off the center screen to the basket. If he does not receive the ball, he steps to the low man in the screen position on the same side as the post. Guard 1 moves low to the wide-lane marker on the weak side. Forward 3 moves his defensive man quickly toward the basket and cuts high to the 3 spot off guard 1's screen. (Diagram 7-1) If the one-cut and two-cut have not pro-

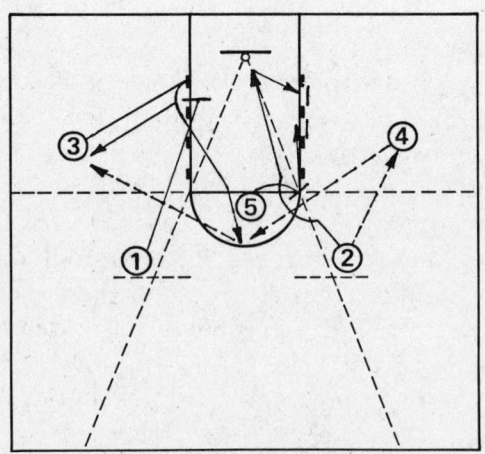

Diagram 7-1
Screening the Same Side

duced a scoring opportunity, forward 4 passes the ball to forward 3 in the three spot, who in turn passes to guard 1, who has popped out to the wing. We are now in the swing-and-cut.

STRONGSIDE SET

The strongside set is probably the simplest and easiest way to get into the offense. It is a different look and can be just as effective. The strongside set can be especially beneficial in the early teaching stages as personnel may be placed in a set position, eliminating a screen, four cuts, and one pass. (Diagram 7-2) One quick pass to the weakside wing and the initial move is executed off of a double screen. The strongside set also offers a one-man front, which has certain advantages that will be elaborated upon later in this chapter. It also enables the personnel to be placed advantageously, enabling your best shooter, strongest cutter, or best one-on-one player to take positions that will bring immediate strength to the attack.

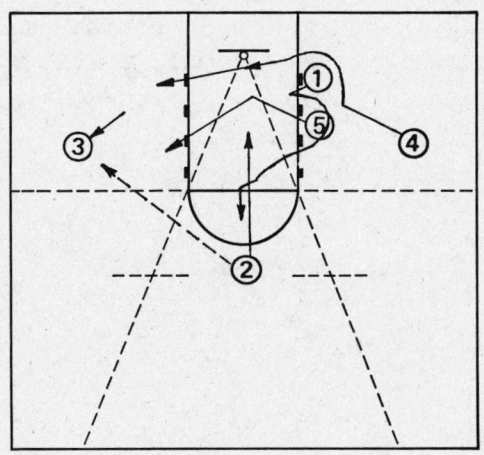

Diagram 7-2
Strongside Set

Guard 2 becomes the point guard operating in the three spot. Guard 1 sets up at the low position of the double screen. Forward 4 takes his position one step below the foul line extended and ap-

80   offensive entries — multiple sets

proximately two and one-half steps in from the sideline. The post man assumes his position as the high man in the double screen.

Guard 2 ignites the swing-and-cut action by passing to forward 3, who is cutting out to the normal wing position. Forward 4, timing his cut, cuts over or under the double screen at the exact moment forward 3 receives the pass. Guard 1 fakes to the inside and cuts to the top. The post man 5 cuts across the lane to daylight. The swing-and-cut continuity is now in motion. (Diagram 7-2)

ONE-MAN FRONT

I have just discussed a one-man front possibility and will mention several others as I discuss the stacks and double post. However, I think of the one-man front most seriously from a 1-3-1 set. (Diagram 7-3) Bear in mind that there are other options from all of these sets should the defense respond unfavorably or in a way we don't anticipate.

Guard 2 will again be the point or ball-handling guard. In this set we usually place our strong forward, forward 3, on the low post position with his inside foot on the wide-lane marker. Forward 4 will take his normal position, except he will be one step

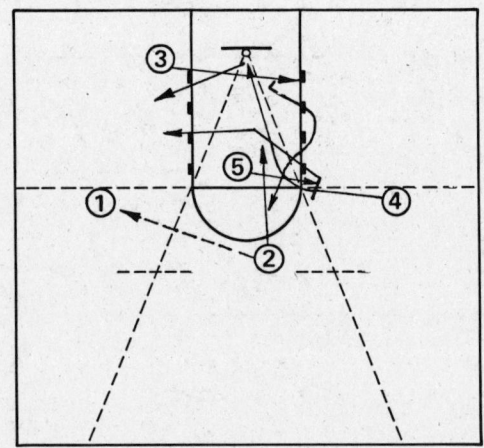

Diagram 7-3
One-Man Front or 1-3-1

above the foul line extended. Guard 1 will position himself in the same position as forward 4 on the opposite side of the court. Post man 5 will take his position on the high post in the center of the free throw line. (Diagram 7-3)

Guard 2 may pass to guard 1 or forward 4 on the wings, or to post 5 at the high post position. As the pass is made to either wing, post 5 will screen opposite just as he does in the normal pattern. Guard 2 has passed to guard 1 on the wing. Post 5 now screens opposite. Forward 4 will cut off the post screen to the basket. Forward 3, in the low post position, will cross the lane to the opposite side, clearing the area for the cut of forward 4, and placing himself in a position as the back-side rebounder. Guard 2 moves low to the basket. Forward 3 cuts to the top. Post 5 cuts to the ball and the swing-and-cut is again in motion. (Diagrams 7-3 and 7-4)

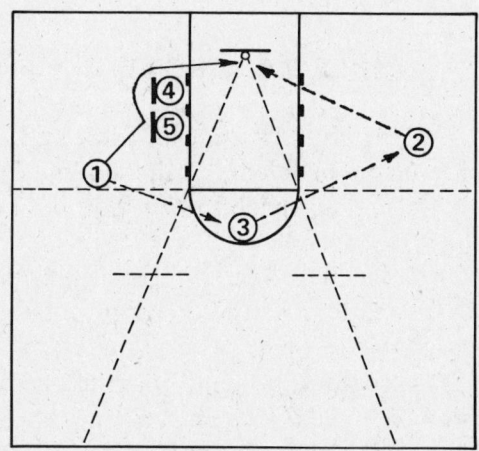

Diagram 7-4
Return to Swing-and-Cut

If pressure is being applied to the wings, guard 2 may choose to pass to post 5. Normally the defensive men would slough off the wings when this happens, enabling the post man to pass laterally to the wing of his choice. On completing this pass, he would immediately screen opposite and the continuity would be exactly as described in the previous paragraph. (Diagram 7-5)

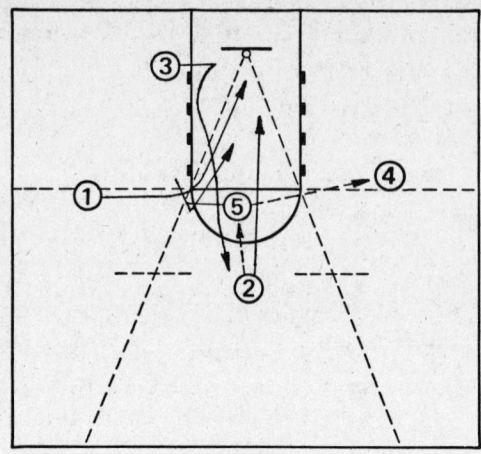

Diagram 7-5
1-3-1 Initial Pass to Post

THREE-MAN FRONT

The three-man front gives us another look and adds an additional pressure tactic to the problems of the defense by using three simple maneuvers: flash post, backdoor action, and a simple cut over the ball.

Guard 2 again is the ball handler. He attempts to start the action as close to the middle of the court as possible and about three to five steps above the top of the foul circle. The outside players, guard 1 and forward 4, position themselves approximately 15 feet on either side of guard 2 and one and one-half to two steps in front of him. The posts, forward 3 and post 5, place their inside foot on the wide-lane marker. (Diagram 7-6)

On a signal, either verbal or recognition from guard 2, the double posts, forward 3 and post 5, will flash forward to the corners of the free throw line. They may use straight quick cuts, crosses, or fake crosses. Guard 2 will pass to the post that is open, post 5 in this case. At the exact moment the ball touches the hands of post 5, forward 4 cuts backdoor from the three-man front position. If he is open, the post will pass him the ball for the lay-up. In the meantime, guard 2 has faked away and now cuts over the ball for the basket. Post 5, upon handing the ball off to guard 2, rolls

offensive entries — multiple sets 83

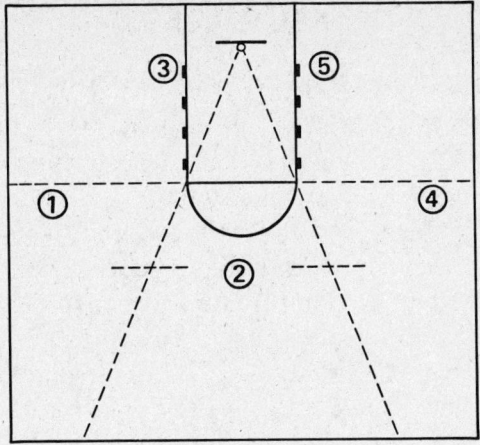

Diagram 7-6
Three-Man Front

to the basket. If none of these options is available, guard 2 passes to guard 1, who is now at the point or three spot. Guard 1 swings the ball to forward 4, who was the backdoor cutter. Forward 3 crosses the lane to become the low man in the screen. Post 5 takes the high position in the screen and the swing-and-cut is operative. (Diagram 7-7)

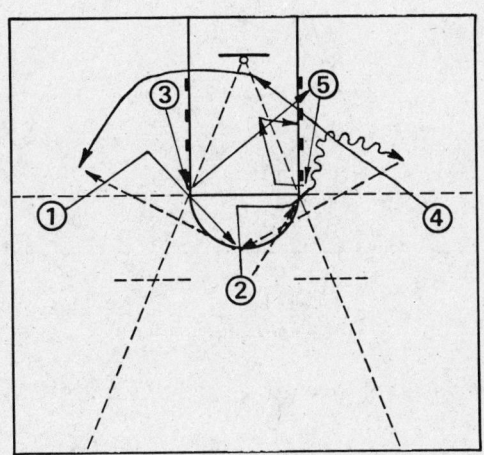

Diagram 7-7
*Three-Man Front
into Swing-and-Cut*

84   offensive entries — multiple sets

HIGH STACK

The high stack offers virtually no change but definitely a different look. Forwards 3 and 4 and post 5 assume the exact positions they do in the normal set. Guard 1 positions himself directly in front of post 5 facing the ball. Guard 2 is now in a one-man front. (Diagram 7-8) Guard 2 takes the key for his initial pass from the way the defensive man is playing guard 1. He may pass to either wing accordingly. For the sake of convenience we will assume the defensive man is playing guard 1 high right, and guard 2 chooses to pass to forward 4. Guard 1 immediately pivots tight and quickly off post 2 and cuts to the basket. Post 5 will aid the cut by sliding to the ball one big step, thereby obstructing guard 1's defensive man even more. All other personnel will move to the normal swing-and-cut moves. (Diagram 7-9) Guard 1 and post 5, by working together, can possibly free guard 1 for one or two baskets a game.

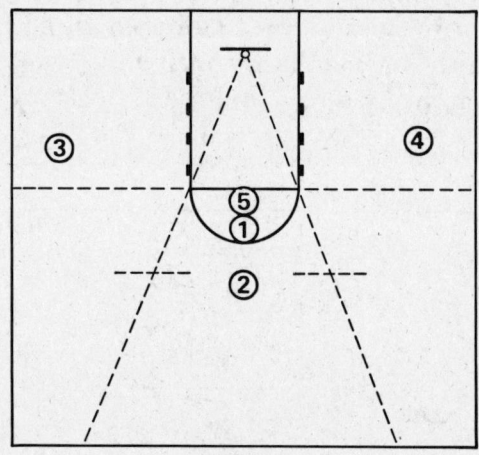

Diagram 7-8
High Stack

Another simple yet somewhat confusing set, when looking at it defensively, is an adjustment from the high stack. Forwards 3 and 4 set themselves low with their inside foot on the wide-lane markers. Using good timing with guard 2, they either cross or straight cut to their normal positions. The high-stack action, previously described into the swing-and-cut, follows.

offensive entries — multiple sets   85

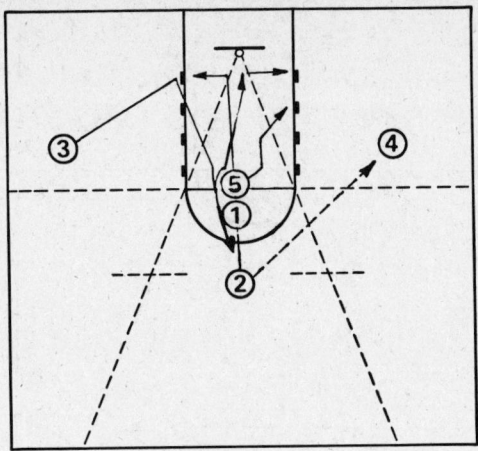

Diagram 7-9
*High Stack
into Swing-and-Cut*

LOW STACK

Stack action has a tendency to present problems for the defense. Although I did not discuss stack action in the chapter on relieving pressure, stack action does provide techniques that are most conducive to relief moves. Many teams stack regularly to avoid pressure tactics or to discourage pressure by the defense. Stack methods are very successful at freeing the forwards and inside players. Stack action is another look, another recognition for the defense, and another adjustment to cope with. These techniques are so simple offensively that they add no problems whatsoever. A team may use any combination of stacks and place personnel in the desired positions to attack the defense effectively with a minimum of ball handling.

I use the low stack to add an additional offensive entry into our basic swing-and-cut pattern. Guards 1 and 2 line up just as they do in the normal swing-and-cut set. Forwards 3 and 4 place themselves with their inside foot on the wide-lane markers. (Diagram 7-10) Post man 5 will line up directly behind either forward. In this case, he is lining up behind forward 3. (Diagram 7-10) Using good timing with the ball handlers, forwards 3 and 4 cut to their normal swing-and-cut positions. Post man 5, at the same

offensive entries — multiple sets

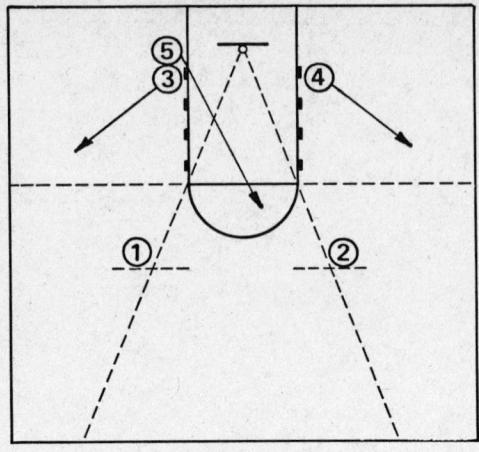

Diagram 7-10
Low Stack

moment, will cut to the high center post, or if the ball handler has already indicated his preference, to the screen position at the corner of the free throw line away from the ball. All personnel are now in their normal swing-and-cut set and the offense is ready to proceed.

LOW STACK AND CROSS

The low stack and cross will find our personnel positioned exactly the same as for the low stack. The maneuver is simple. Forward 3 cuts behind forward 4 and moves quickly to the normal forward position. Forward 4 cuts behind post 5 to the opposite forward position. Post 5 delays until the forwards clear him and then cuts to the high post as in the low stack. The ball handlers choose the side they deem most effective and initiate the swing-and-cut. (Diagram 7-11)

LOW DOUBLE STACK

The low double stack finds us again in a one man front. Forwards 3 and 4 and 5 line up exactly as they do in the low stack. Guard 1, usually the big guard, will set himself behind forward 4.

offensive entries — multiple sets   87

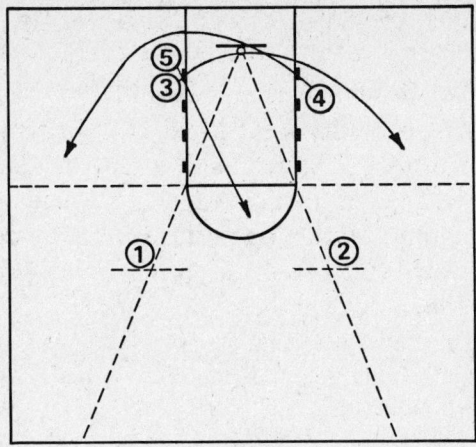

Diagram 7-11
Low Stack and Cross

(Diagram 7-12) Guard 1 will make the long cut high to his normal guard position, receiving a pass from guard 2 as he clears his defensive man. Forwards 3 and 4 flash to their normal wing or forward positions, and post 5 flashes high. Guard 1, upon receiving the pass from guard 2, passes to forward 3 flashing out. The swing-and-cut, through yet another simple set, is in action again. (Diagram 7-12)

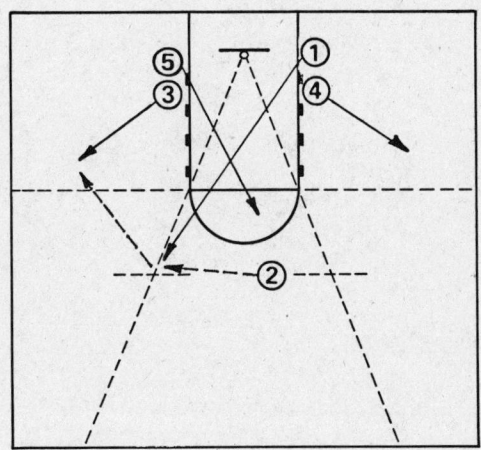

Diagram 7-12
Low Double Stack

GUARD-FORWARD INTERCHANGE

Another very effective entry, originating with a normal set, yet offering an entirely different look, is the guard-forward interchange. The majority of the teams preparing to defend the swing-and-cut will do so against the normal swing-and-cut alignment with the guards out front and the forwards inside. The defensive guards will be better prepared to face the initial cut off the post screen. They are prepared to slide through, loop, or switch. We sometimes use the guard-forward interchange to initiate the action, thereby possibly forcing defensive personnel into positions that they are not familiar with. We interchange the guards to the forward positions and the forwards out front to initiate the action. (Diagram 7-13) We find most defensive forwards have more difficulty with the initial cut than the quicker backcourt men who are more familiar with these techniques. The defense would have a most difficult task in attempting to drill every defensive man in every position in pregame preparations. When you find the defensive forward who cannot adjust to the back screen set by the center, you are ready and capable of exploiting his weakness. I recall one particular game where one of our forwards had six uncontested lay-ups because his defensive forward had trouble with the center screen.

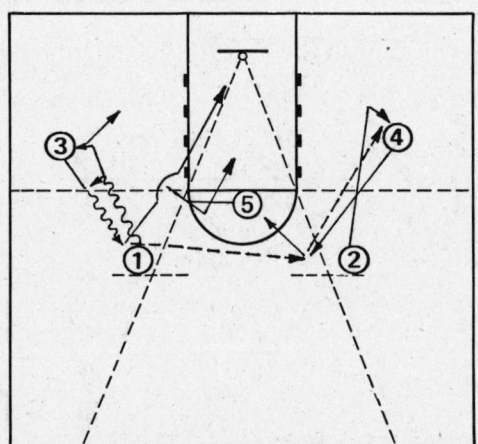

Diagram 7-13
Guard-Forward Interchange

If we take the normal set into consideration, these different sets afford a team about ten possible different entries into the swing-and-cut pattern. If the methods of relieving pressure are included, about five additional ones can be added. I would not suggest that a team attempt to prepare all of these entries for immediate use. In fact, this would be foolish, since it would be impossible to attempt to saddle a team with so much material. I do suggest that you not show the same approach each time down the floor. This enables the defense to adjust too easily to your pattern.

Multiple entries will also afford you the opportunity to place your personnel in strategic offensive positions and to bring superior personnel into focus more quickly and effectively.

Evaluate your personnel, analyze the defensive strengths of your opponent, and select the offensive entries that will be most suitable for your game plan.

8

counteraction

Counteraction is a must in any offensive plan. It is designed to take advantage of the defense if they should attempt to move too quickly to reinforce the point of attack, or to overplay leads and force the offense out of their normal routine. The execution of the play or the offense is exactly the same up to the point of the counteraction. We believe the defense will be confused if they are denying the normal pattern. The need for counteraction is indicated when the defense continues to overplay or to adjust drastically to the point of attack, thereby restricting offensive movement.

The very nature of the swing-and-cut pattern provides us easy adjustment to counteraction and allows the offensive continuity to proceed should the counteraction be unsuccessful. Counteraction, even if it fails in the scoring attempt, can be effective in the overall offensive plan by forcing the defense to play honest.

GUARD COUNTER

We use the guard counter as a very effective called play when we need a quick two points. This is an excellent play to call immediately after a time-out because all personnel can be reminded of their assignments. The guard counter is run only from the normal set or the drive through. We use only these two methods, so our personnel will not have too many techniques or detail to confuse their execution. We like to select the guard with the best shooting touch, as this play presents a finesse shot and should present an unmolested attempt when properly executed.

The play is initiated opposite the guard selected to take the shot. Guard 2 passes to forward 3 and moves away as in the normal first cut. Guard 1 cuts off post 5's screen to the basket and to the low position in the double screen. Forward 4 fakes low and cuts high to the three spot. Post 5, after screening for guard 1, cuts to his position as the top man in the double screen. (Diagram 8-1) Forward 3, cutting high to the three spot, must get himself open. This is a must. Forward 4, who has the ball, passes sharply to forward 3 at the point. He immediately cuts between guard 1 and post 5 in the double screen. Post 5 starts his normal cut across the lane. Guard 1 fakes two steps to the inside and cuts quickly back off forward 4's movement. Guard 1, on clearing forward 4, should curl slightly toward the point and forward 3 with the ball. Forward 3, on receiving the ball from forward 4, makes an exaggerated fake to guard 2, who has flashed out to the normal wing position, and quickly passes to guard 1 for an eight to twelve-foot jump shot off the glass. (Diagram 8-1)

In the event the shot does not materialize into a high percentage attempt, guard 1 can dribble out to the normal wing position. Guard 2 cuts off the double screen by post 5 and forward 4 and the swing-and-cut continuity is sustained.

THREE-CUT COUNTER

Many teams switch or zone the weakside action of the swing-and-cut. When the point man passes to the weakside wing, which in essence converts the weak side to the strong side as a result of the cutting action to the ball, the interchange between the point man and the weakside wing coming to the point is quite often zoned or switched. If this presents a problem in making the pass to the point or the three spot, the three-cut counter can be most effective.

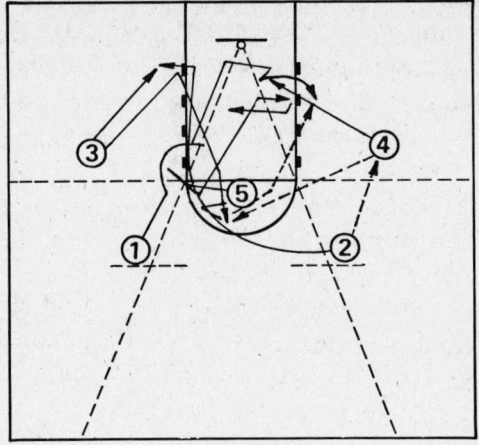

Diagram 8-1
Guard Counter

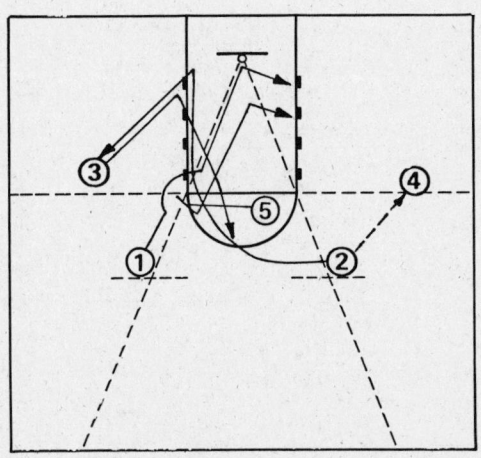

Diagram 8-2
Three-Cut Counter Strong Side

The initial pass has been made. The strong side with the double screen set low has been established. (Diagram 8-2) The zoning or switching is presenting a problem. Forward 4 passes the ball to forward 3, who has moved into the three spot at the point. Forward 3 swings the ball to guard 2 on the wing and starts his move toward the basket. Post 5 cuts to the ball. Guard 1, realizing the switching or zoning is causing a problem, counters this by faking two steps in his normal cut toward the top, forcing the defense into their zoning or switching action. He quickly changes his direction and cuts quickly and tightly under the double screen to the ball side. Guard 2 passes the ball to guard 1 as he clears the screen for a quick ten- to twelve-foot jump shot. In the event the jump shot does not materialize, and to clear the area for guard 1, guard 2, the moment he passes the ball, rubs off the double screen to the basket looking for an overthrow. (Diagram 8-2A) If the swing-and-cut continuity must be maintained, forward 3 rolls back to the top in the swing position, and guard 2 prepares to cut out to the weakside wing.

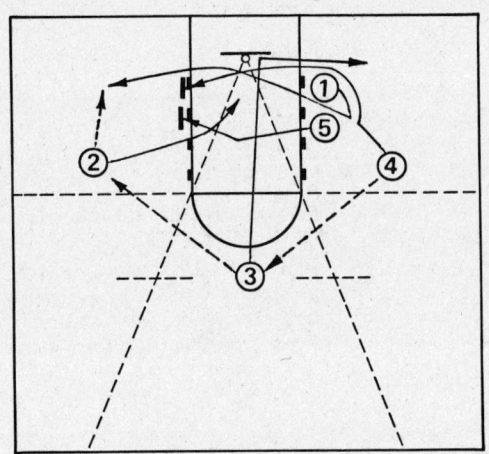

Diagram 8-2A
Three-Cut Counter

SWING-PASS COUNTER

The swing-pass counter is very closely related to the guard counter, except that it is spontaneously executed when incorporated into the swing-and-cut continuity. The responsibility for effective execution of the swing-pass counter rests with the low man in the double screen and the man on the point. I must emphasize once more that the swing-pass counter is a *spontaneous* reaction within the confines of the swing-and-cut continuity. When we feel the swing-pass counter will be an effective countermove, it is a definite adjustment to the continuity. The adjustment is executed by the low man in the double screen. Guard 1 is the low man in the double screen, and post 5 is the high man, as normal. The ball is in the hands of forward 4. Forward 3 is on the point and guard 2 is on the weak side. (Diagram 8-3) Forward 4 passes to the swing man, forward 3, on the point and quickly makes the undercut off the double screen. Post 5 makes his normal cut across the lane. Guard 1 in the low position takes one step toward his normal cut to the top and quickly backs out two steps. (Diagram 8-3) Forward 3 in the swing position has received the pass from forward 4, makes an exaggerated fake to guard 2 on the weak side, and quickly and sharply counters to guard 1 who should have a short jump shot of about 12 feet.

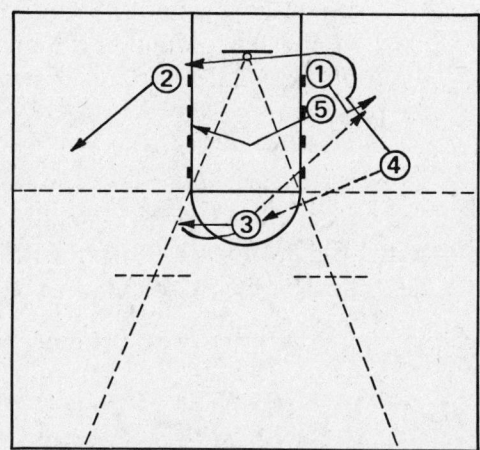

Diagram 8-3
Swing-Pass Counter

If the counter attempt is not successful, guard 1 simply cuts wider to the normal forward position. At that point he receives the pass from forward 3 and the continuity continues. Faking the counteraction allows forward 4 and post 5 to assume the same positions they would have if forward 3 had swung the ball to guard 2. This places guard 2 in position to cut off the double screen should the ball have to be countered wide.

96 counteraction

Remember, when in the swing-pass counter pattern, the low man in the double screen on each swing takes one step toward the top and then steps wide two steps.

POST COUNTER

The post counter is a most effective scoring play. We list this play on our game plan chart as a high percentage success factor. The post counter is similar to the swing-pass counter with adjustments by the post man, the low man in the double screen, and a slight adjustment by the strongside wing. The post counter is most proficient when we have lured the defense into vigorously attempting to defend against and deny the regular swing-and-cut attempts. The offense is initiated through the normal set or any of the multiple sets. All personnel have made their initial cuts on the pass to forward 4. Forward 4, after looking at the one cut and the two cut, will pass the ball quickly and sharply to forward 3 cutting to the three spot at the point. Immediately upon releasing the ball, forward 4 cuts quickly over post 5, who is the top man in the screen. Post 5 starts his cut across the lane as in the normal pattern immediately as forward 4 clears. Post 5 steps into the lane with his high foot, in this case his right. He crosses over with his left, followed by the right. As the right foot is planted on the third step,

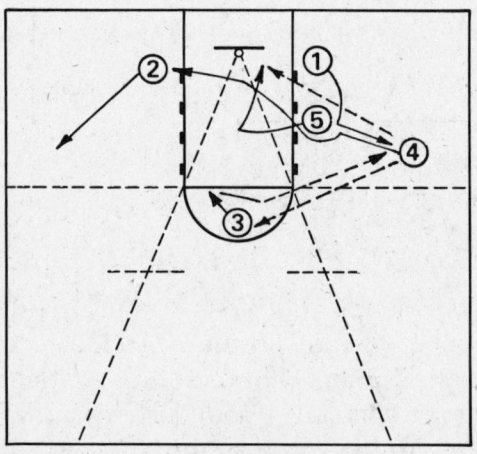

Diagram 8-4
Post Counter

post 5 takes a deep drop-step with his left foot and crabs toward the basket. Guard 1 takes one step toward the top and quickly cuts to the forward position vacated by forward 4. Forward 3, upon receiving the ball from forward 4, fakes the ball to guard 2 on the weak side using an exaggerated fake. He then quickly counter passes to guard 1, who upon receiving the pass, immediately flips it to post 5, who has crabbed low. This gives post 5 a short hook or power move with the defense behind him. (Diagram 8-4) In the event the defense is not influenced and the post is not open, forward 4 will cut back across the lane to form the double screen with post 5. Guard 1 will pass to forward 3 at the top, who in turn will swing the ball to guard 2 on the weak side. This brings us quickly into swing-and-cut action.

LOB COUNTER

The lob counter can be a demoralizing, intimidating play if it is attempted with the right personnel in position for the counteraction. The lob counter is not a frequently used play, but carefully blended into the offense it can prove to be most effective. It is especially helpful in keeping the defense honest and forcing them to play it straight.

The lob counter is effective when the three cut is being denied and the defense is switching on the interchange. Guard 2 passes to forward 4 and moves away and low. Guard 1 and post 5 set their normal double screen. Forward 3, cutting to the top, is being overplayed. Forward 4, seeing this, fakes forward 3 to the basket, and counters with a lob pass over the defense. (Diagram 8-5) Let me reiterate, percentage is with the big forwards or exceptionally good jumpers. It is important that the ball is lobbed about two feet in front of the basket so that it may be easily handled for an easy two-hand tip-in or a stuff shot.

As forward 3 cuts to the three spot, it is very important that he plant his right foot at least one step above the top of the key. It is also important that he does not extend his cut above this point. If the cut is too short, the timing of the lob pass from forward 3 will have to be rushed, and the defense will be confined to an area so tight, that a quick reaction could break up the play. If the three cut is overextended, it forces forward 4 to hold the ball too long

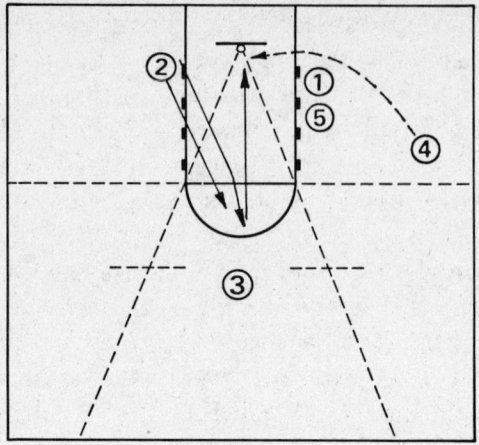

Diagram 8-5
Lob Counter

and affords the defense the opportunity to recognize the attempt. It is very important that forward 3, on planting his right foot one step above the circle, cuts directly to the basket, preparing to extend himself upward to receive the lob pass and lay the ball in the basket. The straight cut will also insure against the defensive man on guard 2 switching to the inside, as guard 2 will be slightly outside the lane. The lob counter is equally effective against an overplaying, switching defense, or an overplaying straight man-for-man. The straight man-for-man is vulnerable to the quick cut. The switching defense is vulnerable to confusion on the switch.

If the defense reacts unfavorably, forward 3 will pass to guard 2 coming to the top on the interchange and the swing-and-cut continues

9

post series

Post play is an important and effective part of every offensive plan. Post players with good size, strong hands, quickness, mobility, and jumping ability determine the success of the post action in relation to the level of their ability. Stand-up post play, even with athletes of exceptional ability, has become less and less functional as a result of more sophisticated defensive plans. Movement, alternating posts, and counteraction will increase post-play potential for the defense. Teams that are not blessed with super talent will gain positive results when applying the aforementioned techniques to post action.

The swing-and-cut relies heavily on strong post action as a basic element in making the swing-and-cut a versatile attack. The extent of the post emphasis, of course, is based on the ability of the personnel available. The versatility of the swing-and-cut allows anyone in the lineup to become a post player. The movement allows this action to be disguised. Alternating post men is beneficial when such a play is possible. A small forward or guard can be forced to play the defensive post if his offensive opponent quickly assumes a post position. This places the defensive man at a distinct disadvantage when forcing him to play a position he is not well-rehearsed in, is not used to playing, and probably does not relish the idea of playing. Post play probably draws more defensive fouls than any other position; therefore, alternating posts enables the offense to exploit an opponent with excessive fouls.

POST ACTION OFF THE PATTERN

The basic swing-and-cut continuity provides constant, moving post action. This action, bolstered by the one cut, and the five cut, provides us with the necessary inside phase of the offense. The ability of the post man determines the ability with which this action may be sophisticated. The two cut, coupled with the rollback following the five cut, provides constant post action.

Post play off the basic swing-and-cut pattern is predicated on what we call cutting to daylight. The two cut following post 5's screen for guard 1 is based entirely on the action of the defense. If the screen is successful and a switch results, center 5 should cut straight to the basket. (Diagram 9-1) With the defensive man at his back, this should enable him to receive a quick pass from forward 4 for a lay-up or a lob pass to the basket. In the event the defense prohibits these passes, guard 1, realizing the defensive center has been forced to switch, should move to the corner. This enables center 5 to post the smaller guard unmolested. If the defensive center refuses to follow guard 1 to the corner, forward 4 will pass to guard 1 in the corner, forcing the defensive center to move out on him or give up a corner shot. If he does move out, of course, guard 1 will now feed post 5. (Diagram 9-1)

Another simple and always present post technique is what we call the *gut* play. This action takes place as forward 4 passes to forward 3 at the point and prepares to cut over or under the double screen. As forward 3 receives the pass, and depending on defensive deployment, center 5 quickly and forcibly steps back into the middle with feet well spread, hips low, and hands and arms extended toward the ball. This crabbing motion will enable forward 3 to quickly dump the ball to him right in the gut of the defense for his choice of moves and shots. (Diagram 9-2) Not only is this an effective scoring play, but it makes the defense work exceptionally hard at defending every offensive move, thereby preventing help with other cutters and setting up counteraction.

post series   101

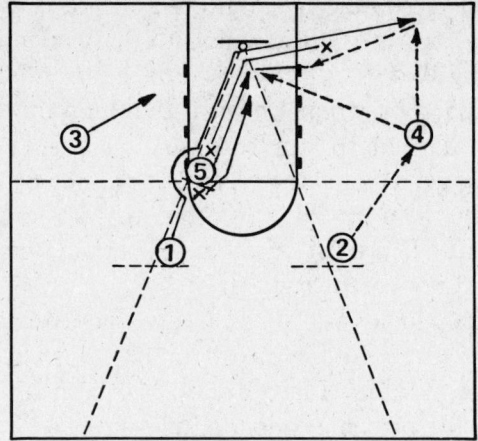

Diagram 9-1
Post Play—Two Cut

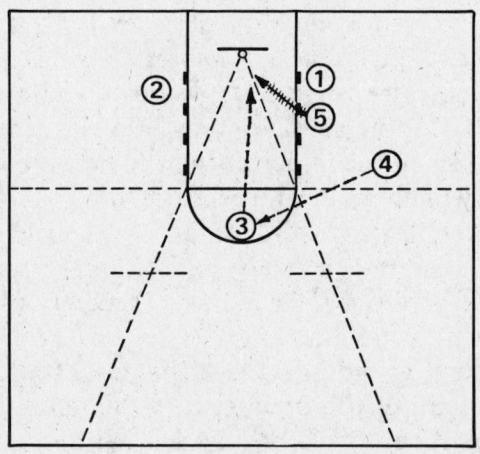

Diagram 9-2
Gut Play

SINGLE POST

Basic single post action is one of the oldest methods of attack and is extremely effective with the right type of personnel. The single post is by no means our primary set attack; however, with proper personnel it should be exploited to its fullest. Incorporating the single post into the swing-and-cut concept can be extremely rewarding. We may switch to the single post occasionally for a change of pace or when we have five men on the court who are particularly adapted to this offense. We keep it simple with very few options; we do not devote an abundance of time teaching it. However, I should point out that the most important and basic single post techniques are found in most every style of play and in actuality are taught and rehearsed daily.

Most of the single post techniques incorporated into our swing-and-cut concept are a result of my association several summers with Tex Winters. I have found his philosophy, ideas, and techniques involving post play most enlightening.

We seldom set up in the single post and operate exclusively from this set. We will, on numerous occasions, go into the single post through swing-and-cut action (as will be explained and illustrated in Chapter 10); or we may set up in the single post, look at the single post power momentarily, and revert to the swing-and-cut (as described and illustrated in Chapter 11).

The operating rules for the single post attack are explained and illustrated in Chapter 11. (Diagrams 11-1, 11-2, and 11-3) The line of deployment and the importance of forward 4 looking down the line of deployment and reading the defense should be continuously emphasized. (Diagrams 11-4, 11-5, 11-6, and 11-7) The number two pass by forward 4 actually initiates the offense. The pass from guard 2 to forward 4 (Diagram 11-2) merely places the ball in position to start the action.

Normally when we go into the single post attack through the swing-and-cut, we are of the opinion that the defensive setup will enable us to exploit the single post attack. With single post action as our immediate offensive objective, we have seven options in mind to combat the defensive strategy. It is of the utmost importance to rehearse your team to the point where they will always deploy themselves accurately, thus enabling you to read the defensive strategy accurately. An accurate evaluation of the defense is essential to successful execution.

pass to the post

The first option, of course, is forward 4 immediately looking down the line and passing immediately to the post, if the defensive post is playing behind or siding from the right or left side. (Diagrams 11-4, 11-5, and 11-6) If the defensive post is playing on the low side or the right side looking in, the ball will be fed to the right hand of the offensive post, as explained and illustrated in Chapter 11. (Diagram 11-5) If the defense is playing high on the left side as we look in, he will receive the pass to his left hand. (Diagram 11-6) If the ball is passed to the post man off the line of deployment, (Diagrams 11-5 and 11-6) this indicates the post man's offensive move to that side.

The defensive post man is now playing behind the offensive post. This normally tells the post man that since the ball is passed to him on the line of deployment, he is to help someone else with a pass, which brings into focus our second, third, and fourth options.

single split

The second option involves a simple screen down for the guard in the corner, freeing him for a quick jump shot over the screen. (Diagram 9-3) Forward 4, seeing the post man being played behind, passes him the ball and immediately screens down for guard 1. Guard 1 fakes a cut along the baseline and cuts back over the screen by forward 4 to receive a short pass from the center or post man, for a 12- to 15-foot jump shot.

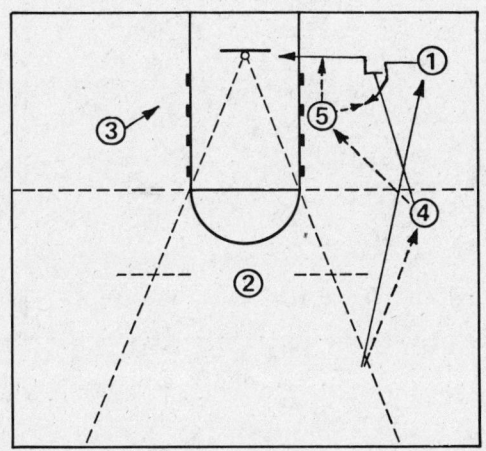

Diagram 9-3
Screen Down and Cut Away

cutaway

We will pick up the third option as forward 4 sets the screen for guard 1. (Diagram 9-3) A good screen should force a switch in defensive assignments. If the switch does occur, forward 4, immediately as guard 1 cuts over him, back pivots on his inside foot, uses a deep drop-step with the outside leg and foot, and immediately, as the outside foot is placed on the floor, cuts away to the basket looking for a flip pass from the center. This is an effective play and at times we actually call it from the bench. We call it cutaway.

double split

A fourth option occurs when the defense nullifies the single split and the cutaway. Guard 2 continued his cut to the center of the foul line where he sets a screen for guard 1. Guard 1 has either faked away or has driven his defensive man up into the key. His cut is over the screen of guard 2 to receive a short pass from the center for a 12- to 15-foot jump shot. (Diagram 9-4) We refer to this as our double split. The slight delay action makes it very effective

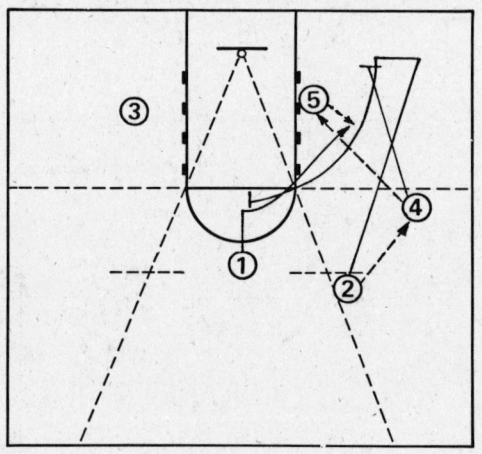

Diagram 9-4
Double Split

backdoor

The fifth option, what we refer to as our backdoor action, is in my opinion a key factor to how successful the single post can be. This technique is one of my favorite plays in basketball. We use the technique effectively in many phases of our offense. The backdoor option depends almost entirely on the weakside forward's ability to read the defensive coverage of the offensive center or post.

The ball is in the hands of forward 4, who is attempting to make the number two pass. Guard 1 is in the corner. Guard 2 is at the top of the key. Center 5 is in his normal single post position. Forward 3 reads the fact that center 5 is being fronted. He recognizes this as an automatic, fakes to the basket, and cuts to the ballside corner of the free throw line. Forward 4, with the ball, is aware that center 5 is being fronted, and he now looks for the defensive action on forward 3. If forward 3's defensive man is guarding him closely, forward 4 will overthrow to center 5, as illustrated in Diagram 11-8 in Chapter 11. If the defensive man guarding forward 3 falls off to protect against the overthrow, forward 4 will pass to forward 3, who will immediately face the basket. Center 5 has now stepped into his defensive man, placing his low foot wide and high. If the defensive man guarding forward 3 moves up to stop the shot, forward 3 quickly passes to center 5, stepping to the basket. If the defense doesn't come up, he has a 15-foot jump shot. Guard 2 also cuts backdoor to add an additional scoring possibility.

pinch post

Some defenses will front the post, cover the overthrow with the weakside defensive forward, and deny the backdoor area with the guard sloughing off of guard 2. When this situation occurs, forward 4 will pass quickly to guard 2 at the top of the key. Weakside forward 3 will move up to the corner of the free throw line where guard 2 may pass to him and pinch off for a drive, jump shot, or check pass as forward 3 rolls to the basket. He may choose to immediately drive hard off the screen by forward 3. (Diagram 9-5)

post series

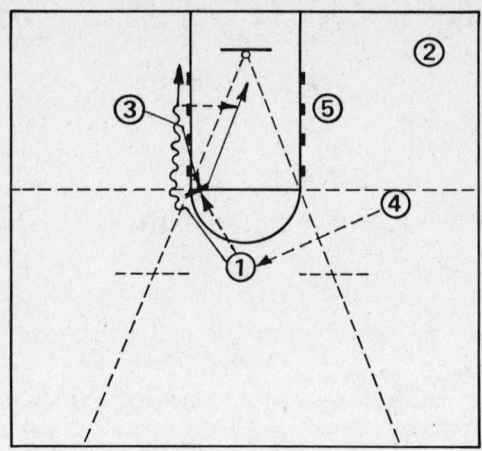

Diagram 9-5
Pinch Post

penetrating dribble

The penetrating dribble comes into effect when forward 4 looks down the line of deployment and finds center 5 being played behind. Forward 4's defensive man has sloughed back to prevent a pass to the post. Guard 1 is being overplayed in the corner. Guard 2 is being overplayed at the point. Upon recognizing this strategy, forward 4 takes one dribble directly toward the basket, thereby occupying his defensive man. Center 5, recognizing the dribble action, moves up the lane, places his high foot at the end of the foul line, and sets a screen for forward 4. Forward 4, after his one dribble toward the basket, changes direction to dribble over the center screen at the corner of the free throw line. As forward 4 clears this screen there are five options available. (Diagram 9-6) Forward 4 may take a jump shot. He may drive. He may check pass to center 5 rolling to the basket. He may pass to forward 3 cutting backdoor, or guard 2 may fan outside the foul line.

This penetrating action, as any penetrating movement does, draws defensive help, therefore creating numerous assist or check-pass opportunities.

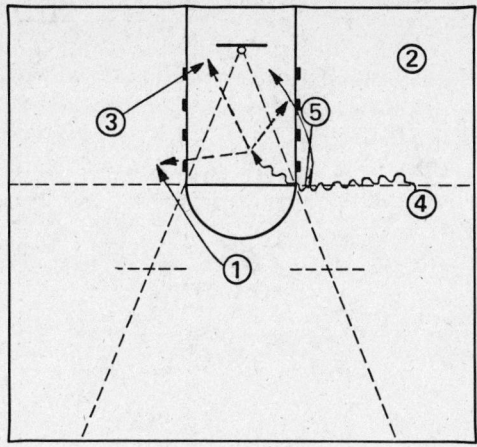

Diagram 9-6
Penetrating Dribble

CHOKE POST

The choke post may be incorporated into our regular swing-and-cut continuity. This enables us, in actuality, to post any player in our lineup. It is especially effective to post strong forwards and big guards with the posting action camouflaged through motion. It is an extremely effective inside maneuver disguised by the defense's efforts to combat a moving pattern.

The choke post position is taken each time the ball is swung. For example: forward 3 is at the point and has just swung the ball to guard 2 on the weakside wing. Forward 4 cuts off the double screen to the ball. Center 5 rolls back to the ball. Forward 3 cuts directly down the middle to the basket as guard 1 replaces him at the top of the key. Forward 3, upon reaching the basket and always facing the ball, pivots and steps outside the lane as he would normally do. As the ball is passed back to guard 1 in the swing position, forward 4 steps over his defensive man with his inside foot, crabbing into the middle of the lane. Guard 1 immediately passes him the ball to his outside hand. (Diagram 9-7) He is now in position for a short hook shot, power move, or short turn and jump shot.

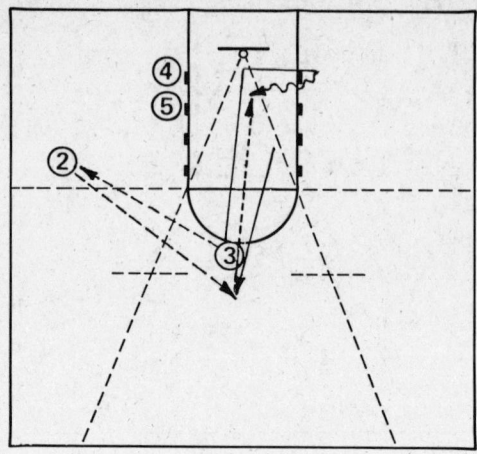

Diagram 9-7
Choke Post

If the defense does not allow the ball to be passed low to forward 3, he quickly cuts out to the wing position, receiving the swing pass from guard 1 and the continuity continues. Guard 1 will now become the choke post as forward 4 comes to the top.

The choke post technique, as incorporated into the pattern, may leave all personnel assuming the choke post position, or it may designate one or two competent players to post each time they move into this position. The other personnel will follow their normal swing-and-cut movement.

POST COUNTER

The post counter has already been explained and illustrated in Chapter 8. (Diagram 8-4) It is such an essential part of our post offense and especially our inside series that it must be mentioned in the chapter entitled post series.

We have scored at least two baskets a game with the post counter technique in every game since we added it to our offensive scheme. It has been an added dimension in our offensive plans since it forces the defensive post man to play honestly or cautiously. This makes our normal post cut more effective.

The post counter will not be effective unless much time and effort is spent on perfecting the post man's techniques. It is of the utmost importance for post 5 to make his initial move blend in perfectly with the normal swing-and-cut move. If the defensive post man has been normally fronting the post cut, the counter play is a must. If he is not fronting and the post man has been producing points, this success should set up the post counter adequately.

A key point in the success of the post counter, second only to the rehearsed techniques of the post man, is the ability of forward 3 to get open in the swing spot at the top of the key. Under normal conditions we do not screen down to free the three cut. When the post counter is called, guard 2 in this case will screen for forward 3 cutting to the top. (Diagram 9-10) In the event of switching defenses or zoning the back-side, guard 2 will move inside the switch, set the screen and cut back to the end of the free throw line on the ball side. He will receive the pass from forward 4, fake to the weak side and quickly pass to guard 1 popping out to feed post 5. (Diagram 9-8)

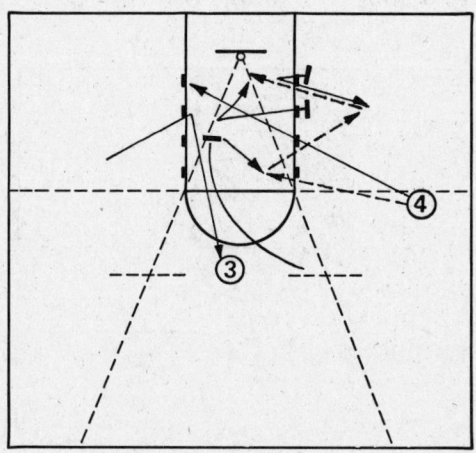

Diagram 9-8
*Post Counter
When Being Overplayed*

COMBINATION POST

We use the combination post as an auxiliary offense in three ways. We go into the combination set through the swing-and-cut.

post series

We set up in the combination and revert to the swing-and-cut, and we use it as a set pattern.

The combination will be explained here as a set pattern. The name *combination post* is a result of four definite posting actions: a regular low power post, a pinch post and two post men crabbing to the inside. We find the technique especially effective because it gives us the opportunity to exploit a strong post man as we relieve defensive pressure with motion, quick passes, and several other posting opportunities.

Going into the combination set, we find guard 1 at the point with the ball. Guard 2 is at the end of the foul line ready to cut out to the wing position. Forward 3 is the low man in the stack with center 5. Forward 3 has his inside foot on the wide-lane divider. Forward 4 is in the screen or pinch post position on the weakside end of the free throw line. His inside foot should be just above the free throw line and just inside the circle. His outside foot should be outside the circle. The body should be low with feet well-spread in a good screening position. (Diagram 9-9)

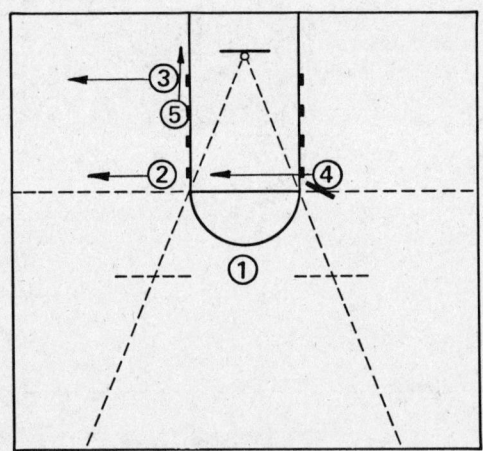

Diagram 9-9
Combination Post Strongside Alignment

The first option will find guard 1 passing to guard 2 on the wing, and forward 3 cutting to the corner facing inside. Guard 2, upon receiving the ball, immediately looks to post man 5. If post 5

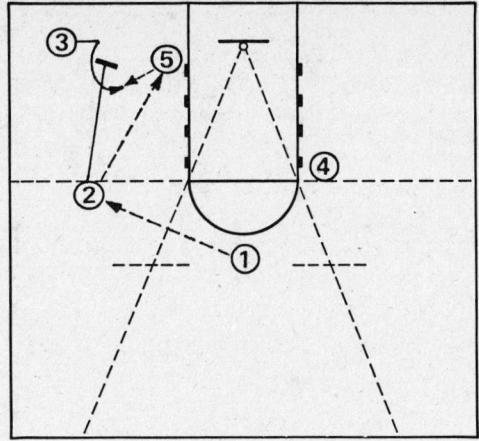

Diagram 9-9A
Combination Post—Screen Down

is open, guard 2 passes to him immediately and screens down for forward 3. (Diagram 9-9A) This should give post 5 an inside move or a quick pass to forward 3 coming off the screen by guard 2 for a 15-foot jump shot. If guard 2 finds the pass to post 5 too congested, he willl pass to forward 3 in the corner. Forward 3 will immediately look to the post, who has stepped high to position his defensive man. This should give forward 3 position for a baseline side pass and a strong power move. Forward 3 should screen high for guard 2 immediately upon releasing the ball. (Diagram 9-9B)

If forward 3 finds post 5 being fronted, he will look immediately to the backdoor area for forward 4. Forward 4, seeing that post 5 is being fronted, crosses to the near side of the free throw line looking for a pass from forward 3 or guard 2. This should also take out the back-side coverage. As forward 4 crosses the free throw lane, guard 1 will fan to the weak side. If forward 3 or guard 2 passes to forward 4, he immediately faces the basket for a quick flip to post 5. Post 5 has positioned his defensive man or a facing 15-foot jump shot in the event his defensive man does not move up. (Diagram 9-9C) If forward 4 is being denied, an overthrow to post 5 from forward 3 should be available.

In the event none of these possibilities exist, the ball will be passed back to guard 1 at the point, who will drive off the screen

112 post series

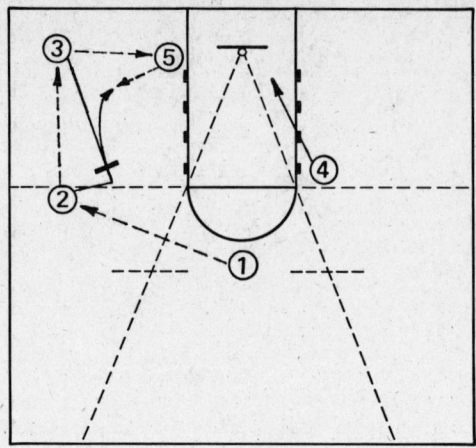

Diagram 9-9B
Combination Post—Screen High

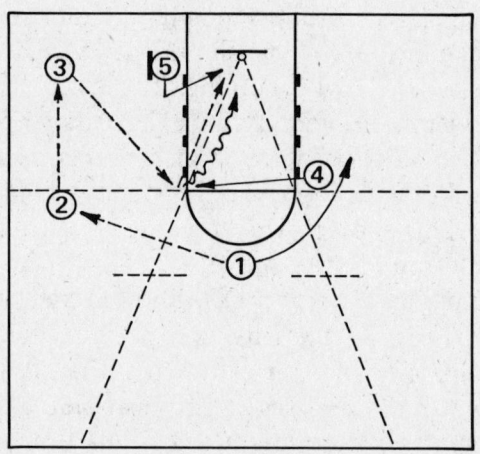

Diagram 9-9C
Combination Post—Post Fronted

by forward 4. Forward 4 will quickly roll out to the basket. Guard 1 is first looking for a drive to the basket, a jump shot, or check pass to forward 4 rolling to the basket or posting. (Diagram 9-9D) If guard 1 finds no openings, he quickly reverses the ball to forward 3 who has cut to the top. Forward 3 immediately looks inside for post 5 or forward 4 crab posting to the inside or a quick

post series   113

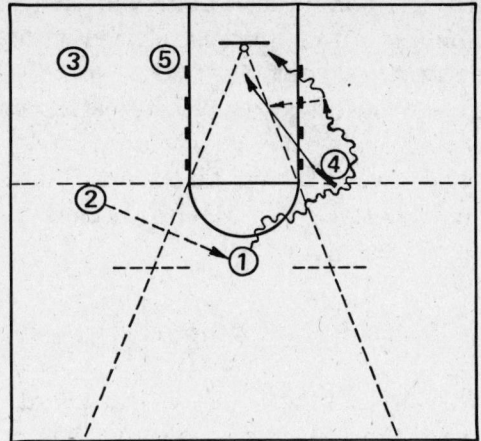

Diagram 9-9D
Combination Post—High Screen and Roll

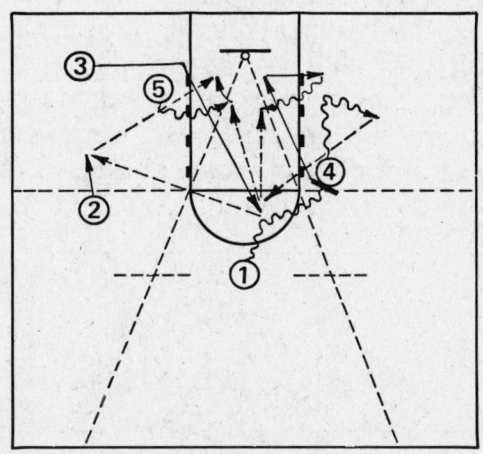

Diagram 9-9E
Combination Post—
Reversing Ball to Top and Looking Inside

pass to guard 2 or guard 1 on the wings who immediately feed the post men. (Diagram 9-9E) With the motion involved and the strong crabbing techniques to the inside, the feed from forward 3 or guards 2 and 1 should be highly successful.

Guard 1 has the option to drive immediately off the pinch

screen by forward 4. I should also point out that all or any segment of the combination post may be utilized with an immediate transition into the swing-and-cut.

The combination post is also a very effective measure against zone defenses as it provides the strongside triangle, high post or backdoor area attack, swing or overthrow possibilities, and movement. The four inside attack points with the movement involved are usually effective.

DOUBLE FLASH POST

In utilizing the double flash post we set guard 1 at the point with the ball. Guard 2 and forward 4 occupy the normal wing positions. Post 5 and strong forward 3 position themselves low with the inside foot on the wide-lane divider. (Diagram 9-10) Upon a verbal, eye to eye, or timing signal, both post men use straight, crossing, or fake crossing cuts and flash forward to the ends of the free throw line. Guard 1 will choose the open man, who for illustrative purposes is forward 3. At the moment forward 3 receives the ball, forward 4, quickly and at full speed, cuts to the basket. Forward 3 passes to him on the backdoor move if he is open. Guard 1 has now moved slightly away and up to the free throw line. Since forward 3 did not pass to forward 4 cutting backdoor,

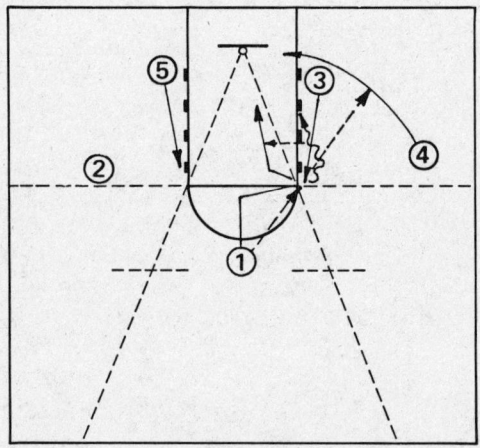

Diagram 9-10
Double Flash Post

guard 1 will cut quickly over him for a drive, jump shot, or check pass to forward 3 rolling to the basket. (Diagram 9-10) Post 5 will move across the lane to the backdoor area. This will provide an overthrow to forward 3, a check pass to forward 3, or a 15-foot jump shot for post 5 in the event forward 3 is being fronted.

I should point out that many times we use this set and look at these options and go right into our swing-and-cut pattern. Guard 1 simply passes the ball to guard 2 who has cut to the top. Guard 2 swings the ball to forward 4 who has cut through. Post 5 slides down and guard 1 cuts off the double screen.

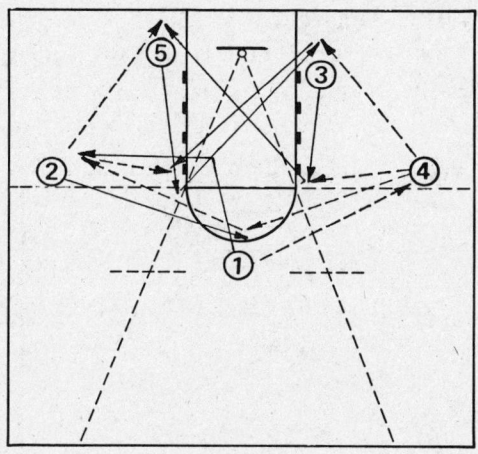

Diagram 9-11
Double Post Cuts

If the post is denied by either the defensive men or by the wings playing tight to the inside to prevent the pass to the post man, guard 1 will pass to wing forward 4 on this occasion. Post 5 will quickly cut low using a straight cut or rollback. (Diagram 9-11) Forward 4 will look for post 5 cutting low. Forward 3 is already in the backdoor area in the event post 5 is fronted, creating the possibility of an overthrow, a pass to forward 3 for a check pass to post 5, or a jump shot. If forward 4 does not like any of these possibilities, he quickly passes to guard 2 at the point, who has interchanged with guard 1. Guard 2 swings the ball to guard 1. Forward 3 cuts to the low post, and post 5 cuts high. (Diagram 9-11)

SNEAK POST

We have yet another simple posting opportunity from our regular swing-and-cut set. Guard 2 passes to forward 4. Post 5 screens away for guard 1 as in our normal continuity. Guard 1 cuts off the screen and on to the corner. Guard 2 moves away and starts low, as in the normal swing-and-cut. Forward 3 moves his defensive man low, takes two sharp steps toward the top as he normally executes the three cut, plants his right foot, and quickly cuts back to the basket and wide-lane divider area. This should produce a quick posting pass to forward 3 from forward 4 or an overthrow possibility. (Diagram 9-12) Post man 5, after setting his screen, moves straight across the free throw line in an effort to keep his defensive man high, or to establish a backdoor area condition.

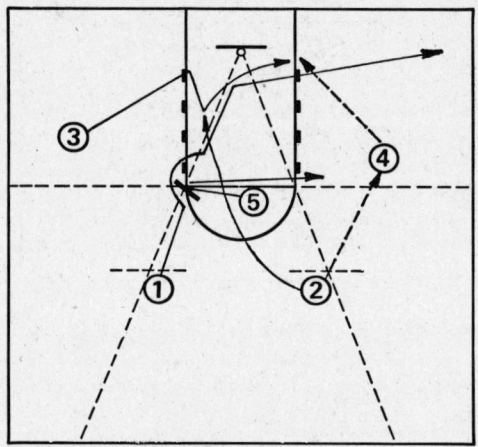

Diagram 9-12
Sneak Post

10

swing-and-cut into other patterns

While it is extremely important that you have complete confidence and faith in the primary offensive system you decide to use, if you want to teach it with conviction, you must realize that style or system is not the most important thing. The important thing is to be certain that your teaching tactics are based on sound, valid basics and principles. It is also important to realize that outstanding features of other systems and other sets may be incorporated successfully into your basic offense.

When using other sets, we have chosen to keep them as closely aligned to our basic swing-and-cut as possible. We feel this maintains an element of confidence in our personnel. In the event of an unsuccessful attempt, the fact that it is possible to move right in to what we know best is reassuring. We believe that teams preparing to defend against us are primarily concerned with our swing-and-cut attack. Therefore, going into an auxiliary set through the swing-and-cut gives us an element of surprise and adds additional pressure and problems for defensive preparation. The same philosophy is applied in Chapter 11 as we go through other sets into the swing-and-cut.

We like to prepare for every game both offensively and defensively, but especially offensively, by disguising our basic attack. In other words, we like to give the opponent's defense a look they have not prepared for and yet not try to become too sophisticated and stray from our basic strengths. Many times this can be accomplished with multiple sets into our basic pattern. An unusual personnel alignment is often effective. We find, however, that going through our swing-and-cut into other patterns and looking at the strengths of other patterns, as explained in Chapter 11, is most effective. Teams that have prepared extensively for the swing-and-cut motion can be lured into mistakes by the change of emphasis. Let me reiterate: this is not complicated or an effort to be highly sophisticated. Our philosophy is simplicity. Yet, as simple as these approaches might be, I would recommend that the relief moves and options of the swing-and-cut be taught, rehearsed, and understood to perfection before any extras are attempted.

SWING-AND-CUT INTO THE SINGLE POST

When using the swing-and-cut as our initial set and initial motion through which we go into the single post, we follow the basic swing-and-cut alignment described in Chapter 2. (Diagram 2-1) The initial move is exactly like the regular swing-and-cut, one cut described in Chapter 4. (Diagram 4-1) Guard 1 must first remember that the one cut is of foremost importance as the cut is being executed. Guard 1, as his first priority, must execute the cut precisely and look for the ball. If he is open, forward 4 will always pass him the ball. It is very important that guard 1 does not make this a mechanical move to single post alignment. If guard 1 is not open, instead of moving to his normal position as the low man in the double screen, he cuts to the ballside corner. Center 5 rolls back as in the normal swing-and-cut move, but he takes his position astride the second-lane divider from the baseline, thus establishing the line of deployment with forward 4. Post 5, guard 1 in the corner, and forward 4 with the ball have formed the single post strongside triangle. Guard 2, after making the initial pass, has moved away and down, and forward 3 has moved to the basket and cuts off guard 2's screen to the top or three spot. This forms our basic single post alignment as described in Chapter 11. (Diagrams 11-1, 11-2, and 11-3)

If we think it wise to keep forward 3 on the front line, we simply move guard 2 down as far as the free throw line and cut him back to the point. We move forward 3 under, start his cut to the top, and step him out to the weakside forward position, thus forming the basic single post alignment. (Diagram 10-1) These swing-and-cut maneuvers have now placed us in position to bring the single post advantages into action. These possibilities are described and illustrated in Chapters 9 and 11.

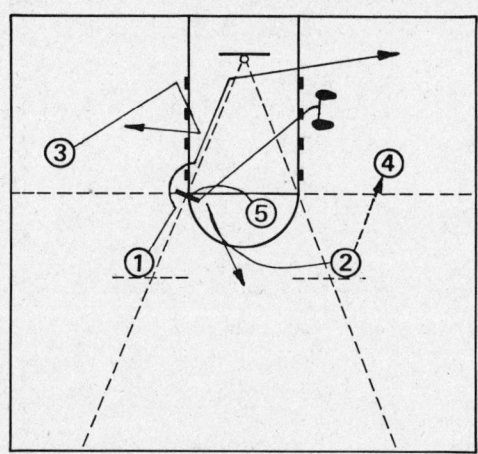

Diagram 10-1
Swing-and-Cut
into Single Post

SWING-AND-CUT INTO THE DOUBLE FLASH POST

The swing-and-cut is now the initial set through which we are going into the double flash post. The entry is through the normal swing-and-cut set. The one cut, two cut, three cut, four cut, and five cut are exactly the same as described in Chapter 4. (Diagrams 4-1, 4-2, 4-3, 4-4, and 4-5) It is important to initiate the offense to the forward or wing you plan on becoming your second post man, in this case, forward 4. The one, two, three, four and five cuts have been completed. Guard 2 has the ball on the left wing. Forward 4 has made the five cut and is now in the low post position on the left side of the lane. Guard 1 is at the top of the key. Forward 3 has moved low and out to the right wing. Center 5, after forward 4 cuts off the double screen, takes one step into the lane to clear for guard 1 cutting to the top, and then steps back to the low post position on the right side of the lane. (Diagram 10-2)

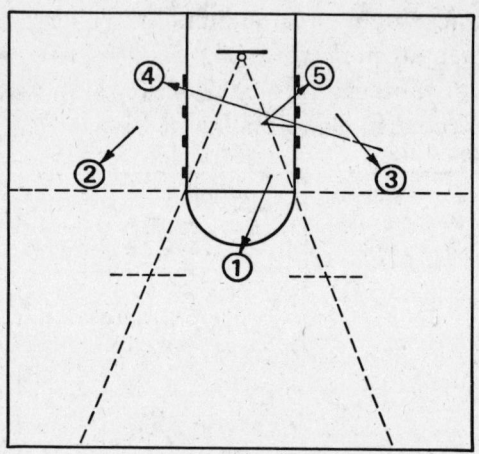

Diagram 10-2
*Swing-and-Cut
into Double Post*

Guard 2 passes the ball to guard 1 at the top of the key. We are now in the double-flash post set. We are ready to bring into effect one of the double-flash post techniques as described in Chapters 9 and 11.

SWING-AND-CUT INTO THE COMBINATION POST

The combination post is a very productive supplementary offense. This is probably the auxiliary offense we use best, especially when we have at least two players who are skilled in the post techniques. This enables us to strengthen our inside attack, and yet present the pressure and movement of the swing-and-cut in the initial phase.

In order to go through the swing-and-cut into the combination set with a minimum of ball handling, we initiate the swing-and-cut opposite the forward we intend to have perform at the pinch post and low post positions, forward 3 in this case. Guard 2 passes to forward 4 and the one cut, two cut, three cut, four cut and five cut are executed as described and illustrated in Chapter 4.

At this point, with only three perimeter passes involved, forward 4 cuts to the corner. Post 5 slides down to the low post. Forward 3, after swinging the ball to guard 2, starts his cut down the lane and quickly steps back to the end of the free throw line. (Diagram 10-3) This places him in a position to step across to the backdoor area, in the event the low post is being fronted, or step back to the corner of the free throw line to screen for guard 1 driving off the pinch post action. As guard 2 receives the swing pass from forward 3, we are in the combination set. He immediately looks at the low post, passes to the corner for a low post entry, or returns the ball to guard 1 for the pinch post, roll out, and low post action on the weak side.

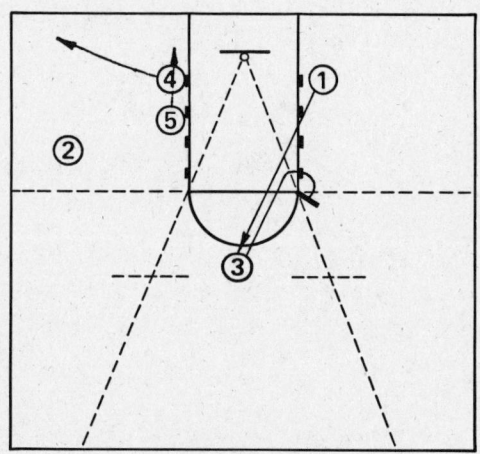

Diagram 10-3
*Swing-and-Cut
into Combination Post*

The complete combination post possibilities are described and illustrated in Chapter 9. (Diagrams 9-12, 9-12A, 9-12B, 9-12C, 9-12D, and 9-12E)

You might feel that this presentation is overly sophisticated. Let me assure you that it is not. I am presenting the possibilities that exist. I am presenting opportunities to camouflage a point of attack. It is feasible, according to personnel and circumstances, to pick one technique in these auxiliary moves to exploit. It could behoove you to change the methods of exploitation. There is an old saying, "he went to the well too often." I believe by simple variations and disguises a bread-and-butter play may be used proficiently throughout a contest.

11
other patterns into the swing-and-cut series

There exists in the mind of every coach the need for additional maneuvers to supplement the basic offense. Many times it is prudent to look at another set or movement from another set. We, at times, like to go into the swing-and-cut through another offensive pattern without changing our overall offensive objective. If this does nothing else, it will challenge the defense and make them face sets they are not prepared for. This creates moments of doubt or indecision that will possibly cause defensive lapses that will make the basic pattern more effective when you return to it. Football teams show varied sets to execute the same basic offense; basketball teams can also use this to a definite advantage. In order to get the most from your basic pattern, disguises may be employed. Whether or not the defense can adjust to the offensive movement effectively is a matter of speculation, but will continually keep them off-balance.

All patterns have basic strengths. These may be incorporated into your offensive philosophy, making both more effective.

SINGLE POST INTO THE SWING-AND-CUT

If you are fortunate enough to have a strong post man, the single post set would be a wise initial move. Look at your power first. After the first pass to the wing and as he prepares to make the second pass to the post, your post man has the possibility of at least five effective single post options—straight post play, overthrow, split, cutaway and backdoor. The penetrating dribble and choke post options could also be used. This depends on how the defense is playing and how well we recognize the possibilities.

Many times we set our offensive strategy for a particular game around one play from the single post or another pattern and move right to the swing-and-cut if this does not prove efficient.

Without going into the entire single post offense, I deem it necessary to describe and diagram the single post cuts we are most concerned with and put the most emphasis on. Our first concern is normally the post play. The post play and the other options are determined by how the defense is playing when the forward receives the ball and looks down the line of deployment. The number two pass keys the option selected or changes the pattern from the single post to the swing-and-cut.

Operating Rules for Single Post

1. Guards should be about fifteen feet apart and should start about six to eight feet above the free throw lane. (Diagram 11-1)

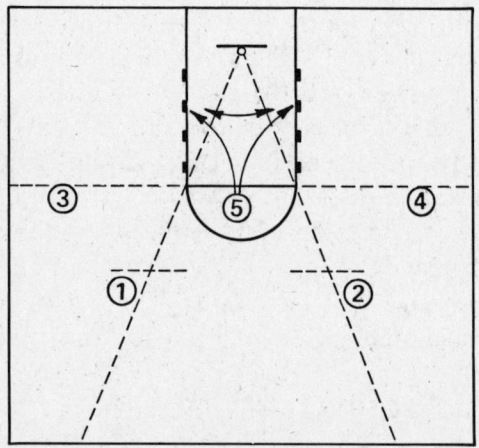

Diagram 11-1
Single Post Alignment

2. Forwards should position themselves one step above the free throw line extended, at a distance from the sideline great enough for the guard to cut comfortably from behind to the corner (approximately two steps from the sideline). (Diagram 11-2)
3. All positions should establish themselves so as to keep approximately 15-foot passing lanes enforced. (Diagram 11-3)

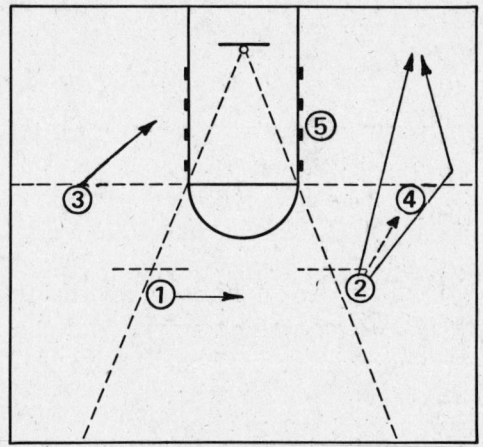

Diagram 11-2
Single Post Alignment

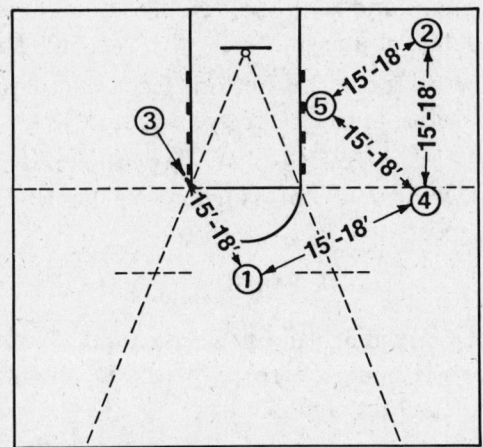

Diagram 11-3
Single Post Spacing

126 other patterns into the swing-and-cut series

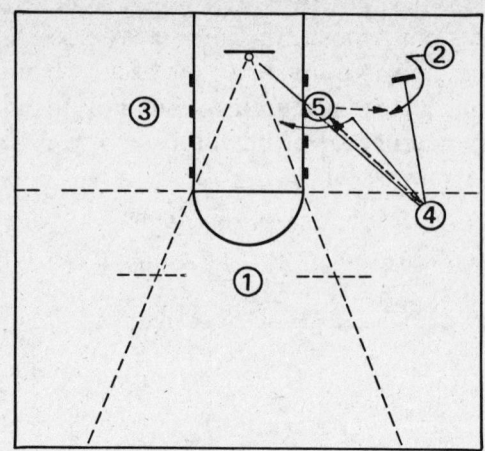

Diagram 11-4
Line of Deployment

4. The post should position himself on the line of deployment directly between the forward and the basket. (Diagram 11-4) The third-lane divider down should be directly between his feet.
5. The number two pass is the key in initiating the offensive action. This triggers the offensive tactic.
6. It is very important that the forward or the player in the forward position receiving the first pass look down the line of deployment and read the defenses quickly and accurately, as this determines the offensive action. (Diagram 11-4)
7. Do not try to force this action. Read the defense. Let the defense determine the offensive action.
8. First read the defensive post play; this as a rule will key the offensive action. This is where we want to go if the opportunity exists.

Automatics

1. *Backdoor.* Anytime the post is being fronted and the point guard is being overplayed, the weak forward should be alert to cut into the backdoor area.
2. *Overthrow.* Any time the post is being fronted and the backdoor area is cut off, the post will position quickly for overthrow.

3. *Penetrating dribble.* If the forward defense is sagging, this affords the opportunity for the penetrating dribble.

It is very important that the post man establish himself firmly on the line of deployment and give the forward a strong target in accordance with the position the defensive post man takes. If the defensive post plays behind the offensive post, the pass will be directly down the line. This usually signifies that the offensive post will be looking for straight cuts or splits between the strongside forward and guard. (Diagram 11-4)

Should the defensive post side low, (Diagram 11-5) the offensive post should give a right-hand target and receive the pass off the line of deployment on the high side. This should place the post man in a position for a short left-hand hook shot, short turn and jump shot to the inside, or possibly an inside power move.

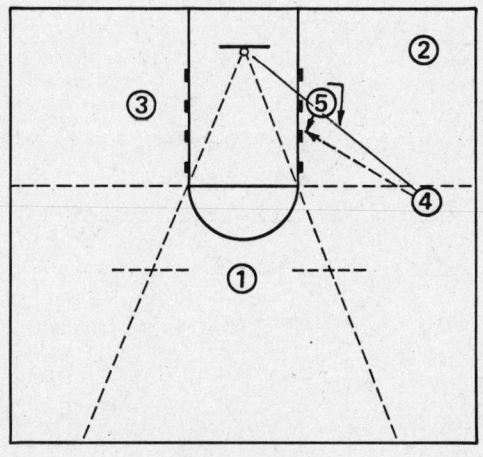

Diagram 11-5
Side Low

Should the defensive post side high, (Diagram 11-6) the pass should be to a left-hand target off the line of deployment, which indicates a strong power move to the baseline, short right-hand hook off the board, or short turn and jump off the board.

If the post man is being fronted, (Diagram 11-7) the offside forward will cut to the backdoor area, taking the defensive man with him and clearing the back-side. The forward will then overthrow to the offensive post. Other options, of course, may be obtained by passing to weakside forward, cutting to the backdoor

128 other patterns into the swing-and-cut series

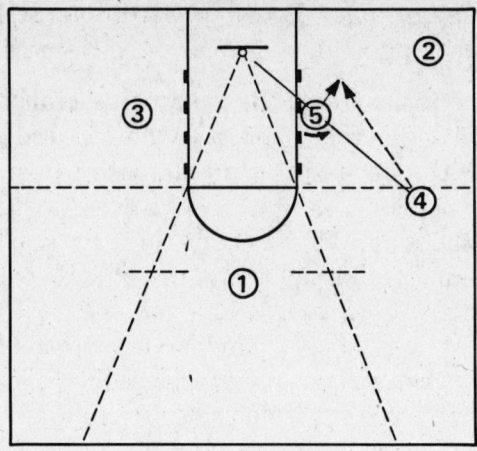

Diagram 11-6
Side High

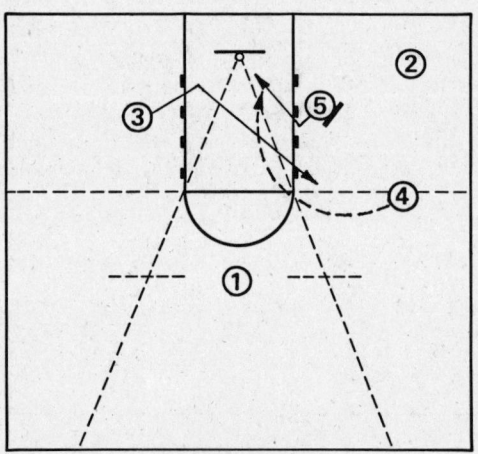

Diagram 11-7
Fronted Overthrow

area where there is the option to face and shoot, checking inside to the post man, or moving backdoor to the point guard. (Diagram 11-8)

These options are all keyed off the number two pass. If a suitable move does not materialize, the number two pass will go to the point guard, who will quickly swing to the weakside forward. This swing places us in our swing-and-cut offense. (Diagram 11-9)

other patterns into the swing-and-cut series 129

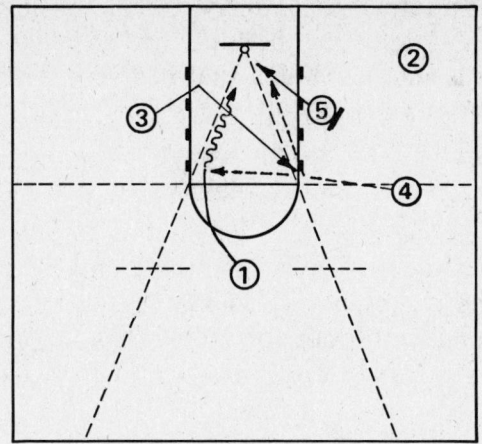

Diagram 11-8
Fronted Pass to Backdoor Area

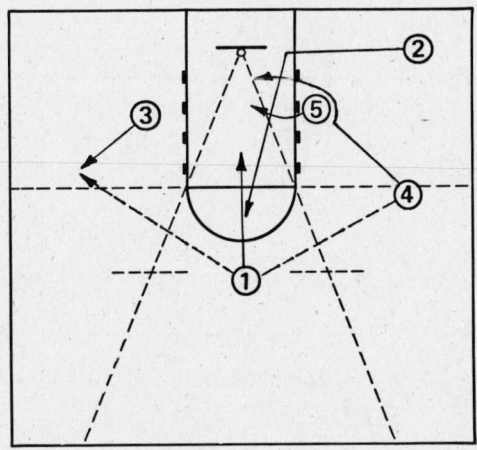

Diagram 11-9
Transition into Swing-and-Cut

DOUBLE FLASH POST INTO THE SWING-AND-CUT OFFENSE

We find the double post set an effective entry into the swing-and-cut pattern on numerous occasions. This set provides many challenges for the defense and enables us, at times, to capitalize on defensive indecision.

1. It gives us another set or entry into our basic pattern. This gives the defense something else to consider and yet the maneuver is simple enough that it does not add additional complexity to the offense.
2. It provides us with a one-man front, while enabling our lead guard more maneuverability and preventing double-teams.
3. It lets us flash both post men high and establish a quick hitter. The guard passes quickly to one of the post men who immediately looks for the wings going backdoor or a quick two-man play with the point guard. (Diagrams 11-10 and 11-11)

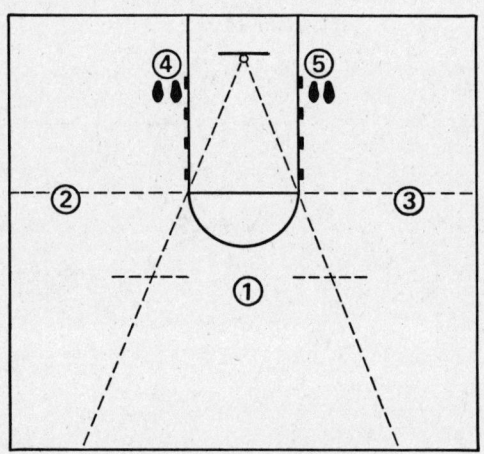

Diagram 11-10
Double Post—Basic Set

4. It enables us to use two post men as we go into our attack, creating a quick posting possibility.
5. It lets us attack either side of the floor quickly, enabling us to take advantage of defensive lapses.

The post man and the strong forward position themselves with the inside foot on the wide-lane divider. The wings should be two to two and one-half steps in from the sideline and one step below the foul line extended. The lead guard attempts to stay in the exact middle of the floor. He passes to the posts flashing or to the

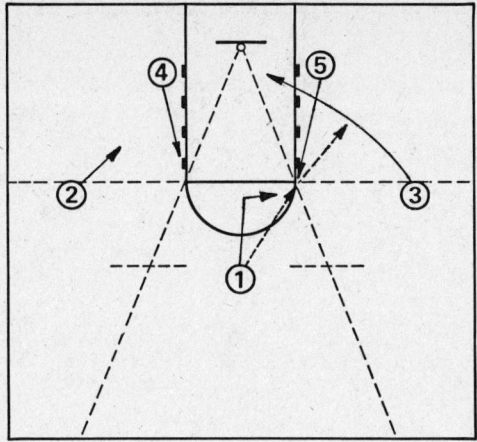

Diagram 11-11
Backdoor Cut

wings. The pass should be made from four to six steps above the top of the key. (Diagram 11-10)

flash post

As the lead guard brings the ball into the attack area, both post men flash forward to the corners of the foul line on either a visual or verbal signal. They should receive the pass as they move forward on the exact moment they reach the corners of the foul line. The exact moment the ball touches the hand of the post man, the wing to the post man's side cuts quickly to the basket establishing a quick backdoor maneuver. (Diagram 11-11) If the backdoor move does not materialize, the point guard fakes away or forces his defensive man forward, and cuts hard off the post for a drive to the basket or a check pass to post rolling back. (Diagram 11-12)

We have now taken a look at two quick hitters. If we fail to find an effective move, the guard keeps the dribble alive and curls back to a wing position. The opposite post crosses over to the strong side for a double screen. The offside wing fakes low, cuts low and to the top, and receives a pass from the lead guard, swings it to the wing who initially cut backdoor, and the guard cuts off the double screen into our swing-and-cut pattern. (Diagrams 11-13 and 11-14)

132 other patterns into the swing-and-cut series

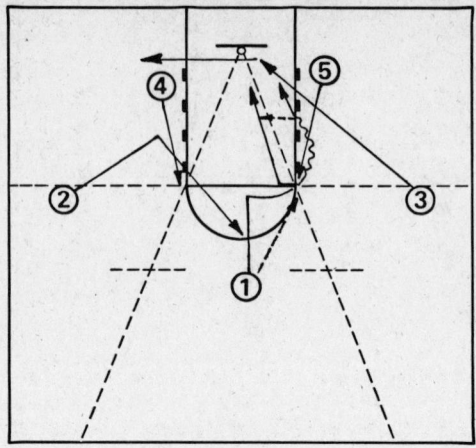

Diagram 11-12
Cut—Drive—Roll

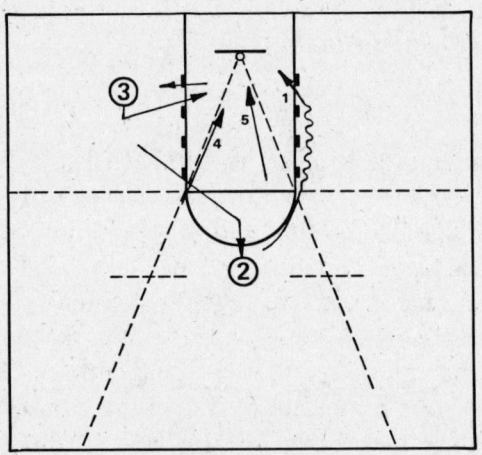

Diagram 11-13
Position of Personnel after Cut, Drive, and Roll

pass to the wing

In the initial stage of the attack, the lead guard indicates he wants the post men to stay low. The first pass will go to a wing who looks to the post and passes the ball to him if at all possible. (Diagram 11-15) This is the post man's play one-on-one; however,

other patterns into the swing-and-cut series 133

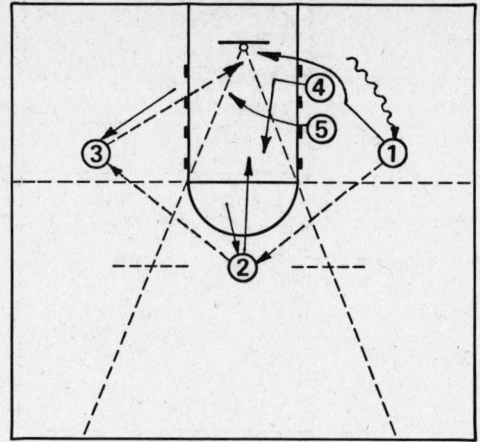

Diagram 11-14
Into Swing-and-Cut after Backdoor Cut, Drive, and Roll

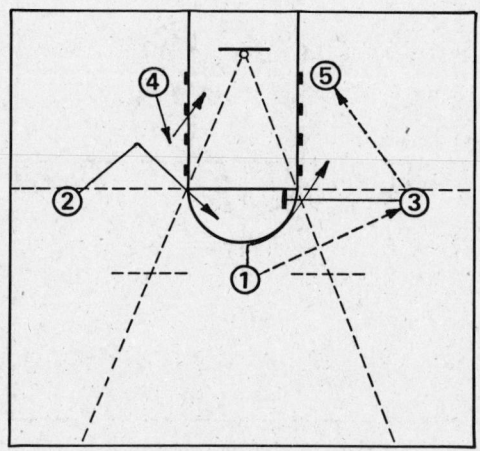

Diagram 11-15
Straight to Post

the wing will cut or screen for point guard to keep the defense occupied and to give the post a pass if he so desires.

Should the post man be fronted, the opposite post man will cut to the backdoor area to clear the back-side for an overthrow. (Diagram 11-16) If the defense does not clear, the pass will be to the post, cutting to the backdoor area. He has the option to face

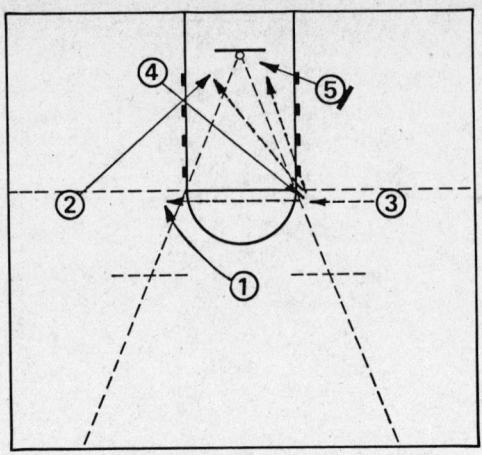

Diagram 11-16
Post Fronted—Pass to Backdoor Area

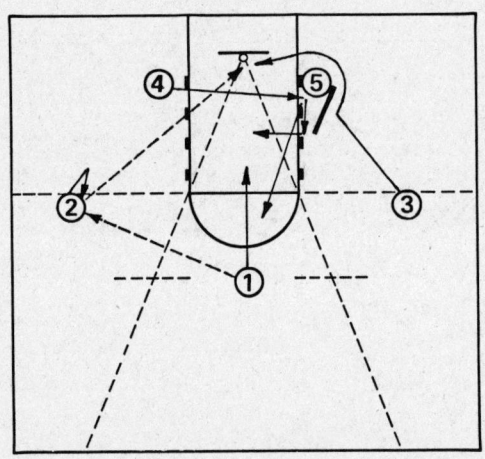

Diagram 11-17
Double Post Straight to Swing-and-Cut

and shoot, check to low post stepping to the basket, or pass to the weakside wing cutting backdoor or the point guard fanning. (Diagram 11-16) If the wing cannot get the ball to the low post or backdoor area, the post in the backdoor area slides down to form the double screen. The wing passes to the point who swings the ball to the weakside wing. The strongside wing cuts off the double screen into the swing-and-cut. (Diagram 11-17)

1-3-1 INTO THE SWING-AND-CUT

The 1-3-1 pattern affords us the opportunity to show the defense yet another pattern. We make no attempt to emphasize the entire 1-3-1 philosophy, but rather only two or three key maneuvers that could possibly score quickly and that concern the defense.

The 1-3-1 pattern affords us:

1. A one-man front with three possible lead passes to the two wings, 2 and 3, and the high post, 5.
2. A method to present an entirely different defensive challenge on the initial move.
3. An opportunity to attack from the middle by placing a highly skilled individual on the high post (shooter, passer, penetrator).
4. Excellent offensive rebounding opportunities with four people in position to move to the boards.

We normally play our strong forward on the low post simply because his defensive man, as a rule, has not defended this position as regularly as the defensive post. He should take his position with his inside foot on the wide-lane divider. The post man should take his position on the high post. We like to use our regular post man here as he is normally our tallest man and gives us somewhat of an edge to pass to. The wings should be two to two and one-half steps in from the sideline and one step below the foul line extended. The point guard should attempt to initiate the action from approximately three steps above the top of the key. He should also give himself latitude of at least 12 feet and not try to force everything directly from the middle. (Diagram 11-18) If we were using the 1-3-1 as our basic offense, we would give the point guard even more latitude.

pass to high post

Normally, when we initiate our offense with a 1-3-1 set our emphasis is to the high post man for a quick hitter. We feel the high post will not be too aggressively challenged and our pass will go directly to him from the point guard. He will immediately face the basket and look for the power forward, crabbing quick, tough, and low to the ball and to the middle of the lane. The high post

136 other patterns into the swing-and-cut series

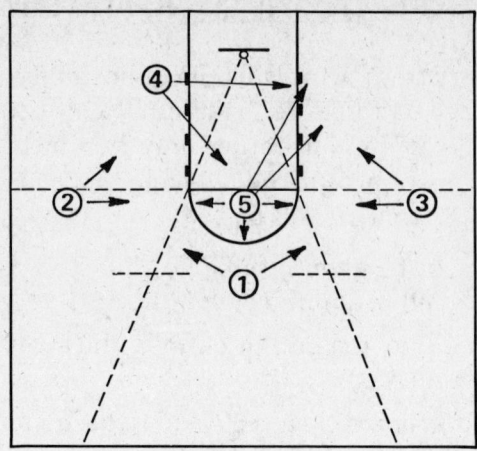

Diagram 11-18
1-3-1 Basic Set

hits him quickly and allows him to use his individual one-on-one move to the basket. Should the high post find his defensive man playing off to prevent a pass to the low man, he will have a 15-foot jump shot. As the post man receives the ball from the point guard and faces the basket, both wings will fan toward the basket. This movement will occupy their defensive men, and should the defense overslough, short jump shots off the board will materialize. (Diagram 11-19)

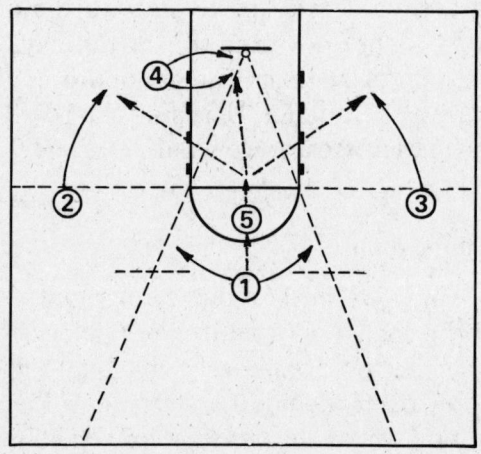

Diagram 11-19
Pass to High Post

other patterns into the swing-and-cut series   137

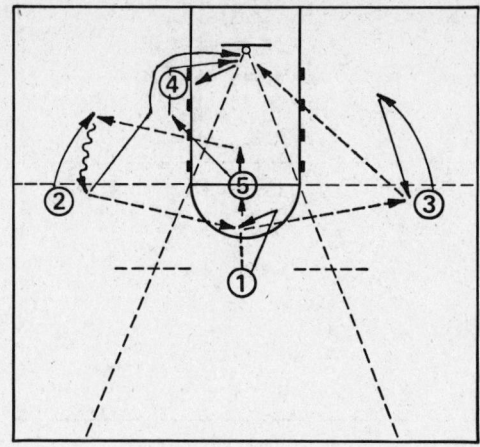

Diagram 11-20
1-3-1 Transition into Swing-and-Cut

In the event the high post finds no opportunity, he can pass to either wing and have both post men move to the side of the ball, which sets up the swing-and-cut pattern. (Diagram 11-20)

pass to the wing

The point guard may elect to pass to the wing opposite the low post man, in which event the low post attempts to position quickly at the basket for a quick pass or move to the low post position on the lane for a quick pass. (Diagram 11-21) If he receives the ball, a power move, short hook, or short turn and jump should be forthcoming. In the event the low post is fronted, the high post will quickly step into the backdoor area for a pass from the wing. He has the option of facing and shooting, checking to the low post stepping to the basket, passing to the back-side wing, or cutting backdoor or to the point fanning to the corner of the foul line. (Diagram 11-22)

In the event of no opportunities, high post 5 slides down to form a double screen. Wing 3 passes to point 1, who swings the ball to the back-side wing 2, as wing 3 cuts off the double screen to activate the swing-and-cut offense. (Diagram 11-23)

Our favorite maneuver from the 1-3-1 is established by the point guard waving wing 3 through and having high post 5 step out and set a screen. Point guard 1 will set his defensive man up and

138   other patterns into the swing-and-cut series

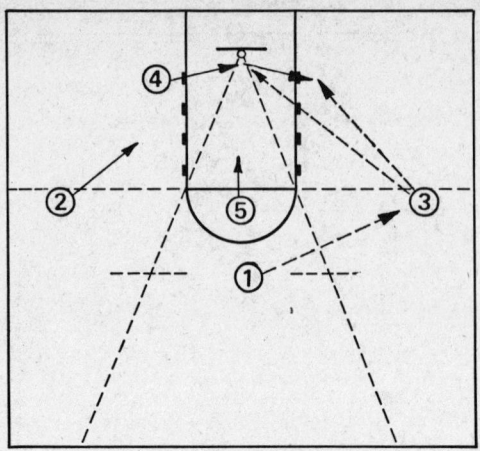

Diagram 11-21
Pass from Wing to Low Post

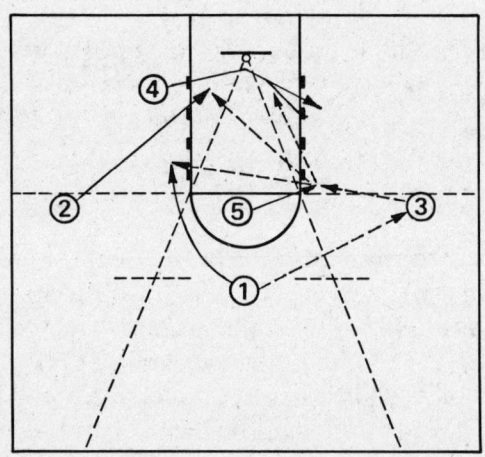

Diagram 11-22
*Low Post Fronted—
High Post to Backdoor Area*

drive off the screen for the basket. High post 5 will roll to the basket. Guard 1 has the drive or check to the high post rolling options. (Diagram 11-24) Should a shot not materialize, guard 1 will keep the ball alive, curl back, and look for the wing 3. Wing 3 has continued through and cut to the top off the double screen of the low post 5 and the weakside wing 2 screening down. As wing 3

other patterns into the swing-and-cut series 139

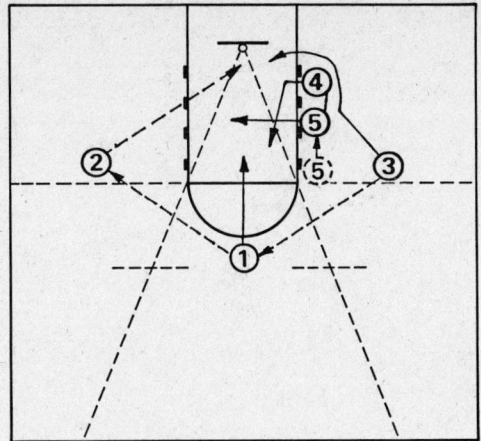

Diagram 11-23
Transition into Swing-and-Cut

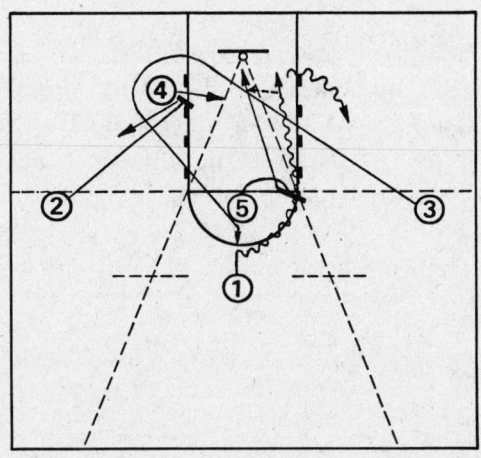

Diagram 11-24
Wing Through High Post Screen

cuts to the top, he should be thinking shot, as his cut around the low double screen is a very effective move. If the shot does not materialize, wing 2 pops out, and low post 4 crosses the lane to form a double screen with high post 5. Guard 1 cuts off the double screen as wing 3 swings the ball to wing 2 and we move very easily into our swing-and-cut pattern. (Diagram 11-25)

140 other patterns into the swing-and-cut series

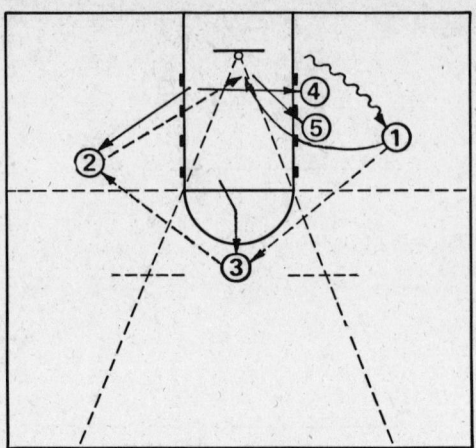

Diagram 11-25
Transition to Swing-and-Cut

high post screen low

Occasionally, point guard 1 will pass to wing 3 opposite the low post. The high post will screen low for the low post. (Diagram 11-26) If the low post is fronted, the high post who sets the low screen will flash into the backdoor area. (Diagram 11-27) Upon receiving the pass, he has the option of facing and shooting, check-

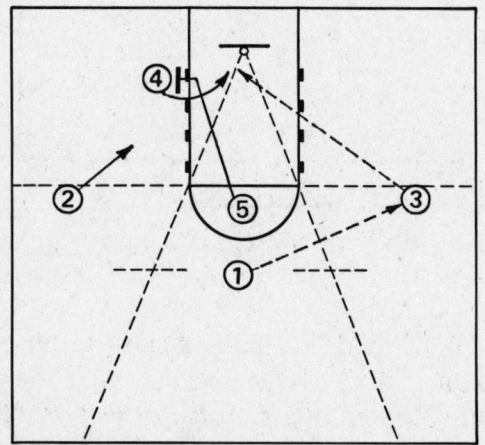

Diagram 11-26
Screen Low

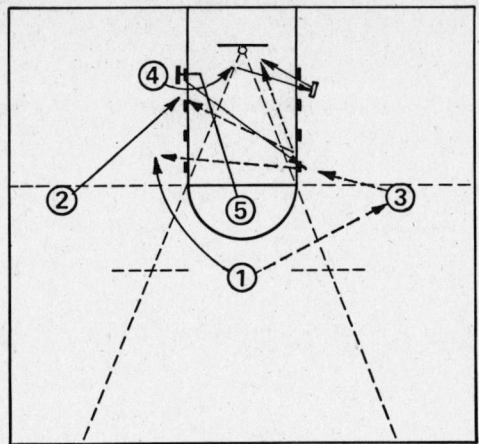

Diagram 11-27
1-3-1 Low Post Fronted

ing to low post stepping back on pass to fan or backdoor maneuvers on the back-side.

Any of the three offenses we have just touched upon, as possible preludes to the offense we have chosen, are proven effective patterns and have been so for many years. I have chosen a few quick hitting maneuvers from each set that will keep the defense challenged, taking advantage of defensive indecision and possibly creating additional scoring opportunities. Methods used in creating scoring opportunities vary with coaches. I think, however, all coaches would agree that it is not the system that is important. We seek, through the knowledge and repetition of the simple basics and minute details, the proper execution required. Attention to these basics can be the difference between a winning team and an average or losing team.

The fundamentals of the few maneuvers from the single post, the double post, and the 1-3-1 correlate very closely with the basic elements of the swing-and-cut. This approach gives us additional offensive possibilities and creates additional problems for the defense; yet, the simplicity still exists.

12 / the swing-and-cut offense versus the zone

It is said that every team must have a special offense to use against a zone defense, or else the zone in effect will take away the offensive potential. I agree with this to a point. There is no question that certain adjustments are necessary. I believe, however, that a team should remain as closely aligned as possible to its basic attack, and that the adjustments should be built around its basic attack. In following this philosophy, changing defenses will not necessarily upset the team's momentum or confidence.

It is impossible to have a different zone attack for the multitude of different zone defenses found in the game today. There is not enough time available to prepare an attack for each zone, especially when you may be preparing for a defense that you will see only once or twice a season. It is more important to perfect the fundamentals involved with your basic or everyday attack, and to make your adjustments from this point.

There are two important facts you must remember in preparing your team's adjustments for a zone attack. First, you must remember that all zones are based on the same principle of playing the ball and area rather than the man. The exception is when the ball is in your area. This necessitates man-for-man coverage. Second, when the ball is on the low side or the corner, all zones are virtually the same. Whether the zone is playing inside out or outside in, the defensive men are in the same general area. The philosophy around which you prepare your adjustments should be built around these facts.

In my opinion the zone set is of little importance. You should work to get penetration, have your zone adjustments in mind, and start your motion. The teams that are bothered the least by zones or changing defenses are those teams who stick close to their basic philosophy. When asked what his team did against zones, I once heard a coach say, "We ignore the zone." For a team exceptionally prepared and rehearsed in the basic fundamentals, this may not be bad advice. We have all seen teams drastically change their offense each time the defense changes. For this to be effective it takes a very experienced, poised, and talented team. Too many teams attempting to follow this philosophy spend more time changing offenses than they do playing basketball.

There are many thoughts and ideas on how to defeat zone defenses. Many of these go as far back as the origin of the zone and are still applicable. Some of them are: fast break against the zone, move the ball rapidly, no dribbling, quick reversals, comeback passes, keep cutting toward the basket to set up the outside shooters. I think all of these elements are incorporated in most good zone attacks. Our basic swing-and-cut offense is predicated on: (1) an inside phase, (2) an outside phase, (3) movement, (4) a quick swing or reverse, (5) penetration, and (6) floor balance. We feel that these elements should be just as effective against a zone, with a few slight adjustments. You must read the defense. Let the defense name the play in the zone just as you do in the man-for-man attack.

The greatest asset of any successful endeavor is *preparedness*. It instills poise, intensity, and confidence. We feel that by staying close to our basic offensive attack and employing the tactics we work on daily that our confidence and poise should never be lacking.

One of the greatest advantages of a zone defense is the element of surprise, which can be a tremendous psychological factor. Confidence in your overall attack can reverse a negative psychological picture to a positive one.

the swing-and-cut offense versus the zone   145

The swing-and-cut offers the offensive opportunities essential to attacking successfully any defensive alignment, maintaining confidence and poise in the players, and sustaining the necessary intensity.

NORMAL SWING-AND-CUT VERSUS ZONE

As previously mentioned, the swing-and-cut is our basic attack against any zone. We do make adjustments, usually influenced by the defensive alignment. However, three slight adjustments are always prevalent in the initial set and initial cut. First, the wings, forwards 3 and 4, line up one step above the foul line extended instead of one step below as in the normal set. (Diagram 12-1) This gives us better spacing in the strongside triangle. It creates some indecision on the part of the defensive point, wing, and low men as to how the strong side will be covered on the initial move. Second, we give post man 5 the option of screening opposite the way he does in the normal swing-and-cut, or of immediately cutting to daylight. (Diagram 12-1) Normally the screen is ineffective. Occasionally, however, we find a team matching up and following the first cutter through. An effective screen might possibly free the first cutter for an easy basket, especially if the low man is matched up with our wing receiving the first pass.

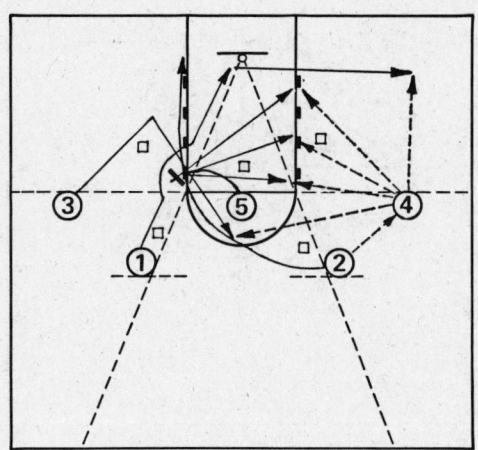

Diagram 12-1
Swing-and-Cut Alignment Versus Zone

146   the swing-and-cut offense versus the zone

Third, the first cutter, guard 1, first cuts to the basket looking for the ball. The moment he determines the pass will not come to him he cuts quickly to the corner (Diagram 12-1), thus establishing the strongside triangle. We place additional emphasis on post 5 cutting to the open spot or forcing the defense to concentrate on defending an area with force. The initial move of post 5 could be from the end of the free throw line to the low post position. These three adjustments are normal procedures when facing any zone.

movement and swing

The effectiveness of the normal swing-and-cut attack against the zone defense is predicated on movement and the quick swing to the weak side. Each time the ball is swung or reversed we have five-man movement on the turnover. (Diagram 12-2) Forward 4 cuts under or over post 5 to the basket and then the corner. Post 5 cuts to daylight. Guard 1 moves up the baseline to the wide-lane marker and cuts to the top. Forward 3, on swinging the ball to guard 2, moves down the lane to the basket looking for an overthrow and steps out to the weak side. This swing provides us with three cutters coming to the ball and forces the defense to deny hard an area from the basket to the top of the key, or a distance of approximately 22 feet, plus defending a possible overthrow.

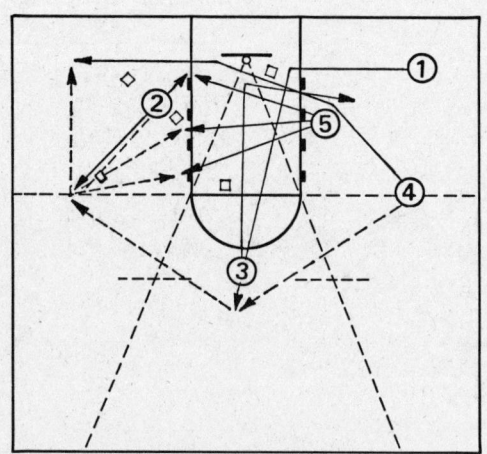

Diagram 12-2
Swing-and-Cut Alignment
Versus Zone, Movement, and Swing

The motion aspect creates a difficulty for the defense to point or emphasize coverage on an especially good outside shooter because they find him in so many different positions.

Patience, poise and confidence in the continuity of motion will normally provide a high percentage shot.

bringing in the back-side

One of the first defensive attempts to thwart this attack is to deny the swing pass, thus forcing the ball to remain on the strong side, preventing the cutting action. When faced with this defensive adjustment, we ask our point man to move a step higher and our post man 5 to use the low post area, thus forcing the defense to front him or drop off deep. This extends the line of coverage three or four feet. At this point we bring in back-side guard 2 to the backdoor area in the vicinity of the corner of the foul line. (Diagram 12-3) Forward 4 will pass to guard 2. Guard 2, upon receiving the pass, immediately faces the basket and has the option of check passing to post 5 if he is being fronted, taking a jump shot, or passing to forward 3 who has fanned to the back-side. Forward 3 could possibly have a 15- to 18-foot jump shot. If not, he dribbles to the wing, guard 2 either moves down and out or steps out to the top, and the cutting action takes place and the offense is sustained.

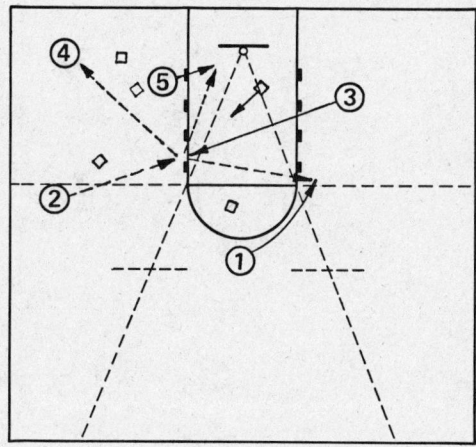

Diagram 12-3
Bringing in the Back-side

148 the swing-and-cut offense versus the zone

Points of Emphasis

1. Cut sharp and fast.
2. Don't ignore the corner. Always pass or fake to the corner before reversing the ball.
3. The post man must be active and cut to daylight.
4. The post man must remember the defense is going to swarm him. If he doesn't have the shot, he should quickly throw out the back-side.
5. Be aware of the long pass across the zone. This makes the defense move with maximum effort and distance and will still maintain the continuity and balance.
6. Be patient.

ATTACKING THE SEAMS

We find it prudent on occasions to adjust slightly from our basic spots and attack what we call the *seams*. This, in essence, means we do not have a point man. Instead, the point man is positioned approximately ten to twelve feet to the weak side and approximately three feet above the foul line extended. This places him approximately 18 feet from the basket. (Diagram 12-4) We

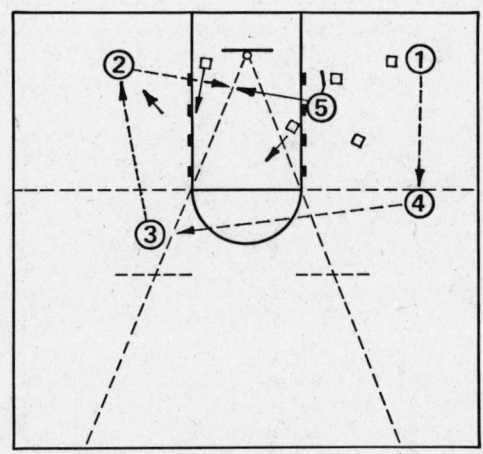

Diagram 12-4
Attacking the Seams

emphasize the seam concept in most cases when the zone is playing the ball intensely and sloughing the other four men deep to the inside. This enables forward 4 to make a longer flat pass to forward 3. When this pass is made, it immediately creates pressure and indecision on the defensive point man and the back-side defensive wing as to who will cover forward 3 in the seam and guard 2 on the back-side. It also creates maximum distances for defensive coverage. This should provide an open shot as a result of a direct pass to the seam or of a two-on-one situation on the back-side. (Diagram 12-4) With two defensive men forced to move quickly and at a maximum distance, it is very possible to pull the zone apart and make available some inside opportunities.

movement and continuity

The movement and continuity are essentially the same as the normal swing-and-cut movement. In fact, in the seam concept it is a good tactic at first to cut to the normal spots and move out to the seams.

When forward 3 in the seam does not have the shot and passes to guard 2, also on the back-side, guard 2 has a shot or drive, or the cutting action begins. Forward 4 cuts to the basket and then to the corner. Post 5 cuts to daylight. Guard 1 moves up the baseline and cuts to the top or the opposite seam. Forward 3 moves down and away. In the event nothing positive has occurred, we pass immediately to the opposite seam and attack from that side.

penetrating the seam

It is very effective on occasion to penetrate the seams, especially from the front or a high wing position. Different zones present different seam opportunities. With the ball in the corner the seam concept is practically eliminated as the baseline and congestion reduce the possibilities. Zone penetration should be used wisely. It can be an effective weapon or grossly misused. Zone penetration is normally effective as a result of penetrating the perimeter defense, forcing the inside defense to pick up the penetrator, and checking to the open man. Short jump-shot opportunities also occur.

The seam occurs when the defense is forced to move maximum distances and when indecisions occur. The point of attack should be exactly the halfway point between two defensive players. The spots on either side of the key, ten to twelve feet from the point and about three feet above the foul line extended, will always present seams. These, in effect, are between defensive positions or will be with motion.

SCREENING THE ZONE

On occasion we find a measure of success using screens on the back-side of a zone. This is especially effective when we find a zone taking away the inside game. It gives high percentage 18-foot shots and has a tendency, if the outside shooting is effective, to pull the zone apart and make the inside play more effective, as the defense begins to cheat back in an attempt to get through the screens.

The swing-and-cut presents us with an effective screen on the initial pass and enables us, if the first screen is unsuccessful, to counter quickly behind a double screen.

Guard 2 passes to forward 4. Post 5 either screens opposite and cuts back, or simply rolls down to the low post. Guard 1 cuts to the basket and continues on to the corner. Guard 2 moves away and down as he normally does. Forward 3, instead of moving low and cutting to the point, moves down and sets a screen on the low man in the zone. (Diagram 12-5) Guard 2 cuts out at a 45-degree angle 15 to 18 feet from the basket. Forward 4 passes the ball across the zone to guard 2 behind the screen. This pass must be sharp and crisp and yet it must be high enough to prevent an interception. If the defensive man fights through the screen, forward 3 should turn immediately and take a low posting position looking for a check pass. In the event these options are thwarted, post 5 holds his position and screens the low man in the zone on the back-side. Forward 4, instead of cutting off the screen, moves in and sets a double screen with post 5. Guard 1 moves toward the basket and then cuts out at a 45-degree angle approximately 15 to 18 feet from the basket. (Diagram 12-6) Post 5 and forward 4 should turn and post up in the event the defense overcommits themselves to get through the screen and stop the shot.

If a shot or check pass does not result from the double screen, guard 2 will by this time have moved to the point. Guard 1

the swing-and-cut offense versus the zone 151

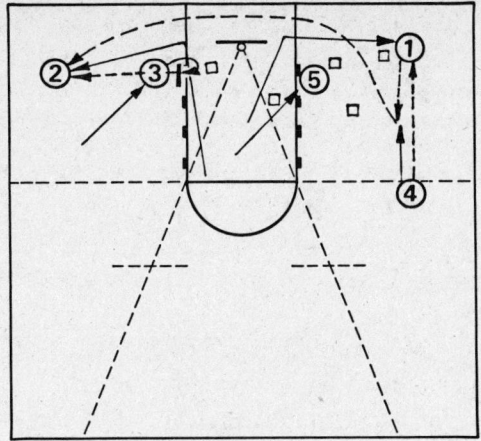

Diagram 12-5
Screening the Zone

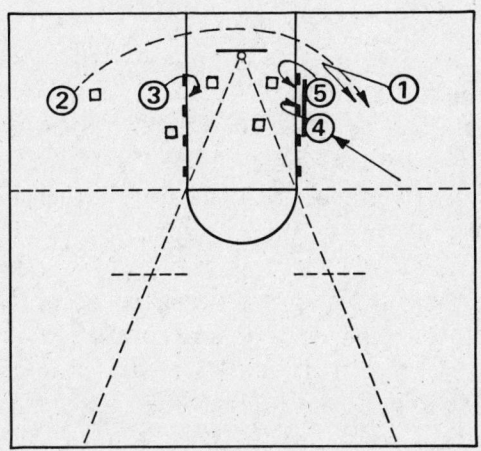

Diagram 12-6
Screening the Zone

will pass to guard 2. Guard 2 will swing the ball to forward 3 cutting out to the wing. Guard 1 will cut off the double screen. We have now turned the offense over, and the screening action may start again.

It is possible at times to throw the ball across the screen several times in a row if the desired shots have not materialized. In doing this, don't lose sight of inside possibilities. The defense has to move maximum distances with maximum effort and is very susceptible to mistakes.

SWING-AND-CUT INTO THE COMBINATION POST VERSUS THE ZONE

We find it especially effective to blend the screening effort with the combination post.

When a zone defense enables us to get the ball inside we find the combination post techniques most proficient. The execution is similar to that of the combination post versus man-for-man defense, as explained and illustrated in Chapter 9. (Diagrams 9-9, 9-9A, 9-9B, 9-9C, 9-9D, and 9-9E)

The zone, however, adjusts easier than the man-for-man to the various options. We have found it wise to show the swing-and-cut and quickly establish the combination post off the swing-and-cut motion.

Guard 2 passes to forward 4 and the swing-and-cut motion off the initial pass is executed. Forward 4 passes to forward 3 at the swing point. Forward 3 swings the ball to guard 2 on the weakside wing. Forward 3 moves into the foul line and curls back to the corner of the free throw line. Guard 1 cuts to the top of the key. Guard 2 immediately looks to the post, or passes to forward 4 in the corner, or quickly passes back to guard 1 at the point. Forward 3 reads the post defense and reacts just as explained in Chapter 9. (Diagram 9-9C) If guard 1 receives the ball back at the point, he immediately drives off the screen by forward 3. (Diagram 9-9D) Forward 3 rolls to the basket and posts low. Guard 1 should attempt to get as much depth as possible, which will be more difficult agiinst the zone. If forward 3 has posted successfully, guard 1 passes to him. If not, he passes to forward 4 at the top, who immediately looks for post 5 and forward 3 crabbing to the middle. If this is unsuccessful, he swings the ball to guard 2 on the wing, who passes to post 5 on the low side. (Diagram 12-7)

The pass from forward 4 at the top to post 5 or forward 3 crabbing in, or the quick swing to guard 2, or return pass to guard 1 on the wings for the post feeds are usually productive as we catch the zone moving and many times off-balance.

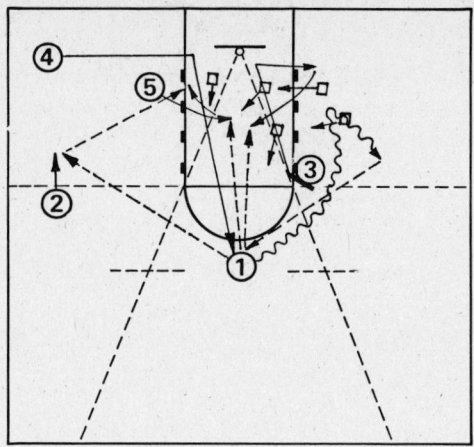

Diagram 12-7
Combination Post Versus Zone

Points of Emphasis

1. Read the defensive post play.
2. If the post is fronted, look to the backdoor area.
3. When the point man drives off the screen he must get some depth toward the baseline.
4. When the ball is returned to the top, the post men must crab aggressively to the ball. This sets up the pass from the wing.
5. The inside men must want the ball and work to get it.

13 offensive rebounding from the swing-and-cut alignments

There is an old saying in basketball that "the team that controls the bank boards controls the game." I believe this to be true in every sense of the word. There are, of course, many other factors involved, but a team that is aggressive enough to control the boards will be the winner in most cases.

There are many other factors involved in rebounding. Jumping ability, of course, is one of the most important assets, but this is not enough in itself. Perhaps timing should be placed above jumping ability, because the sense of timing is most valuable. Good judgment is important and should be used in determining the flight of the ball as to where the shot was taken and the likely rebound area. Courage and aggressiveness are most essential because many boys shy away from board play. With all of this we should blend some quickness; quickness of hands and feet and reaction. This quickness could very well be the most important factor. So, what do we have? Jumping ability, timing, judgment, courage, aggressiveness, and quickness: put them all together and you have an excellent rebounder and basketball player.

Everyone will probably agree that tall boys have an outstanding rebounding advantage, but there are also many excellent rebounders among the smaller players because they apply the above mentioned ingredients. I think it absolutely essential that rebounding techniques be drilled into every player, whether he is large or small.

position and form

The first step we take in teaching rebounding is to get a floor position that will be advantageous. We insist that our rebounders work toward never getting too far under the basket. In our rebounding drills we insist that the defensive rebounders in the side positions never have their feet completely inside the free throw lanes. We mark the floor six feet in front of the basket and instruct the front man not to get inside this. This, of course, is until the ball hits the board or rim. At this moment he should explode up and toward the ball with arms fully extended. From this position the smaller man, using the block out, places himself in a position equal to the taller man. If the smaller man lets the taller man force him under the basket, he does not have a chance at the rebound, since the taller man only has to outreach him for control of the ball. Even in the case of the tall man being forced under by the small man, he is at a definite disadvantage on the long rebound as the smaller man may force him in and step out for the ball. Any ball rebounding lightly goes to the inside man. This is where the block out and the aggressive move to meet the ball is most effective.

Proper rebounding form is important. We spend an adequate amount of time tossing the ball high against the board and having all players rebound for form against no opposition. The players should be instructed to jump as high as possible, to time the flight of the ball as expertly as possible, and to grab the ball with both hands. The moment both hands are firmly placed on the ball it should be snatched 12 to 18 inches in a downward motion that will free it from the hands of the opponents. The player's elbows should be forced out as the ball is brought in to the rebounder's chest; this will add extra protection. The legs should be spread as wide as possible as he comes to the floor. He should land in a decided crouch, feet spread, elbows out, ball into the chest in a protective cup. This entire action should be executed with determination, vigor, and enthusiasm. We tell our players to make this a savage motion.

blocking out

Although this chapter emphasizes offensive rebounding, I think it important to discuss blocking out. Teams that are well-drilled in the blocking out technique will always get their share of the rebounds. There are many blocking out opportunities on offense if the offense will work for position. When your players are more than six feet from the basket and if you have inside position, ask them to take one step back in the direction of the basket when the shot is taken. This will enable you to control the position of your rebounders and to prevent them from chasing their opponents. Chasing or lunging at your opponent is one of the biggest mistakes made in blocking out, because it gives your opponent an opportunity to outmaneuver you as you chase or lunge, and it also takes you away from the rebound area. After you step back, if the opponent is crashing the board, the blocker should turn into him with a body check and maintain this contact until he releases to the ball. Always turn into the opponent.

The technique is very similar to that of a front pivot. By turning in you always have your eyes on the opponent in case he fakes one way and crashes another, and you can very easily compensate for the move. For example, if the opponent crashes to your left, you will pivot on your left foot, cross over with the right and body check with the right hip. If he fakes left but crashes right, you will quickly compensate by stepping aggressively with your left foot and riding him off with your left hip.

We don't like to use a back pivot and turn our heads. This causes us to lose sight of the opponent and the first fake can defeat our efforts. If a player finds himself only six or seven feet from the basket when the shot is taken, he must disregard the step back and turn quickly into the opponent in the method previously discussed. If the player finds himself inside of six feet, he must force out to the six foot mark immediately on the shot and not get smothered.

It is important that every player anticipate a jolt as he attempts to block an opponent out. The players should be ready to meet force with force without losing their balance and falling back when no contact is made. They should not let the opponents force them under.

judging the flight of the ball

Many players get so preoccupied with blocking out that they forget about the ball, and it may fall loosely behind them or at their feet. Good judgment should be used when playing against an opponent that seldom crashes the board, one who moves too slowly to be effective, or one who tries to fake several times. (Usually more than one fake is ineffective.)

Emphasis should be placed on the flight of the ball. A player has no more than one second to step back, block out, and go after the rebound. A player should leave his opponent when he has determined the ball will hit the rim and rebound quicker and more effectively than any blocking action.

A simple drill for this is to place five men in a normal defensive pattern. We have another player to shoot different types of shots. The defensive men judge the flight of the ball and turn quickly into rebounding position the moment they think the ball will hit the rim. A few minutes of this each week will prove most beneficial.

going up to meet the ball

It is very disheartening to see a player doing an exceptional job of blocking out, judging the flight of the ball perfectly, and then letting an opponent reach over him and slap the ball away because he did not go up to meet it.

This is a very simple but important maneuver, and it should not be taken for granted. The body and feet, occupied with blocking out, are already in favorable position. Perhaps the feet at the last moment should be brought a little closer together in order to gain momentum for the upward thrust. In general the feet should be parallel, spread a little wider than shoulder width, and positioned about six feet from the basket. The body is balanced low in a deep crouch in order to absorb the shock of the opponent crashing. From this position, with good timing, a very explosive leg thrust should drive the body quickly and powerfully forward and up to meet the ball.

Height, jumping ability, and timing are all determining factors in how close to the rim or board this forward thrust will carry you. In every instance however, the player must be encouraged to meet the ball at the maximum height of the jump.

snatch and control

As the hands close in on the ball they should be placed a little to the top of the ball as the direction of the action is down. A good firm hand position is an important factor in controlling the rebound.

As the hand position is obtained and as the ball is captured at the heighth of the jump, we instruct our players to snatch the ball down with quickness and power for a distance of 12 to 18 inches. This teaches a boy to get the ball quickly out of the many hands that are reaching for it and to bring it into his own control. It helps to eliminate the slow hands of many big boys who simply try to get their hands on the ball by outstretching the other players. It adds aggressiveness and determination to rebounding.

The body is also another excellent control measure. As the ball is snatched down, it should be brought into the chest, the legs spread-eagled, and hips and body in crouched position. The elbows should be extended, back straight, head up and erect. These moves should be quick, aggressive, and commanding.

OFFENSIVE REBOUNDING

The first portion of rebounding dealt mainly with basic fundamentals and blocking out. When we mention blocking out we immediately think of defensive rebounding, and rightfully so. However, there are many opportunities for an offensive team to block out if they are alert and aggressive. There has never been a great deal written or even discussed on the offensive part of this important action. This is due in part to the fact that it is very difficult to plan an organized approach to this action. If the opposing defense and rebounding techniques are up to par, the offensive rebounder will find himself, in most cases, on the outside and being blocked away from the basket. It is difficult under the circumstances to have a planned organized strategy. I have at times attempted such strategy, only to find I was confusing the issue and getting no results. Our main objective now is to endow our offensive rebounders with an idea of the area they should be responsible for and the determination and ability to move aggressively to the board. *Aggressive movement is to offensive rebounding what blocking out is to defensive rebounding.*

We instruct the offensive rebounder to first test the player who is blocking him out. Many times this blocker can be easily forced under the basket and out of position. He should find out how quick his opponent is and how good his execution is. Many times quickness and know-how will do the job. Try the force, the fake, and just plain quickness, but get inside.

From every offensive pattern we attempt, we advise our personnel as to the correct rebound position and area. We try always to have three men on the offensive board. It is a must to get to the back-side of the basket. Since many more shots are overshot rather than undershot, we would like to get our best rebounder to this spot. The next area we want to cover, if possible, is the front of the basket. Finally, to complete the triangle, a rebounder is placed on the same side the shot is taken from. In many cases this is the shooter, depending on the distance and the type of shot.

As previously stated, movement is the secret to offensive rebounding, just as blocking out is the secret to defensive rebounding. Movement is the secret to offensive board play. We ask our players to keep three things in mind: (1) move to the board with the idea every shot is going to miss and you own the ball; (2) get a hand on the ball or at least knock it loose and keep it in play; and (3) smother the defensive rebounder. In order to present an effective offense, we must be able to keep pressure on the defense. If our offensive rebounders follow the pattern or steps mentioned above they take a huge stride in exerting pressure on the defense in the rebounding stage of the game. As we talk about each of the steps mentioned above, bear in mind that movement is the key to the success of each step.

As we move to the board, many things must be taken into consideration. First, we must be alert to the fact that a shot is going to be taken. As we anticipate the shot the movement begins. Many times just prior to the shot we find an open path to the basket. The quick reaction of the rebounder, along with his knowledge of what his teammate is about to attempt, should find the rebounder getting to the desired position before the defensive rebounders are set. At times a series of stagger steps or fakes will prove valuable in making the defense commit to a point where the offensive man can slide inside for position. Many times the offense can simply force the defense under the board and smother them.

Quickness is of great importance, and a rebounder with quick hands, quick feet, and a sense of aggressiveness is very difficult to block out. All of these steps will help put the player in the rebounding range desired.

After the rebounder gets his desired position and as he starts his maneuvers to get a hand on the ball, he must be forming a judgment as to where the ball is most likely to rebound. This judgment, the position he has obtained and the rebounding fundamentals previously described, will allow him an aggressive moving opportunity to get the rebound or get his hand on the ball, rather than the passive attempt if he allows the defense to control him. Remember, if our rebounders on the offensive level cannot secure the rebound and control it, they must by all means get a hand on it and knock it away so that a teammate using these same maneuvers may have the opportunity to come up with it. If he cannot secure the ball, he must not let the opponent have it.

If by chance our plans do not work out and the opponent does get the ball, we must smother the man with the ball. Here again movement is the essential ingredient. We try to smother the man and not let him get the outlet pass away. We make him turn inside to nullify the possibilities of the fast break. This action will give us the opportunity to get our defenses back and set, and prevent the immediate threat of a fast-break attack. As previously stated, a defense to be successful, must keep constant pressure on the offense. This smothering move will immediately initiate this concept of pressure.

To sum up offensive rebounding, it is a determined scramble to get the best position. It is endowed with *aggressive movement*, desire, and intestinal fortitude. It is based on the offensive pressure placed on the defense, movement to the board, getting a hand on the ball, and smothering the opponent who might come up with the ball.

offensive rebounding techniques

We have discussed the theory and ideas concerning offensive rebounding. It think it wise to mention several skills involved in this phase of the game. These skills will make our carefully prepared plans either pay off with a basket, ball control, or have our efforts fall short because of our inability to execute.

basic rebounding fundamentals

We use many of the basic rebounding fundamentals previously discussed with defensive rebounding. If we accomplish our objective and quickly get the desired rebounding position, we must use all of the basics, beginning with blocking out, that the defensive rebounder is instructed to use.

tipping

The quickest scoring move of the offensive rebounder is tipping. When used by an agile player with exceptional jumping ability and timing, this is most effective and will place tremendous pressure on the defense. Both the one-hand and the two-hand methods of tipping are effective. The two-hand method is more accurate if the opportunity presents itself. Tipping drills are important and should be rehearsed daily.

the power move

Another efficient scoring move after capturing an offensive rebound is the power move. From a good rebounding position we may possibly capture the rebound in two hands at a distance from the rim that the tip would not be a high percentage move. Immediately upon returning to the floor with the ball, a quick, upward move to the basket while carrying the ball up in two hands and using the body for a shield, will gain effective results. Quickness, strength, and size play an important part. However, some small men also use this move productively. This move executed to perfection will also result in many three-point plays. This move at times can be made more effective by adding a fake which, if strategically used the moment the rebounder returns to the floor, has a tendency to get an alert defensive man off-balance and force him into the air. The moment he is off-balance the rebounder continues with the power move to the basket.

reverse power move

The reverse power move is fundamentally the same as the power move, except that the moment the rebounder returns to the floor with the ball, if the defense moves toward him, he will quickly use a low dribble under the basket, using a slide step and one dribble to the opposite side, and from there use the power move.

turn and jump

At times the rebounder finds it necessary to move slightly away from the basket due to the position from which he captured the rebound or the congestion near the board. At this point the turn and jump shot off the board may be exceptionally valuable. This enables the rebounder to move away not more than one dribble and quickly turn and put up a quick, short shot. Our other rebounders are still in the basket area and are in position to follow this shot.

REBOUND AREAS FROM THE SWING-AND-CUT

Rebound areas must be obtained to insure that all three sides of the basket are covered. Rebound areas must be obtained before the basic fundamental of offensive rebounding can be fully applied. It is true that the first fundamental is exercising the proper techniques involved with getting to the proper areas. This appears to be a very simple maneuver, but in reality it is not. The rebounding structure designed for the swing-and-cut to be effective must keep five rules in mind.

Rule 1. We rebound offensively with three and one-half men. This gives us a man and a half in position to quickly get back on defense. The term one-half man means that one of the guards takes the area around the free throw line anticipating a long or tipped rebound and is in position to get back quickly on defense. Against some teams we will rebound with three men and possibly with as many as four at times. Scout reports reveal the opponents' habits and personnel which dictate this strategy.

Rule 2. The center or post is always assigned the front of the basket.

Rule 3. If a guard is the low man in the double screen, he is always the one-half man.

164 offensive rebounding from the swing-and-cut alignments

Rule 4. If there is a guard on the point, the wing guard is the one-half man.

Rule 5. The post and two forwards are always rebounders.

I will discuss and illustrate swing-and-cut rebounding areas with shots from the strong wing, point, and weakside wing positions.

SHOT FROM THE STRONGSIDE WING

Forward 4 has the ball on the strongside wing. Guard 1 and post 5 form the double screen along the lane. Forward 3 is at the top of the key. Guard 2 is on the back-side. Forward 4 takes an 18-foot shot. Post 5 quickly rolls to the front of the basket. Forward 3, at the top of the key, cuts to cover the back-side of the board. Forward 4, who attempted the shot, follows to the near side. Guard 1 rolls up to the one-half man position at the free throw line, and guard 2 moves back as the safety factor. (Diagram 13-1)

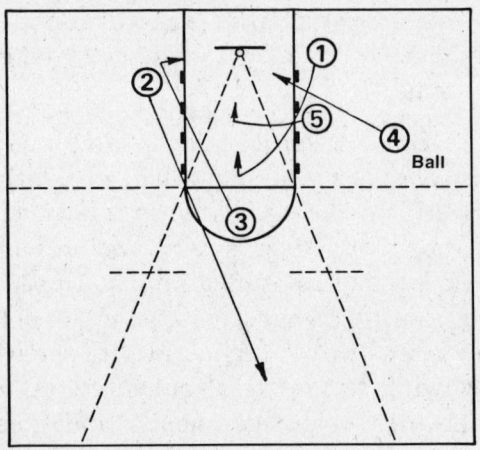

Diagram 13-1
Rebound Shot from Strongside Wing

If the shot is taken from the strong wing by a guard, as it could be on every alternate swing or turnover, we would find forward 4 as the low man in the double screen. Post 5 will be in his normal high position in the screen. Forward 3 has moved down and away and is now on the weak side. Guard 1 has moved to the three spot at the point. As the shot is taken by guard 2, post 5 rolls to the front of the basket. Forward 4 moves to get inside position on the strong side or shooting side. Forward 3 works to get his desired position on the weak side. Guard 2, who took the shot, follows for one or two steps and moves to the long rebound area in the vicinity of the foul line. Guard 1, at the top of the key, moves back a few steps as the safety or floor balance factor. (Diagram 13-1A)

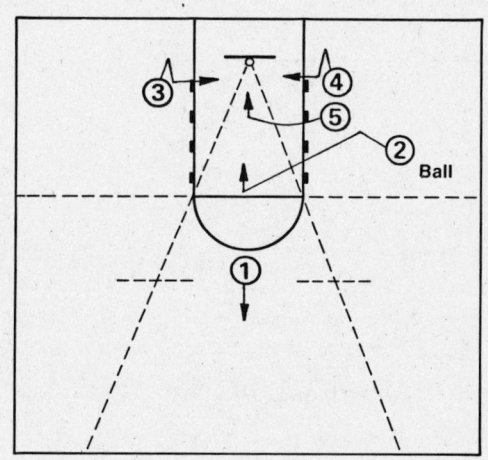

Diagram 13-1A
Rebounding Shot from Strongside Wing

Perhaps I should take this opportunity to explain inside rebound techniques according to defensive adjustments. If the defense plays behind the low man in the double screen, forward 4, and the high man, post 5, will move and work for rebound position, as explained and illustrated in Diagrams 13-1 and 13-1A. This results in the most difficult rebounding task we will find.

If the defensive man halves forward 4 on the low side with a hand across the chest or passing lane, and post 5 finds his defensive man halving him on the high side with a hand across the chest, two quick moves should enable us to block our defensive men out and obtain an excellent offensive rebounding advantage. Forward 4, pivoting on his low foot, the right in this instance, executes a quick, strong, back pivot, blocking his defensive man out of the area. He thereby gains a position that should control the strong side of the basket. (Diagram 13-2) Post 5 executes a strong, quick, back pivot on his high foot, the left in this example, blocking his defensive man out and quickly stepping to the front of the basket. (Diagram 13-2)

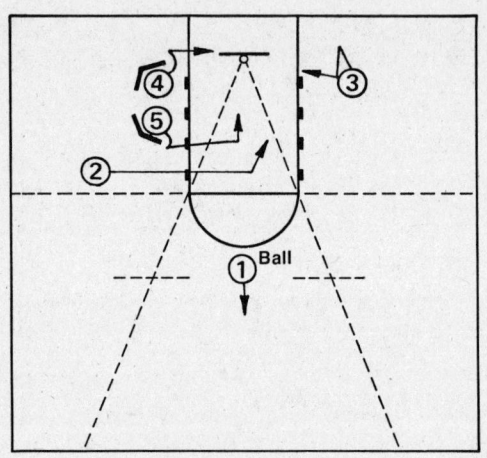

Diagram 13-2
Rebounding Shot from Top of Key

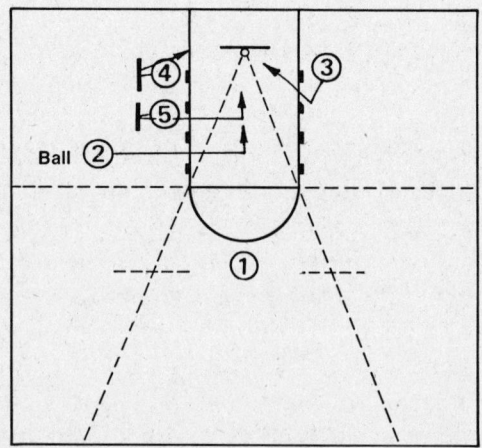

Diagram 13-3
Shot from Strongside Wing

offensive rebounding from the swing-and-cut alignments   167

If forward 4 and post 5 find themselves completely fronted, they are presented with their most advantageous possibilities for obtaining effective rebound positions. Forward 4 simply body checks his defensive man and maintains control of the strongside area. (Diagram 13-3) Post 5 steps sharply into his defensive man, body checks, and moves quickly to the front of the basket. (Diagram 13-3)

SHOT FROM THE WEAKSIDE WING

Occasionally we find our wing putting up a shot from what we consider strictly the weakside position. This usually occurs on a long overthrow or when a four-cut clear out is necessary. The techniques involved here are quite similar to those involved in Diagram 13-1. In this case we would ask guard 1, who is the low man in the double screen, to be a little more aware of the safety factor as he comes to the long rebound area. It is necessary that this emphasis be stressed, as guard 2 is the shooter. Guard 2 should follow his shot one to two steps and then sprint back as the safety factor.

If the weakside shot is taken by a forward, for example, forward 3, post 5 moves as always to the front of the basket. Forward 4 will now strongly hold his position and command the backside of the board. The shooter, forward 3, will follow his shot and become the strongside rebounder. Guard 1 is the safety factor and guard 2 moves to the long rebound area. (Diagram 13-4)

Bear in mind defensive positions utilized by the defensive team must be recognized and dealt with accordingly as explained in Diagrams 13-2 and 13-3.

SHOT FROM THE POINT

If the shot is taken from the point or foul-line area, the rebounding techniques should be closely aligned with those designed in Diagram 13-1. Forward 3 takes the shot from the point or three spot. Upon completely releasing the shot, he follows with strong emphasis to the weak side of the board. Post 5 again rolls to the front of the basket. Strongside forward 4 moves quickly and with strength to the strong side of the basket. Guard 1, the low man in

168 offensive rebounding from the swing-and-cut alignments

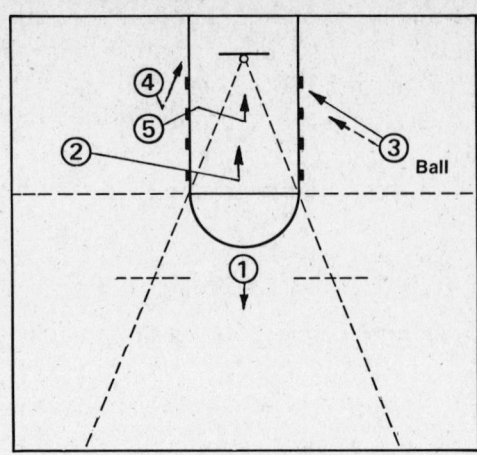

Diagram 13-4
Shot from Weakside Wing

the screen, cuts quickly to the long rebound area, and guard 2 moves back for defensive purposes.

If a guard takes the shot from the point, the rebounding techniques found in Diagram 13-1A are quite similar. Post 5 moves to the middle. The low forward in the screen maintains his strongside position. The weakside forward is responsible for the weak side of the board. Guard 2 moves to the long rebound area and the shooter, guard 1, follows one or two steps and moves back for floor balance.

Pay special attention to Diagrams 13-2 and 13-3. Recognizing defensive positions will simplify rebounding efforts and effectiveness. Do not fail to take advantage of the opportunities presented. Be quick to recognize the more difficult situations. Work and move especially hard to equalize them.

The cardinal sin relating to offensive rebounding is the lack of movement. Don't stand. Some players have a special talent for going to the board, timing the rebound expertly, and forcibly retrieving it. Other players have to be driven until it becomes a conditioned reflex. Instill in all your rebounders the idea that every shot is going to miss and they must get a hand on the rebound. Rehearse it daily.

14

control and tempo change

More players in basketball are getting better at the game they love. Coaches are working diligently to improve their knowledge, techniques, and strategies, to make competition more balanced and exciting. In the next decade we will see an emergence of new coaches challenging the veterans. Some will succeed while others will come up short. Much of the success of coaching, whether newcomer or veteran, relates directly to being able to control the game and change and adjust the tempo.

Control and tempo change covers a wide range of situations. These situations mean different things to different teams. Speaking strictly from an offensive point of view the following situations for controlling the game and changing the tempo must be considered.

1. *Strength of your opponent.* It is obvious the strength of your opponent is going to be an important factor when preparing for each game. The type of game you will play will be predicated on your scout reports and the relative comparisons between the two teams. Records, size, quickness, experience, maturity, and results of previous games all have important bearing. If you are definitely stronger than an op-

ponent, the emphasis would be on executing your basic efforts to perfection with very little pregame adjustment. If, however, you are a definite underdog, it is absolutely essential to have in your game plan some type of equalizing factor.

2. *The opposing coach.* You must know his style, his personality, and his game tendencies. When is he the most effective? Does he bring his team from behind well? Has he prepared for special situations? Is he a competitor? Does he coach well in pressure situations?

3. *Location of game.* Whether you are at home, away, or on a neutral court, the crowd is certainly a factor in a ball game. The design of the building is a possible factor. The lighting could make a slight difference. Have your team in the proper frame of mind so that there are no surprises. Don't let the crowds or facility take away the concentration of you, as the coach, or of your team. These obstacles can be greatly minimized with proper planning. Your success will most likely be related to the time you spent preparing for the occasion.

4. *Opponents' defense.* What defense are you likely to encounter? What elements of your offense are likely to be the most effective? An all-purpose offense such as the swing-and-cut is especially adept at maintaining poise and confidence in unusual or unexpected defensive encounters.

5. *Type of officiating.* Reports and files should be kept on the officials just as files should be kept on your opponents. Know them and their tendencies; plan your strategy around their specific attitudes. Certain officials are noted for their emphasis on a particular foul or violation. Basketball games range from a foul-infested, touch-me-not game to one of vicious physical contact. Coaches often complain after a game about a certain call which they themselves could have anticipated if they had thought ahead as to who was blowing the whistle and had prepared their team adequately.

6. *Substitutions.* The decision as to who is going to play, why they are going to play, and for how long, can be formulated long before game time. The same holds true for your

opponent. If you envision needing someone other than a starter, give him a chance in the early part of the game so he will get a feel for this particular encounter. Substituting is an art that outstanding game coaches use to a great advantage. Substitutions are often the key to victory. Practice the moves and countermoves before game time.

7. *Game plan.* How long do you stay with your game plan? Set some pregame monitors for your strategy relating to time and point spread. An all-purpose offense that requires a slight adjustment has a definite advantage.

8. *Score of game.* The score of the game or the point spread is the determining factor as to game effectiveness. Adjustments must be made throughout the game in an effort to control the point spread. It is essential to maintain a lead and even more essential to control the point spread so you will always be in a position to win.

9. *Time remaining.* The time remaining and the point spread are very closely related. It is extremely important never to let the point spread reach the position in your opponents' favor, so that unnecessary pressure because of time remaining presents an insurmountable obstacle. Many times teams trail for most of the game and prevail victorious at the final gun. This can be accomplished only if the time remaining and the point spread correlate positively throughout the game.

10. *Time outs.* Use them wisely. Tie them into your game plan. You get five in regulation play, plus possible TV's if you are on that level. Also you get an additional one for each overtime. You would never run your practice sessions or practice games without occasionally stopping for critiques. Here is an opportunity for some very important one-minute clinics. The clinic topic will change each time, but an emphasis on poise and confidence should always prevail. You must plan to save time outs. When and for what purpose are you going to use these precious five minutes? Plan and practice the time allotted to your assistants and to your team. The experience and maturity of a team will have a lot to do with the stage of the game your time outs are used.

11. *Key moves.* Mentally practice the key moves it will be necessary for you to make under game time pressures in order to control the tempo of the game effectively. Who takes the last shot? How do we set this shot up? What game tempo must be established? Whom do you foul? There are many key moves for executing situations that should be planned and rehearsed daily.

12. *Game coaching.* The quality of talent is obviously one of the most important factors in determining the outcome of a game. The home-court advantage, the fans, the referees, physical conditions, maturity, and many other factors have been widely discussed. Many of these will eventually equalize themselves over an extended period of time. Game coaching may become, over this same period, the most important factor. You can reach only 75 to 80 percent of your potential as a coach unless you diligently work at this important aspect of the game. Game coaching, once the game has begun, is the ability of the coach to alter the outcome of the game. Many games are won or lost as a result of game coaching strategy. So many teams are capable of victory, especially when they reach the championship level, that without a doubt the eventual champion will be a team that is coached by a man who is able to make the best use of game coaching circumstances.

Both on the high school and collegiate level there has been a definite trend to the delay game. This usually occurs when a team has captured the lead and the opponents are in some type of zone defense. Making the defense come out and play seems to be the prevailing philosophy. This, as a rule, dictates a definite change in offensive tactics. It also forces both the offense and the defense to be more aware of and live within the framework of insufficient action rules. In many instances this has presented as many problems for the offense as for the defense. The fact that a distinct change has taken place, the rules impact becomes a factor, and you begin to draw negative responses from the fans, has psychologically removed the confidence and poise from an otherwise effective team. There are game situations where ball control and delay tactics are necessary.

The swing-and-cut provides flexibility that will incorporate all the necessary ingredients of control, delay and tempo change with only slight adjustments necessary to the basic pattern. No offense is complete without control and tempo-changing possibilities. The very fact that a team may easily establish these ingredients, using the same offensive techniques it rehearses daily, maintains a poise and confidence not otherwise possible. Making these necessary adjustments while staying with your basic attack many times disguises the fact you are indeed attempting to change the tempo, delay or run time off the clock, and/or baiting the defense into allowing you to place them at a disadvantage. These possibilities provide the swing-and-cut with additional offensive weapons as you rehearse daily your total offensive attack.

We think of our offensive philosophy in three phases:

1. Normal Phase

In the normal phase we employ the fast break to its utmost as our basic plan of attack along with our swing-and-cut continuity (as previously explained and illustrated in Chapters 2 through 12). The early stages of the game will determine if adjustments are necessary. Basic cuts, basic relief moves, and basic fundamentals are essential. The defensive alignment and pressure will dictate the basic elements we must emphasize.

2. Control Phase

The swing-and-cut allows us to make positive strategic adjustments if game conditions dictate a control type attack. Our first attempt at ball control is normally with our basic alignment. We designate specific shots and specific shooters. We do not necessarily eliminate the fast break. We do ask for only extremely high percentage passes and high percentage shots. The control phase enables us to place special emphasis on specific cuts and designate specific shooters. In this phase we do not stray too far from our normal offensive philosophy. We simply do not put the ball up as freely. We force the defense to work a little longer and a little harder until we free specific cuts and specific shooters. This also increases offensive rebounding potential as our personnel are more aware of the floor positions from which the shot will be taken.

Reasonable success when using this tactic increases confidence and poise.

Ball possession falls under the control phase in our offensive philosophy. Effective ball possession is eliminating the possibilities of a superior team establishing an insurmountable point spread. This of course will cut down the opponent's shot production and psychologically affect a high scoring opponent. Any effort at controlling the ball will change the tempo, a very vital part of the control phase.

Tempo change is most effective when teams of fairly equal strengths are involved and efforts are made to gain an advantage. Teams with superior personnel normally rely on their power and the aspects of the game in which they are especially proficient. A team with inferior personnel might use a control or delay tactic from the outset of the game, which in essence is tempo change. The strategy is to upset the superior opponents by taking away their power. The swing-and-cut has built-in factors that are positive to ball possession and tempo change necessities. Make your personnel aware that your offense, as it is rehearsed daily, will prepare them to meet and command any situation. This awareness will build the confidence necessary to successful execution.

3. The Delay Phase

We think of our delay game as the semi-freeze and the freeze. The semi-freeze is the most often used. We eliminate all perimeter shots and take nothing but lay-ups or wide open shots off the board six feet or closer, but definitely not beyond six feet. The freeze is exactly what it says: freeze it, don't shoot it, we want the ball, not the points. In either strategy our normal swing-and-cut continuity may be sufficient. The fact that two men are always cutting to the basket, one man always cutting to the top, and one to the back-side of the basket, makes trapping virtually impossible. Someone has to be open if double-team tactics are employed. The quick reverse or swing enables the offense to operate from both sides of the floor. The interchange at the top discourages overplaying.

The two adjustments that we most commonly use when employing control or delay tactics are what we call *high* and *wide* and *high stationary post. High* and *wide* means we execute our normal swing-and-cut pattern, but extend our operating positions. On the initial move we do not ask the guards to attempt to bring the ball to two and one-half steps from the top of the key. They may initiate the action immediately as they cross into front court. We permit the forwards to come as high and as wide as necessary to receive the pass. As the swing is made, we permit the point man to move as high as necessary to receive the pass and to make the swing pass to the wing.

Point of Emphasis: It is vital that, even though the operating positions have been extended, once the swing pass has been completed the cuts must be executed with quickness and precision. Do not stand. (Diagram 14-1)

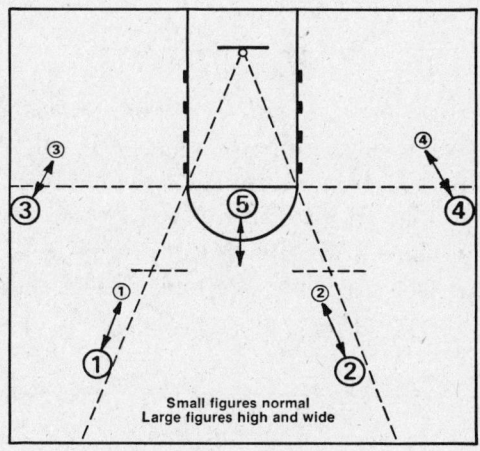

Diagram 14-1
High and Wide

The *high stationary post* may be executed from the normal swing-and-cut operating positions or from the high and wide alignment. The adjustment is simple. The post man takes his initial swing-and-cut position and stays there. Guards 1 and 2 and forwards 3 and 4 execute the normal swing-and-cut continuity. (Diagram 14-2) The advantages of this adjustment are simple. First, the post man maintains his position, thereby being always available to pass to in the event of excessive pressure or quick double-teams.

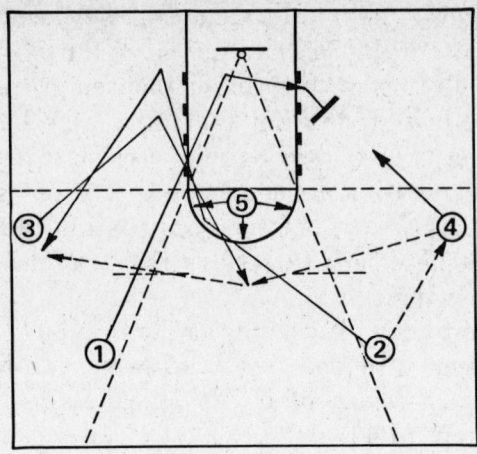

Diagram 14-2
High and Wide Stationary Post

Second, the area under the basket is not as congested and possible quick short shots become more prevalent. Third, the swing man now uses the post as a back screen. (Diagram 14-3) This forces his defensive man to play more cautiously. In the event of excessive pressure, the low man, normally in the double screen, cuts by the post to the top. As he receives the ball, the men being pressured interchange to the operating positions. (Diagram 14-4)

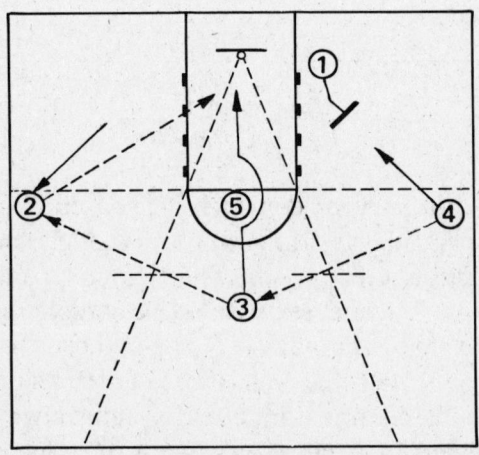

Diagram 14-3
Back Screen by Post

control and tempo change 177

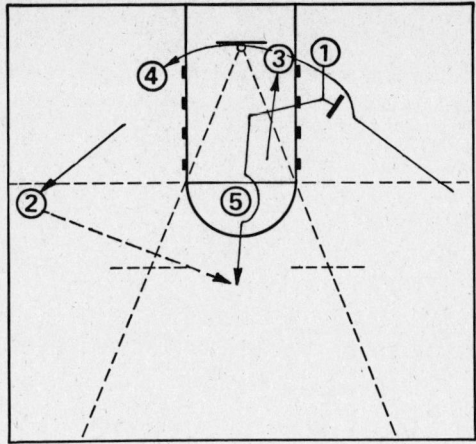

Diagram 14-4
Cut Off Post to Top

When any type of control or delay tactic is necessary, the awareness on the part of the offense that they are prepared to meet and command any situation that might occur instills in them the confidence necessary to successful execution. Meeting these situations with an effective offense rehearsed daily adds to the confidence and poise desired.

15

teaching drills around the swing-and-cut pattern

Drills are excellent. There are drills by which you can teach fundamental basketball that are of the utmost importance to the basics of the game. These drills have very little to do with the continuity and motion of the basic offense. I deem it exceedingly important, especially after the basics are well-taught and rehearsed, to align them as closely as possible to the offensive or defensive situations through which you will put them to use. This philosophy will enable you to rehearse the techniques desired under the conditions they will be realistically applied. Ball handling, screening, cutting, positioning and timing must be rehearsed daily. This can be put into effect and emphasized as you rehearse your pattern, both with and without a defense.

We have all had players who are picture perfect when the basics are taught as a simple, individual maneuver. Yet these same players, when becoming involved with a pattern or versus a defense, are perhaps inept.

The best drills in basketball are those you design yourself and relate directly to your offense, defense, or the situation involving your personnel.

Many coaches ask me for good drills for a variety of situations. This is all well and good. Do not, however, become so drill-conscious that you fail to apply them to game conditions. Drills are not designed as time consumers. Drills are designed specifically to improve the effectiveness of your personnel within the boundaries of what you are attempting to accomplish.

This chapter describes and illustrates some special drills. Notice however, many of our important drills are based around our offensive patterns.

FOUR MAN SWING-AND-CUT

After we feel we thoroughly understand the fundamentals, the four man swing-and-cut is probably the drill we utilize the most. With this drill we rehearse fundamental basketball daily as it relates to our offensive pattern and at the same time emphasize position, spacing, and timing, which are so important to the successful execution of the offense. We use all personnel in this drill, including the post men. This enables us to familiarize our post men with the cuts and moves ordinarily performed by the guards and forwards, thus providing the opportunity to alternate post men without impeding the motion of the pattern.

This drill emphasizes the fundamentals of ball handling, cutting, screening, faking, and timing involved in the basic pattern. It is wise at times to tape or chalk the exact floor positions from which the players are expected to operate. We work in groups of four and designate the number of swing-and-cuts desired before a shot is taken. On the shot, four more players step in.

In utilizing this drill our personnel place themselves in the exact swing-and-cut alignment prescribed for the guards and forwards in Chapter 2. We insist all players get the feeling for positioning themselves and starting from all four positions. In Diagram 15-1, 1 passes to 4 and then cuts through the corner of the free throw line for the basket. When he does not receive the pass he steps out to what would normally be the low position in the double screen. Player 3 moves into the wide-lane marker and quickly cuts to the three spot at the top of the key. Player 2, who made the initial pass, moves away and down. After looking at his first cutter, 4 passes to 3 at the top. Player 3 swings the ball to 2, who

teaching drills around the swing-and-cut pattern   181

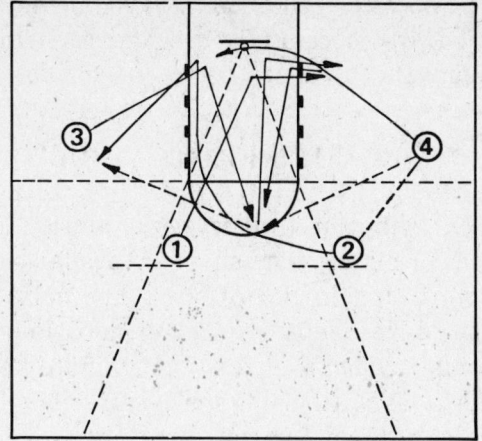

Diagram 15-1
Four Man Swing-and-Cut

has cut out to the wing or forward position. Player 4 cuts off the screen by 1. Player 1 fakes to the inside and cuts to the three spot at the top of the key, replacing 3, who has moved down and away.

Passing, feet positioning, cutting, faking, and screening should be carefully scrutinized and corrected during the process of this drill. This drill may be used without any shooting. The swing-and-cut action will continue until the whistle. A specified number of swings may be designated with a specific shot. You may also terminate the action with a relief move, thereby rehearsing relief moves. It may be used daily as a warm-up drill. Supervision is important. Insist on basic values and precisioned execution.

The four man swing-and-cut may be used most proficiently as a defensive drill. Assign four defensive men and execute; this provides the defense with a team defensive concept. They are exposed to quick cuts, weakside cuts, high cuts, screens, overplaying and one-on-one situations.

On one occasion we used the four man swing-and-cut as an effective deterrent to a box-and-one defensive alignment. We placed the player being pointed out by the box-and-one in the deep corner and used the four man swing-and-cut as our offense, giving the player cutting low the option of cutting to the corner and the player cutting to the point the option of placing himself in the weakside seam.

On another occasion, finding a player being fronted, overplayed and denied, we successfully used the same tactics against a man-for-man defense.

THREE-CUT SHOOTING DRILL

The three-cut shooting drill is very important in the swing-and-cut scheme as probably more shots are available from this spot than any other position in the offense. The very nature of the swing-and-cut persuades defenses to sag and slough inside. The three cut is moving away from the basket and defensive philosophies align themselves with being inside-conscious first. At times we definitely screen down for the three cut, which adds to the possible chances that this shot will be available.

We deem it absolutely necessary to make above 50 percent of our shots from the three spot; therefore, we must constantly rehearse the fakes, cut, position of the feet, body balance and exact spot the ball is delivered to the shooter. One basic mistake could render this move ineffective.

The three-cut shooting drill may be performed with any number of players. I suggest however, no more than six players be involved to insure constant action and ample shooting attempts.

Player 1 positions himself with his inside foot on the wide-lane divider while facing the top of the key. Player 2 positions himself at the top of the key, feet spread about the width of his shoulders, with his body in a slight crouch. Player 3 takes his position on the wide-lane divider opposite 1. Other players line up evenly behind each of these positions. Player 2 initiates the action by passing to player 3 as he cuts to the wing or forward position. Player 2, upon releasing the ball, makes his normal move to the basket, anticipating a short lob. He may screen for player 1, positioning himself for the back-side rebound and in position to cut to the wing if the ball is swung. Player 1 fakes to the inside, cuts to the free throw line and quickly steps to the three spot for the shot. (Diagram 15-2) This shot should never be over 20 feet. If properly executed, the 18-foot shot is ideal. It is also possible to adjust this drill to use only two shooters. Place a player in the number one position and the number two position. Place a coach, manager, or another player on the wing as a feeder. Players 1 and 2 do all of the cutting, screening and shooting. (Diagram 15-3)

teaching drills around the swing-and-cut pattern   183

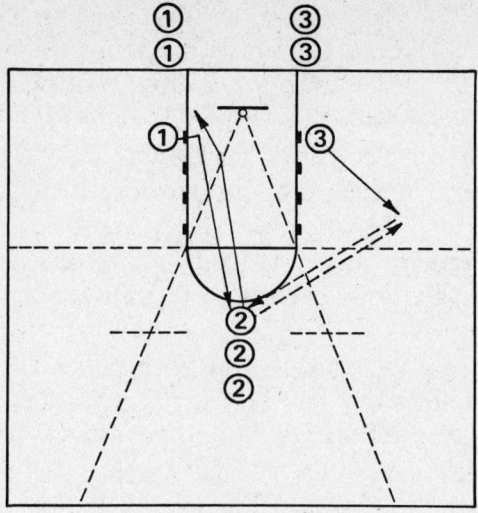

Diagram 15-2
Three-Cut Shooting Drill

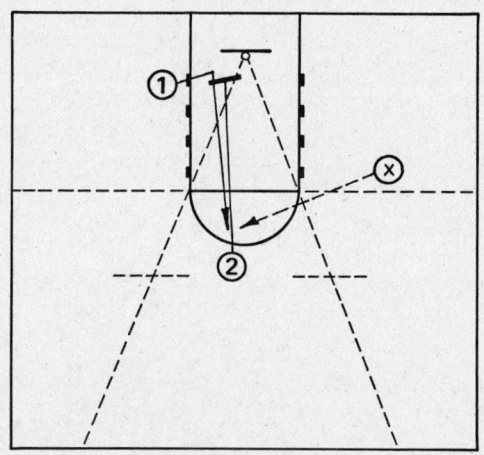

Diagram 15-3
Three-Cut Shooting Drill—Two Players

THE FOUR-CUT SHOOTING DRILL

The swing or reverse factor alone makes the four cut and the four spot a productive scoring opportunity. We add to these possibilities by making the four cut a possible one-on-one move for a talented player. We hold our cutters and allow him to shoot, take his man to the basket, drive, and jump shoot with the entire area cleared out. This is a most effective shooting drill as it brings into focus techniques basic to our swing-and-cut offense, resulting in a specific shot.

In using the four-cut shooting drill the players position themselves in the exact positions as the previous drill. (Diagram 15-2) The supplemental lines are behind players 1 and 3. Again, any number may participate, but I strongly suggest that participation be limited to five or six players to provide sufficient action and shooting attempts.

Player 2 passes to player 3 on the wing and moves down to the basket as in normal procedure. Player 1 fakes to the inside and cuts to the top. Player 3 passes to 1 coming to the top. Player 1 reverses the ball to 2, who has cut out to the wing for the shot or one-on-one move designated. (Diagram 15-4) New players step in the 1 and 3 positions. Player 1 remains at the top and resumes the action as the ball is passed back to him. Player 3 moves to line one and the shooter moves to line two.

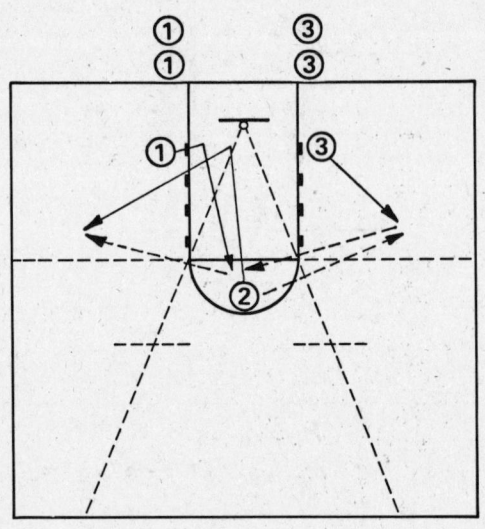

Diagram 15-4
Four-Cut Shooting Drill

CUTTING DRILL

Timing is vital in cutting. It is extremely easy to cut too fast and arrive before the ball can possibly be delivered, thus allowing the defense to catch up. By the same token, a slow cut will not allow the ball to be passed the moment it is received. The cut should be made just as the ball leaves player 2's hands. The ball and cutter should arrive at the basket at exactly the same time. Emphasize cutting to a position from which you can shoot immediately as you receive the ball. The shooting techniques may be a driving lay-up across the front of the basket, a fake and power move, a short turn and jump shot, or a short hook. The cutters should rehearse these techniques at every affordable opportunity to insure comfort and confidence as he receives the pass.

Player 1 positions himself on the left wing, player 2 at the top of the key in the swing position, player 3 on the right wing. Two chairs are placed along the right side of the free throw lane simulating the double screen. The feeder lane lines up with player 1.

Player 3 passes to player 2, who swings the ball to player 1. As the ball leaves the hands of player 2, player 3 cuts under or over the screen. Player 1 passes to player 3 as he clears the screen and comes into position at the basket. (Diagram 15-5) Player 3 now goes behind the line of 1; 2 moves to the position of 1 and the drill continues. It is advisable to use two balls in this drill to speed up the action.

Practically every offensive fundamental is involved in these five drills. All are closely aligned with our basic swing-and-cut of-

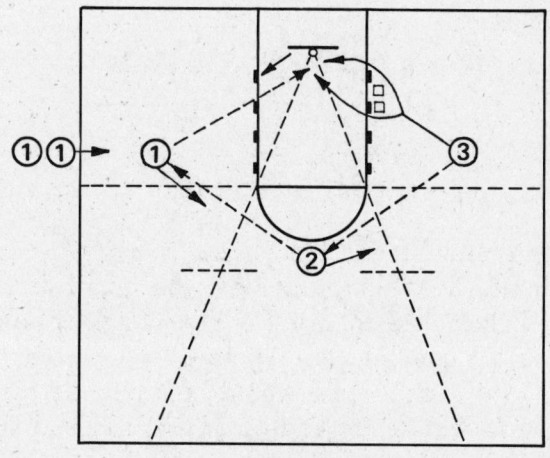

Diagram 15-5
Five-Cut Shooting Drill

fense. Other drills relating to relief moves, interchanges, and rollouts may be easily devised and aligned with our offensive pattern according to necessity. The best drills are the drills you devise to fit specific needs.

Two other drills that we use daily and deem as effective supplements to the swing-and-cut offense are our basic shooting drill and the screen and roll drill.

BASIC SHOOTING DRILL

We call our basic shooting drill the *ten-from-a-spot*. We shoot from six different spots on both sides of the floor. (Diagram 15-6) We use this as our basic shooting drill because it provides us with numerous shooting attempts from practically all of the same areas that the swing-and-cut offense provides.

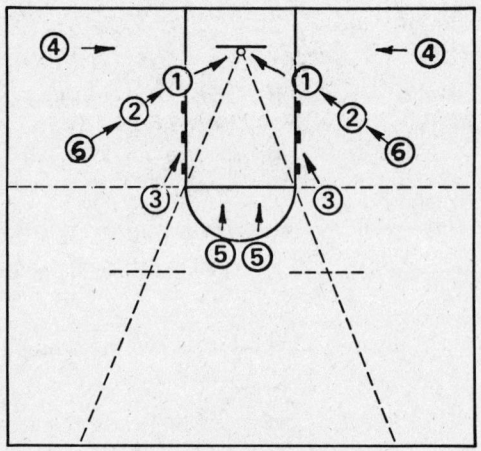

Diagram 15-6
Basic Shooting Drill

The number one spot is at the top corner of the wide-lane markers. This should be a jump shot off the board at seven to eight feet from slightly less than a 45-degree angle. The number two spot is on the same line but 10 to 12 feet from the basket. This is also a jump shot that should be taken off the board. The number three spot is at the end of each foul line about 15 to

16 feet from the basket and should be shot directly into the basket. The number 4 spot is 18 feet from the basket in the corners and should be shot directly into the basket. The number five spot is at the top of the key, slightly inside the free throw circle 18 to 20 feet from the basket. The number six spot is 18 feet from the basket at a 45-degree angle. This is the approximate wing or forward position.

Normally we shoot with a partner and each pair must make ten baskets before moving onto the next spot. Each shooter follows his own shot, passes quickly back to his partner, and cuts back to the shooting spot. It is most important to insist on accurate return passes and quick sound releases by the shooter. When all shots are completed on one side of the floor, the two partners move to the number one spot on the opposite side and complete all six spots. If all shots were made, a shooter and his partner would take 120 shots in this shooting drill; a realistic accuracy would be 80 percent. Therefore, they will be attempting around 145 shots. This entire sequence should take between ten and twelve minutes. Emphasis should be placed on sustaining the movement and concentration related to game situation.

The ten-from-a-spot drill is easily adjusted to emphasize different aspects of shooting. This also breaks the monotony of the daily routine while accomplishing the same effect.

For example, it might be desirable at times to have the shooter step out and raise his hand as he passes the ball back to his partner. This forces the shooter to take his shot over an upraised hand and arm and adds another game situation to the drill.

We sometimes have our shooters position themselves one or two dribbles to the right or left of the shooting spot. When they receive the ball, they take one or two quick dribbles to the spot and quickly shoot the prescribed jump shot. This relates to a shot coming off a screen or defeating your defensive man with quickness.

Yet another adjustment may be brought into focus by having one player stay on the spot and shoot until he has made five baskets. His partner retrieves the ball and passes it back. When the five successful baskets have been made, the partners change places.

It is possible to add a little fun to the drills by occasionally having a contest to see which group finishes first. Have all groups

188 teaching drills around the swing-and-cut pattern

position themselves at the one spot. All groups start shooting on a whistle. Reward the first two or three groups to finish. Assign extra shooting or quickness drills to the last two or three groups.

It is ideal, if enough baskets are available, to assign one group (two men) to a basket. If it is necessary to assign two groups (four men) to a basket, each group will start on the one spots. If three groups (six men) have to be assigned to a basket, two groups will start on the one spots and one group on either of the three spots and proceed in order.

SCREEN AND ROLL DRILL

Setting screens, followed by the quick rollouts, are such a vital part of our swing-and-cut offense, relief moves, and basic offensive basketball, that we find it advantageous to rehearse these simple but effective techniques daily. The position, steps, and movement should be followed exactly as prescribed in Chapter 3, under screens and rollouts. The drill is simple and will require five minutes.

Place a chair at the end of each foul line. The inside leg of the chair should be placed exactly on the end of the free throw line. Players line up behind each chair at somewhat of a 45-degree angle. (Diagram 15-7) Player 1 drives into the middle, stops and

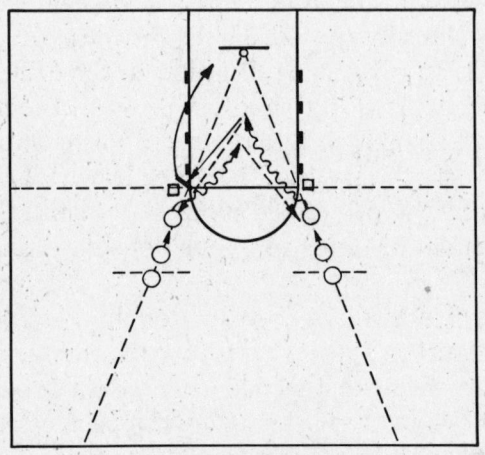

Diagram 15-7
Screen and Roll Drill

passes to player 2, moves up and screens for player 2. He should use all screening techniques as explained in Chapter 3. The moment the screener stops, player 2, who should by now have faked opposite, crosses over with his outside foot directly to the screener's inside foot and drives into the middle toward the basket. The screener, at the exact moment the driver's crossover foot is about to hit the floor, back pivots on his outside foot, making sure his inside foot is placed outside the free throw lane. He takes one step down the lane and cuts to the basket, cuts back outside the lane and goes behind the line on the same side. He must never turn his back on the ball. Player 2, who had driven into the middle, now passes to line 1 and this action continues emphasizing proper technique. In order to insure mental alertness, occasional check passes should be made to the player rolling to the basket.

16

the fast break

The fast break is our initial offensive maneuver and we will make every attempt to capitalize on it. After reading the preceding 15 chapters, you may get the idea that we are a strictly patterned, shuffle-type team. This is absolutely not true. The fast break is our initial attack. The swing-and-cut is our set pattern, our equalizer against all defenses, our confidence builder.

We will make every attempt to capitalize on the fast break. Sometimes our personnel will limit the possibilities the fast break presents, but we will always attempt to use the fast break as our first offensive weapon. Then, if the high percentage scoring opportunity does not present itself, we will resort to the swing-and-cut.

FAST-BREAK PHILOSOPHY AND PRINCIPLE

We always bring the ball down the court as quickly as possible. There are three main reasons for this. First, we attempt to pick up a few baskets by outrunning our opponents. Second, we may be able to catch a defensive man loafing and capitalize on it, and third, we will at least make the defense run hard for 40 minutes to get back up the court, thereby challenging their physical condition. We know we will be conditioned to employ this pace. We look at our opponent's condition as suspect and thus test it.

There are many styles and ideas concerning fast-break basketball. This particular discussion presents our particular style and the reasons for using this style. The fast break deserves an entire book devoted exclusively to the techniques involved. I am devoting only one chapter as the fast break is closely allied with the swing-and-cut when looking at our entire offensive picture. You will notice our maneuvers and techniques are quite simple, and they are taught in simple but emphatic terms.

Fast-break basketball has a tremendous appeal to players and spectators. We occasionally land a fair prospect because our style of play appeals to him. We feel that is for this same reason: the players like it; it is easy to teach; and players look forward to our fast-break drills and style of play. The fast break, when properly executed, is very conducive to good physical conditioning. It develops speed and quickness, and speeds up reaction time and the development of fundamental basketball techniques.

To be successful in coaching a fast-break style of play, you must be a task master. Detail is of the utmost importance. You must also have a certain amount of patience. In a fast style of play it must be recognized that more ball-handling errors will be made, especially in the first stages of development. A coach must have the patience to see this style of play work gradually into a well-planned attack. He must *insist*, as this development is taking place, that mistakes are held to a bare minimum and work diligently each day toward eliminating errors. Fast-break basketball is not a "race horse game"; rather it is a carefully organized attack designed to exploit the basic fundamentals that result in a high percentage scoring attempt.

In our philosophy it is extremely important to keep it simple. We are of the opinion that we can accomplish much more and convince our players more quickly on the important techniques if we do not confuse them, and if they understand at all times what we are attempting to accomplish.

Fast-break basketball, properly executed, is probably the most organized and disciplined of any attack method.

FAST-BREAK OPPORTUNITIES

The most important mental aspect of fast-break basketball is to be sure that your personnel are "fast-break conscious." This means that they are always ready and looking to fast break. I must add here, it is possible to be fast-break conscious and yet not detract from defense and other fundamentals.

Bear in mind that fast-break basketball is a carefully organized attack, designed to utilize fundamental techniques and exploit defensive weaknesses through constant pressure. These factors should result in high percentage scoring attempts. Remember, it is extremely important to keep it simple. We believe we can accomplish much more and sell our players more quickly on the important elements if we do not confuse them, and if they understand at all times what we are attempting to accomplish.

FAST-BREAK SITUATIONS

There are many situations from which the fast break may be ignited. I use the word *ignite* for a purpose. I want our break to literally blow out of there when a fast-break situation occurs. The most important element of igniting the break is that of having your team fast-break conscious. A team must expect and anticipate fast-break situations. This in itself is not too much of a task. It is however, very difficult to instill this fast-break consciousness in your team and not violate defensive and other fundamental principles. We attempt to fast break:

1. after a field goal attempt is missed (Rebound is one of the most effective situations.)
2. after a field goal attempt is made (We move the ball down the side line.)
3. after a free throw attempt is missed (Rebound)
4. after a free throw attemp is made (Move the ball down the sideline.)
5. from a loose ball situation
6. from a stolen ball situation
7. from intercepted passes

8. from jump ball situations at center and backcourts
9. from out-of-bounds in backcourt
10. from opponents' errors

TEACHING PHASES

There are five phases of our fast break to which we give special emphasis. There are some very important fundamentals that must be coordinated into these five phases. Rebounding, good footwork, excellent ball handling, dribbling, running, cutting, and shooting are among the most important.

1. *Condition*—We must be able to rebound, run, shoot, and play defense for 40 minutes.

2. *Rebounding*—We must be able to get position in the rebound area, get the ball off the board, and make an effective outlet pass.

3. *Ball handling*—Without proper and effective ball handling, the fast break is nonexistent.

4. *Floor position*—We must get our outlet receivers, our middle man, and our wings in the proper floor position or our break will be forced out of prospective.

5. *Control*—At a certain point (that practice and experience will recognize) all personnel must come under and maintain perfect body control and floor position both with and without the ball.

PRIMARY IGNITION POINT

We always attempt to bring the ball down the court fast, looking for weaknesses or mistakes by the defense. However, the primary source for igniting the break is the defensive rebound. This is the situation where rebounding strength, sound fundamentals, and fast-break conscious teams gain a vastly superior edge on their opponents. This is the point where it is easy to determine the superior edge in basketball teams. The team with superior rebounding talent, plus the inside position it will normally have on defense, plus positive execution of the rebounding and outlet pass techniques, should establish game control early. A team with less talent may also be effective. However, much emphasis must be placed on blocking out, rebounding, and getting the ball quickly away from the defensive basket.

It is extremely important to establish outlet receivers. The outlet pass should be thrown out as quickly and as far as possible and with accuracy. More rebounds are passed out to the right side than to the left, simply because there are more right-handed players. Ninety-five percent of all rebounds captured in front of or on the right side (the left side looking in) of the basket are outletted to the right side. It is only normal to turn to the strong hand. Passes rebounded on the left side (right side looking in) should be outletted to the left side. Don't throw back into the jam.

A right-handed player should use a right-hand baseball pass, two-hand overhead pass, or two-hand chest pass when outletting to the right side. On the left side we suggest a two-hand overhead pass or a two-hand chest pass, but not a left-hand baseball pass. We do not want our players throwing one-hand passes (especially outlet passes) with a basketball using their off-hand. This leads to errant passes and numerous turnovers.

This part of the fast break, the primary ignition point, deserves an abundance of preparation, rehearsing, and attention if it is to be as effective as it should be.

SECONDARY IGNITION POINTS

The secondary ignition points are not as specifically located as the primary point. The secondary points may come from anywhere in the backcourt, at any time during the game, from any one of the five players. The fact that the secondary points are basically spontaneous implies that schooling in the general basics are essential but it is difficult to elaborate on specific basics.

The secondary ignition points rely extensively on a team being fast-break conscious.

REBOUND POSITIONS

It is imperative that a good fast-break team be a good rebounding team. To be a good rebounding team all the basic

196 **the fast break**

fundamentals must be emphasized to the utmost, especially the rebounding positions. Generally speaking, the center or post should work for a position directly in front of the basket at a distance of six feet from the basket. The forwards on their respective sides of the basket should also be no closer than six feet. This would place them on the free throw lanes after they have blocked their offensive men out. *It is important for the post and forwards to maintain this six-foot position, block out, and then spring up to meet the ball.* Otherwise, they will be smothered under by an aggressive offensive rebounding team. The guards should close in on the shot to a position that will find their high foot on the foul line and the low foot on the free throw lane. This is extremely important. These are control points. Many rebounds come off long and we must be in position to capture them. This is our rebounding area and we must work for these positions. (Diagram 16-1) We must first get the ball before we can fast break.

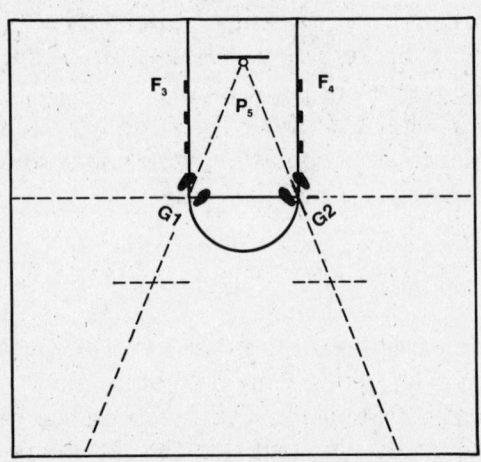

Diagram 16-1
Fast-Break Control Points

FIRST MOVES AFTER CAPTURING REBOUND

Both guards, after seeing the ball is definitely in our rebounder's possession, cross over with the inside foot, take three and one-half steps to the sideline, drop step, cross over and move down the sideline, looking back over the inside shoulder for the outlet pass. If the outlet is not made immediately, the guards must cut back quickly to meet the ball. (Diagram 16-2) Both forwards, on recognizing the post possession, must sprint for the positions in the outside lanes, as indicated in Diagram 16-2.

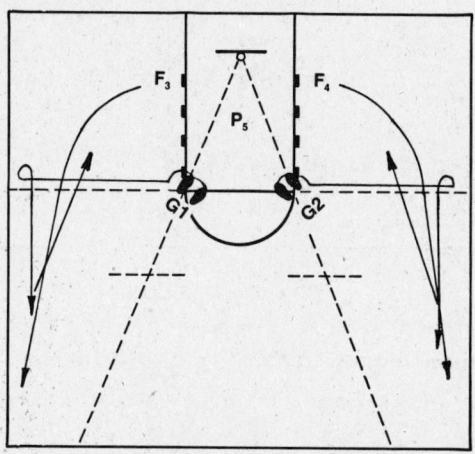

Diagram 16-2
Fast Break—
First Moves After Capturing Rebound

FAST-BREAK POST REBOUND

The post man has captured the rebound. The guards immediately cross over to the sideline. (Diagram 16-2) Both forwards, upon recognizing that the post man has captured the rebound, turn to the outside and sprint outside the guards to fill the outside lanes. In this particular instance the post throws the outlet pass to guard 1 on the right side. Guard 2, upon recognizing the flow of the ball, should cut directly toward the ball until he reaches the middle of the court, and then cut up the middle looking for the pass from guard 1. Upon receiving the pass, he dribbles down the middle or passes ahead to a wide lane, and cuts behind or throws out and maintains the middle lane looking for a return pass. (Diagram 16-3) The strongside lane is not designated. It should be a foot race between the strongside guard and forward. The one that reaches the center line first, fills the strongside lane, with the second man becoming the trailer.

198 the fast break

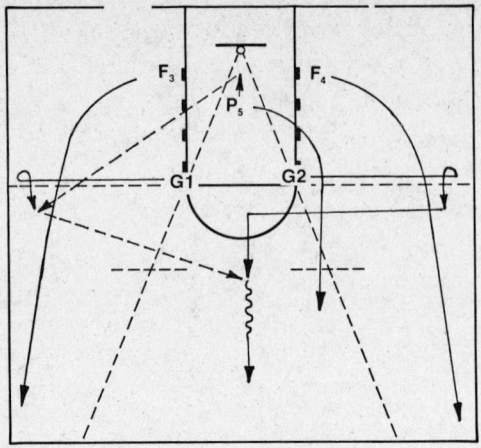

Diagram 16-3
Fast Break—
Getting the Ball to the Middle-Post Rebounds

FORWARD REBOUNDING

All action with the forward rebounding is the same as described for the center rebounding with only two minor exceptions. First, the forward who rebounds the ball passes out to the guard on his side and races to fill the lane. Second, the offside guard, see-

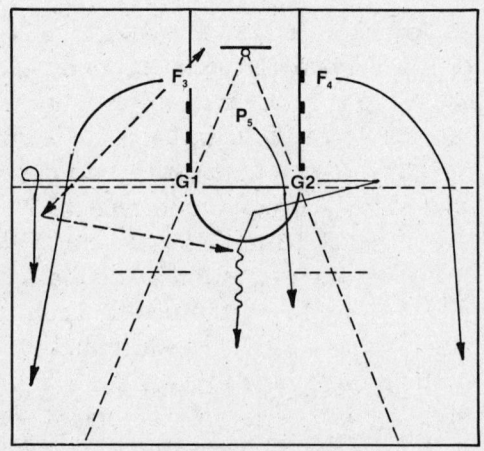

Diagram 16-4
Fast Break—Forward Rebounds

ing the flow of the ball is away from him, does not need to go all the way to the side. Instead, he cuts back torward the strongside guard and up the middle looking for the pass. (Diagram 16-4) Notice the center or post man move in all of these diagrams. Our center sprints from basket to basket with no lane responsibility, except that of a weakside trailer down the center of the court.

COMPLETE FAST-BREAK PATTERN

Diagram 16-5 shows the complete fast-break pattern down to the free throw line. Establishing the strong side is extremely im-

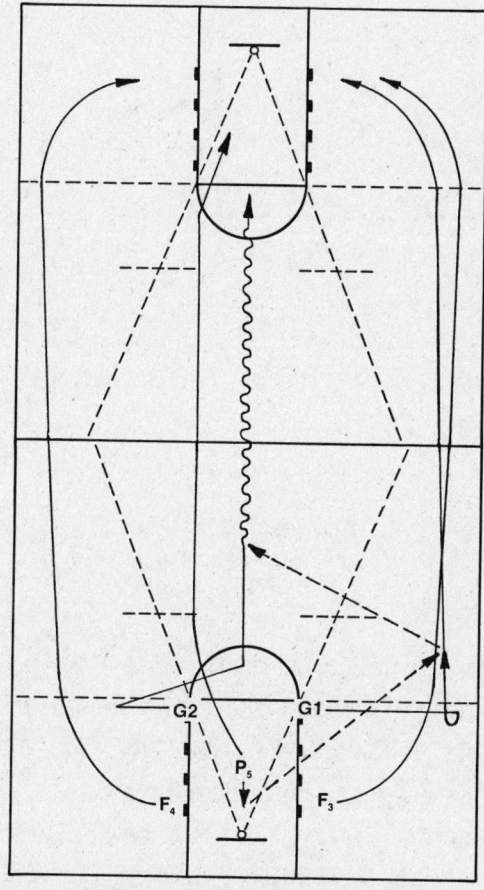

Diagram 16-5
Fast Break—Complete Pattern

portant. The second man across the center line on the strong side is the strongside trailer and should adjust his distance to follow 15 feet behind the front man and verbally and distinctively call strong side. Race for the lanes. Be fast-break conscious.

3-ON-2 OR 3-ON-1

When we find a 3-on-2 or 3-on-1 situation, which we are striving to get, we have six options, four of which are diagrammed here.

1. Pass to wings—Diagram 16-6

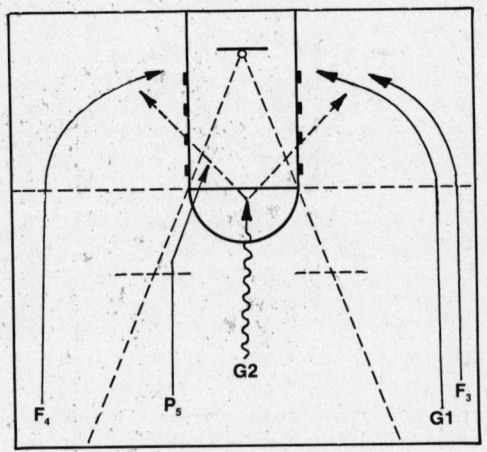

Diagram 16-6
Fast Break—Offensive End

2. Pass to strong trailer—Diagram 16-7
3. Pass to strong wing behind screen—Diagram 16-8
4. Flip to post trailer—Diagram 16-9
5. Middle man hold to receive check pass
6. Middle man penetrate—shoot or check pass

Remember, unless the middle man elects to penetrate he always holds at the foul line and looks for a check pass.

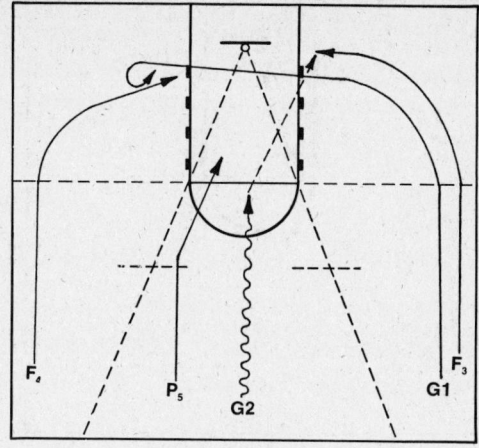

Diagram 16-7
Fast Break—Second Cutter

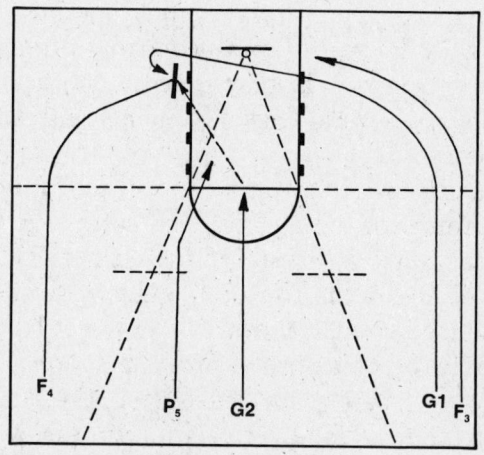

Diagram 16-8
Fast Break—Weakside Cut

FAST BREAK AFTER MADE FIELD GOAL

After a made field goal we attempt to sprint out forwards and move the ball down the side of the court. Many teams after

the fast break

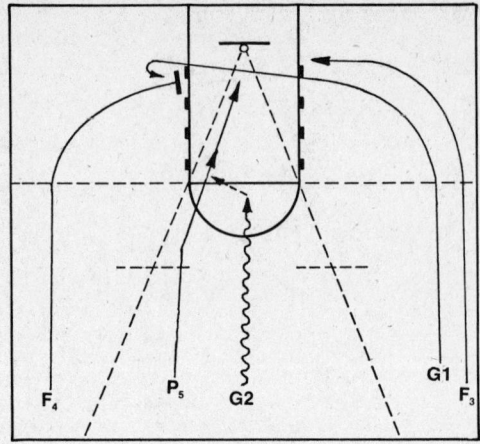

Diagram 16-9
Fast Break—Post Trailer

scoring a basket have a tendency to bunch up and forget the ball momentarily as they make the transition from offense to defense. We feel by getting the ball in play quickly and accurately down the sidelines we score several baskets a game, and we put a lot of pressure on the defense.

We like for our center to take the ball out-of-bounds after a field goal. Both forwards, immediately on seeing the ball enter the basket, turn to the outside and sprint down the sideline, turning in toward the basket about the top of the key, expecting to receive the ball on a 45-degree angle about 15 to 18 feet from the basket.

The guards take their normal outlet positions, and upon receiving the inbounds pass from the center, the guard looks immediately down the sideline, expecting to throw long to the forward on that side. The offside guard cuts toward the strongside guard and up the middle. If the long pass down the side did not materialize, the pass should go to the middle man, who immediately passes to the offside forward.

If the long pass is completed down the sideline and the defense covers adequately, the forward should pass to the weakside guard coming down the middle for a reverse, and around the horn to the weakside forward. (Diagram 16-10)

the fast break 203

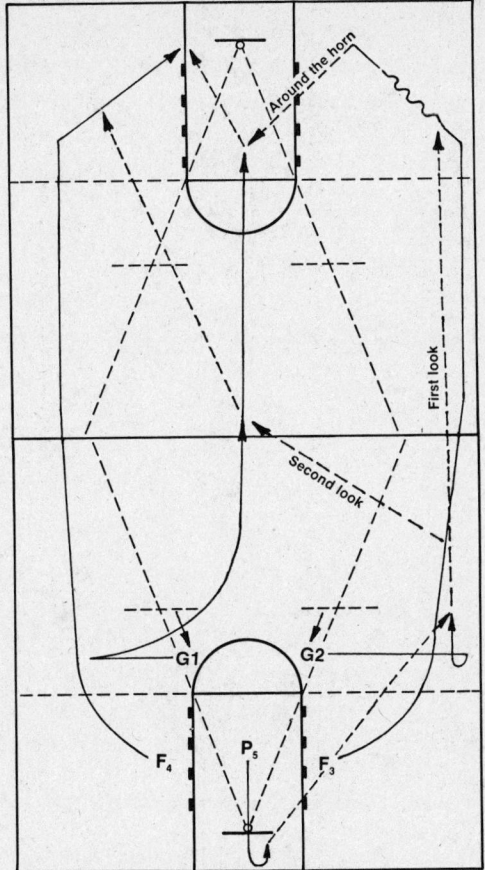

Diagram 16-10
Fast Break—After Made Field Goal

FAST BREAK AFTER MADE FREE THROW

Diagram 16-11 illustrates our fast-break effort after a made free throw. The center or post is assigned the inside position on the left side looking in. Our two best shooters are placed in the third positions on either side. We call these the sprint-out positions. Guard 1 positions himself with his toes slightly behind the free throw circle. The other forward takes the inside position op-

204 the fast break

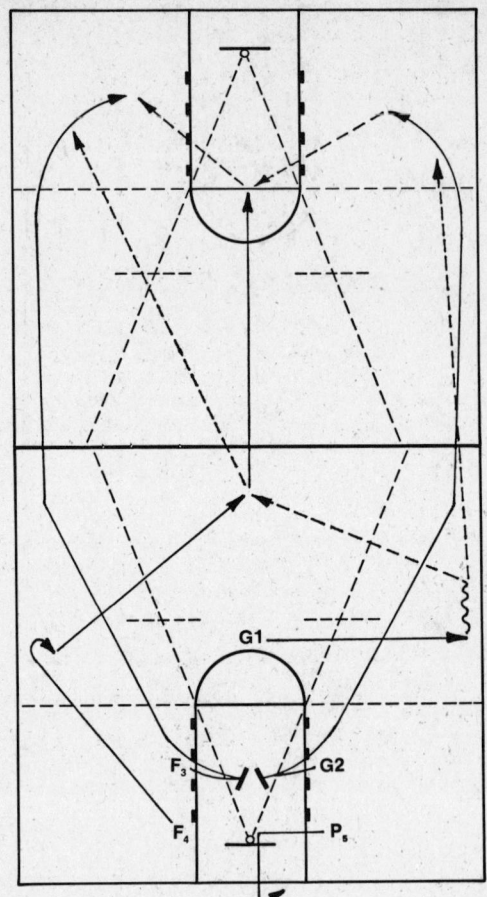

Diagram 16-11
Fast Break—After Made Freethrow

posite the post man. The two sprint-out players step into the lane foot-to-foot. The exact moment forward 4 realizes the ball is entering the basket, he turns to the outside and sprints quickly to the sideline, always to his left. This establishes our outlet receivers. Forward 3 and guard 2, as the ball enters the basket, immediately turn to the outside and sprint along the sideline and into a position 15 to 18 feet from the basket on a 45-degree angle. Post man 5 takes the ball out quickly and passes to guard 1. Guard 1 attempts to pass long to guard 2. Forward 4 cuts to the ball and up the middle. If the long pass is not successful, the same tactics as described in Diagram 16-10 apply.

17 / supplementary drills for improving offensive technique

To supplement our overall teaching techniques, and in unison with our all-inclusive instructional organization, we use two sets of simple drills daily. We firmly believe that these drills are extremely effective elements in our general approach to teaching the fundamental aspects relating to all phases of the game of basketball. These two sets of drills are, in the eyes of many, too elementary and too simple to be included daily.

On many occasions, when I am speaking at clinics or especially conducting basketball schools, I make this statement: "Do not overlook the little things." Mastery of the little things is paramount to making daily progress in basketball or for that matter, any sport.

The first set of these drills we call our *Daily Dozen*. The Daily Dozen, as described and illustrated here, was also published in two parts in the *Basketball Clinic* by Parker Publishing Company.

The second set of drills of equal importance is what we call our *situation drills*. Normally the Daily Dozen is the first thing our players do after they come on the court for practice. The situation drills are also used daily in the early part of the practice but in larger groups.

The little things are the basics, the fundamentals, the foundations of the game. To improve a skill or skills first we must master the fundamental concept of that particular skill. Secondly, we must apply those fundamentals through constant repetition and practice. Knowledge of fundamentals will provide a player with the confidence, poise, and relaxation necessary to get the task at hand accomplished. Repetition or constant practice will insure a higher degree of efficiency.

It is only through the mastery of the "little things" such as passing, jumping, dribbling, faking, footwork, agility, body balance, and shooting that we can have a good basketball team. As coaches, we are not honest with our players, the game of basketball, or ourselves, if we fail to remind our players constantly of daily attention to fundamentals. These two sets of drills employed daily insure that we never neglect this phase of the game.

Our first intent was to make the Daily Dozen the first thing our players did when they came on the floor. This was usually unsupervised because some players reached the floor and completed these drills before some of the others arrived. Even though much emphasis was placed on the importance of this series, we soon found that only a few players were getting the full benefit of these drills, primarily because of the lack of supervision.

We have now changed our thinking and administer the series under a coach's supervision. We divide our squad equally on six baskets and assign two specific drills to each basket. Team members move to the next basket or station upon completion of the two drills at the preceding station. We continue this progression until all players have completed all six stations.

In order to prevent these sessions from becoming draggy or complacent, we attempt to challenge a young man to improve daily on a series of skills that are basic to the game and will eventually endow him with poise, confidence and desire necessary for top-flight performance.

At times we keep accurate charts at each station and rate our players daily or weekly on their efficiency of performance and improvement. Place your first rating on the locker room bulletin board and watch for changes in performance at the next rating period. You will notice individuals working on their own time in weak areas in an effort to move up the chart and replace someone else. We feel that a daily application of these two sets of drills will definitely improve a player's touch, quickness, ball handling, jumping, agility, body balance, hand and eye coordination, and faking. The intangibles involved are discipline, motivation, and challenge.

A VALUABLE LEARNING EXPERIENCE

Teaching and improving skills in basketball closely follow the lines of the association concept of learning.

1. The experience must be presented so that a vivid memory of the facts and details remains.
2. Frequency of application or repetition insures steady progress.
3. The duration of the learning process has a definite bearing on retention factors.
4. Current, fresh application better prepares an individual for sharp, effective performance.

The drills are described and illustrated in the following paragraphs.

DAILY DOZEN

1. *Rim Touchers*—This is an excellent jumping and coordination drill for all players, regardless of their size. (Diagram 17-1) It serves as a good warm-up drill. However, its greatest value lies in the fact that daily we test and challenge our jumping muscles and progress to the most difficult aspect of the jump in the last phase of the drill.

   A. The player faces the basket and jumps to touch the rim five times with his right hand. He may jump from a position in which his feet are stationary, or he may take one step and jump.
   B. The player jumps to touch the rim five times with his left hand, using the same technique as in A.

208 supplementary drills for improving offensive technique

Diagram 17-1

C. The player jumps to touch the rim five times and alternates hands. He starts with either hand using the same technique described in A and B. If he starts with his right hand, the drill will be right-left-right-left-right.

D. The player jumps to touch the rim five times with two hands. This is the most difficult because it follows 15 previous jumps. The important point here is that the upward thrust must come off of two feet. In most instances the upward thrust in the three previous jumps will come off of two feet; however, it is more static when using the two-hand touch.

If a player is too small to touch the rim, or if his jumping ability is inadequate, we ask him to pick a spot on the backboard, use this as his target, and strive to get higher on each successive effort.

I prefer two players to work on this drill at one time, and no more than three. When player 1 completes five touches with the right hand, player 2 steps in and performs the same stage of the drill. When player 2 finishes, player 1 steps back in for five jumps with his left hand. This continues until all four steps have been completed by both men. If they so desire, all 20 jumps may be performed by one individual in succession after the proper techniques have been mastered.

2. *Tapping Drill*—This drill is to help improve touch, rhythm, agility, and coordination. (Diagram 17-2)

Diagram 17-2

A. The player faces the backboard about two steps in front of the board. He tosses the ball onto the backboard and taps it against the board ten times at maximum height with his right hand. He should try to use good rhythm and touch and strive to complete this stage of the drill without a break in the motion.

B. Same as A but with the left hand.

C. Same as A and B but with alternating hands.

D. Same as A, B, and C but with both hands.

The important effect here is rhythm, timing, and touch. A small player may also use the board effectively, but his touch and timing must be excellent in order to accomplish the desired rhythm. The distance between the ball and his hand is greater than that of the tall player or super jumper.

Again, I prefer two players to alternate ten taps each. When an individual becomes exceptionally accomplished with this technique, have him use right hand, left hand, alternating hands and two hands without a break.

3. *Hook Shot Drill*—The player should take a position with his back to the basket. (Diagram 17-3) He should be one step in front of the rim holding the ball waist high with two hands.

Diagram 17-3

He will then take a short step to the right and slightly toward the baseline on his left foot, and shoot a short hook shot with his right hand using the backboard. He must maintain his balance, catch the ball as it comes through the net, (the ball should never touch the floor) and with two short rhythm steps, roll in and shoot a short hook shot with the opposite hand.

He continues the action until he makes 20 baskets. Misses are not counted.

This is an excellent drill for improving agility, rhythm, timing, touch, and concentration. It is a great help in improving the steps and rhythm of the weaker hand.

4. *Flip-Flop Drill*—This drill is executed best with three players: one ball handler, one obstacle, and one shooter. (Diagram 17-4)

supplementary drills for improving offensive technique 211

Diagram 17-4

A. The ball handler stands one step in front of and facing the basket, with the ball in two hands.
B. The player acting as the obstacle should be one step behind the ball handler and facing the basket.
C. The shooter is one step behind the obstacle and facing the basket.
D. On a signal, the ball handler flips or hangs the ball about shoulder height at a 45-degree angle to the determined side. The shooter moves forward, takes the flip, and shoots a lay-up. He immediately comes under control, quickly turns, and cuts behind the obstacle to the opposite side for a lay-up with his opposite hand in a half-circle pattern. This action continues until the shooter has made ten baskets. Misses do not count.
E. The ball handler should never wait for the shooter. Immediately upon catching the ball as it comes through the net, he should flip it as described to the opposite side. It is the shooter's challenge to be there. It is important that a lay-up and not a jump-shot technique be used.

F. When the first shooter finishes, he becomes the obstacle. The obstacle becomes the ball handler and the ball handler becomes the shooter.

The result should improve quickness, agility, touch, footwork, and concentration.

5. *Saddle Drill*—The player stands with his heels on the foul line and his back to the basket, with the ball held waist high in both hands. (Diagram 17-5)

Diagram 17-5

A. Choosing the right side for his first move, he should execute a slight head and ball-fake to his right. At the same time, he should execute a deep drop-step with his left foot, quickly turn to the left foot, and drive hard directly to the basket for a right-hand lay-up.
B. Same action to the opposite side.

The player should complete ten of these moves to each side. On each move, he should strive to make that move quicker than the one before. Improvement in quickness, quick drives, and faking should be noticeable.

supplementary drills for improving offensive technique 213

6. *Two-Ball Dribble*—The player stands at one end line with a basketball in each hand. (Diagram 17-6) Choosing his own pace, the player begins to dribble the two basketballs alternately toward the opposite end line.

Diagram 17-6

Progression will be slow at first, and the player will be prone to dribble the balls simultaneously. As the alternating technique is improved, speed should also improve.

The desired effect is accomplished when the player is able to sprint-dribble to the opposite end line, make the turn and sprint-dribble back to the starting point without losing a ball or breaking the dribble.

This drill is very effective for improving hand-eye coordination, reflex action, agility, and ball control.

7. *Wiggle-Waggle Drill*—The player stands at one end line with the basketball.

A. Choosing his own pace he drops his hips and takes a long step forward on his left foot. With the ball now in his right hand, he passes the ball under his left leg from the inside into his left hand. (Diagram 17-7)

214 supplementary drills for improving offensive technique

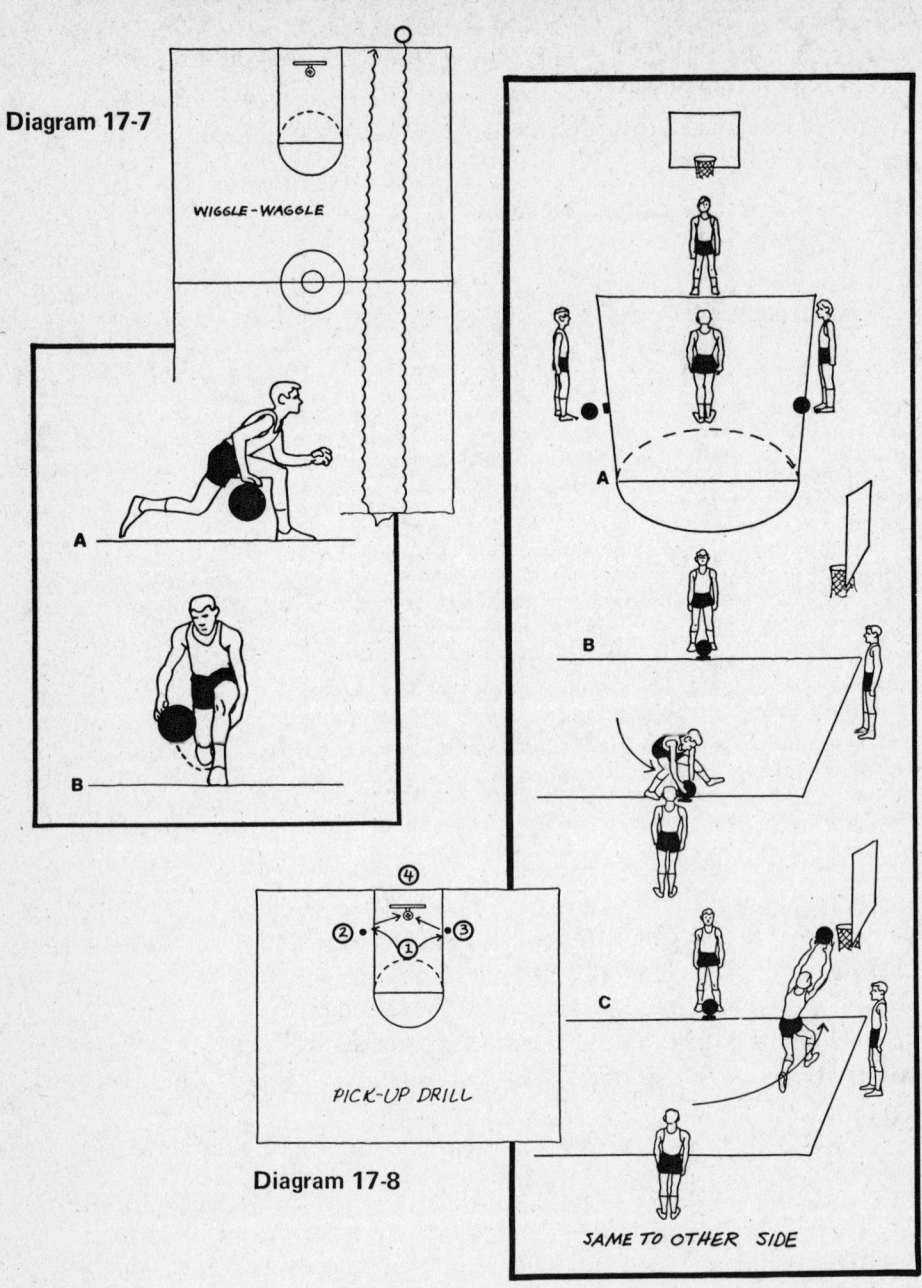

Diagram 17-7

WIGGLE-WAGGLE

PICK-UP DRILL

Diagram 17-8

SAME TO OTHER SIDE

B. Now his right leg has come forward. With his left hand, he passes the ball from the inside under his right leg into his right hand.

C. The player continues this process at his own pace until he reaches the level where he can move swiftly from end line to end line, turn and return to the starting point without an error.

The technique is to keep the hips down and the body low, step long and place the ball with the hands. Players should not attempt to lift their legs to step over the ball. This drill may also be performed by placing the ball under the legs from the outside. It is a slight change and a bit more difficult.

Repetition of this drill improves coordination, agility, body balance, ball handling, and condition.

8. *Pick-up Drill*—This drill must have at least three people involved. It is more satisfactorily performed with four.

A. Place a ball on each wide-lane divider. Place a helper behind each ball and one under the basket. (Diagram 17-8)

B. The player executing the drill takes a position in the middle of the lane between the two balls and facing the basket.

C. On a signal or whenever he is ready, the player steps toward the ball with his right leg. The left leg is extended on the line between the ball and the basket.

D. From this position, the player reaches down and picks up the ball with both hands. He does this without moving his left foot and without turning his body. He drives the ball up toward the basket using the power move technique.

E. The player then quickly steps with his left foot toward the opposite ball using the same technique.

The player repeats these moves, alternating sides, until he has made 20 baskets. It is important that the participant not open his body to the basket. Instead, he should practice the technique of protecting the ball with his body, with his back to the court and a firm grip on the ball.

As technique and form progress, a fifth player may be added as a defensive man to slap at the ball, use some body contact, and increase game type pressure.

This drill is a must for our inside people; however, all players participate during Daily Dozen time. The drill develops strong hands, the power move, agility, and body balance.

216 supplementary drills for improving offensive technique

9. *Shuttle Drill*—The player takes a position on either foul lane marker. One foot is completely outside and the other foot inside.

   A. On a signal or when he is ready, the player positions himself in a parallel or even defensive stance. (Diagram 17-9)

   B. His first step should be a crossover step with the outside leg. The crossover step should be converted into a slide step or series of slide steps that will bring the original inside foot completely outside the opposite lane marker.

This action continues as quickly as possible. The challenge is to cross the lane as many times as possible in 30 seconds. The player may also cross the lane 20 times and time his effort. For a

Diagram 17-9

Diagram 17-10

completed lane crossing, the extended foot must be completely outside the lane marker. Only completed attempts will be counted.

The player should keep his body low and his face and shoulders forward during the entire drill. He should strive for speed, quickness, and agility.

10. *Drives*—Place a chair or other obstacle on each side of the court at a 45-degree angle to the basket and approximately 20 feet away. Line up as many players as necessary behind one of the obstacles (not over three if possible).

- A. Using various stages of the rocker step or the stagger step, the first player will drive to the basket in quick explosive starts for a driving lay-up. All his efforts should be programmed for technique and the attempt to make each drive quicker and faster than the one before. (Diagram 17-10)
- B. After the player completes the drive, he moves to the opposite side and prepares to make his next drive.

Ten drives are expected from each side. Chairs may be moved and starting points adjusted.

The player should always keep speed, quickness, footwork, and ball control in mind and should strive to make each drive quicker than the one before.

11. *Quickie-Touch Drills*—Our eleventh drill is actually a series of quickie drills that we think produce an improvement in touch and ball handling. (Diagram 17-11)

- A. Stand erect, feet together, and "feel" the ball by wrapping it around the body, right hand to left hand. Start at waist level and go as high and as low on the body as possible. These continuous wraps in a circular motion around the body should be performed ten times as fast as possible.
- B. Stand erect with feet spread and the ball held in two hands in front of the body. To begin the drill, drop hips and place the ball between the legs from the inside into the opposite hand. Continue in a figure-eight motion for at least ten complete figures.
- C. Same as B, but each time the ball goes between the legs it

218 supplementary drills for improving offensive technique

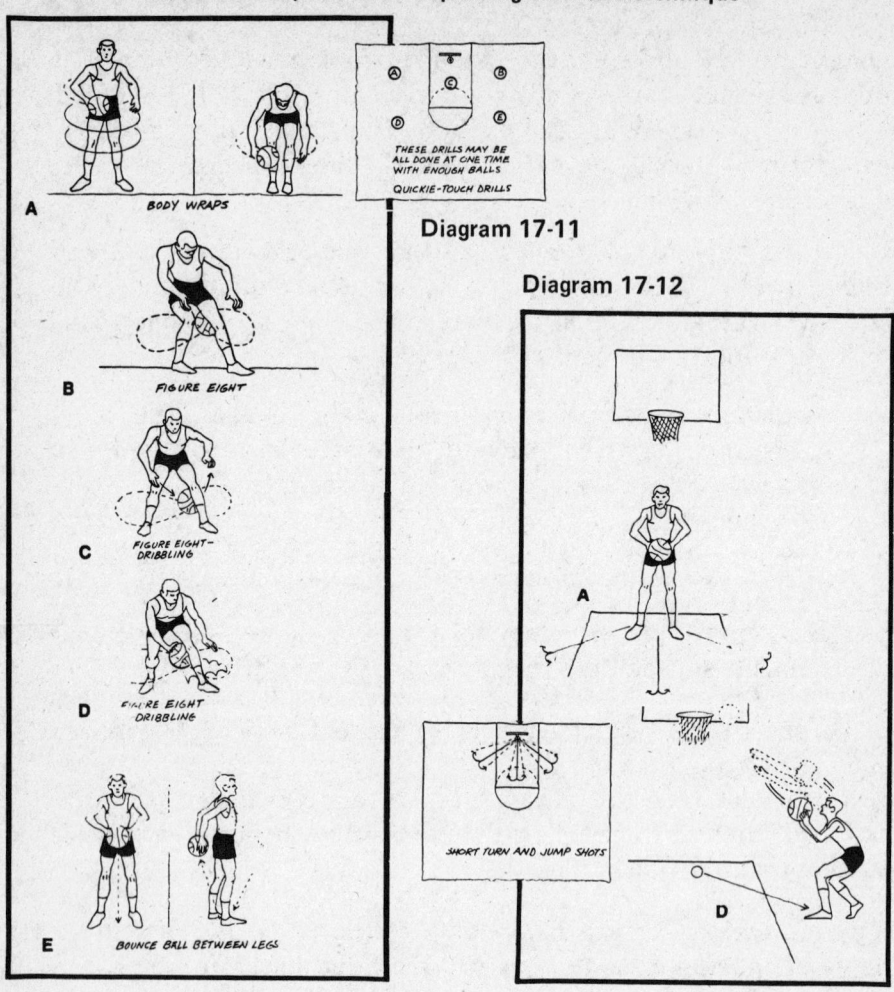

Diagram 17-11

Diagram 17-12

should go with a short bounce from one hand to the other. Ten complete figure-eights with two bounces to each figure.

D. Same position as B and C, but this time dribble the ball in the figure-eight motion ten complete figures. The dribble should never be broken.

E. Stand erect with feet spread. Hold the ball in two hands in front of the body. Bounce the ball with two hands between the legs and catch it with two hands behind the back. After catching the ball behind the back, bring it to the front. Do this ten times. Work to bounce the ball harder and faster.

12. *Short Turn and Jump Shots*—We find this drill good for improving the short high-percentage finesse shots close to the basket. These important shots do not present themselves to all personnel too often, but a team must be successful when the opportunity does arise. This drill gives us daily contact with such shots. (Diagram 17-12)

    A. The player should stand directly under the basket with the ball in his hands.

    B. He takes one hard dribble away from the basket at a 45-degree angle, turns and jumps using all the techniques of the jump shot, and banks the ball off the board into the basket. He repeats this until he has made ten baskets.

    C. The player dribbles straight forward and lifts the ball over the rim. Finesse is important.

    D. The player dribbles to the right at a 45-degree angle and uses the backboard.

The player must make ten successful baskets from each of the three positions. The goal of the drill is good shooting form and technique, quickness, and accuracy.

A working squad normally has between 10 and 15 players. With this group divided between six baskets, using the station method, the Daily Dozen can be completed easily in 20 minutes. I think most coaches will agree this is 20 minutes well-spent.

I have not emphasized the value of the Daily Dozen as warm-up drills or as conditioners, but check your players after a few days of the drills. I think you will be pleased.

SITUATION DRILLS

The situation drills are always set up under strict supervision and in groups no larger than eight players if possible. There are 22 of these situations. Groups of eight doing each situation two times at a maximum of 20 minutes is needed to complete the entire series. It is permissible however, to do a smaller number of these, such as twelve one day and ten or eleven the next day.

The situation drills cover practically every possible offensive situation with the exception of post play. Pass and cut, give and go, change direction, fakes, screen and rolls, check passing, dribble and hand off, pass and cut behind, backdoor the forward, backdoor the guard, drive, guard around, forward to guard screen and roll, jump shooting and check passing off the jump shot are all included.

We name and number these situations. We want our personnel to be thoroughly familiar with them so we will not have to explain them over and over. Proper execution, speed, quickness, the basic fundamentals, and agility will always be emphasized with perfection insisted on.

For all but five of these drills we place line 1 at the top of the key, toes touching the circle. Line 2 is in the normal forward position.

1. *Pass and cut*—Line 1 passes to line 2 and quickly cuts directly to the basket for a return pass and lay-up. (Diagram 17-13)

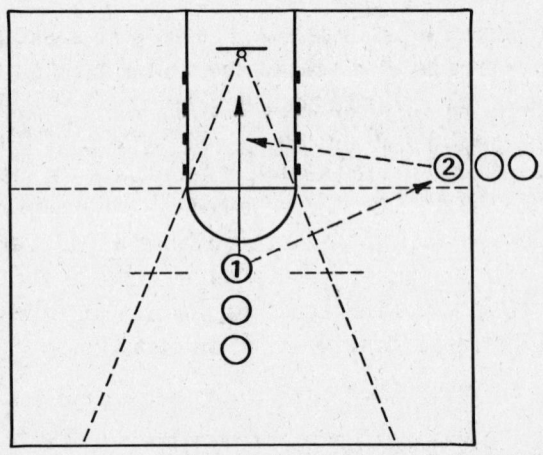

Diagram 17-13
Pass and Cut

2. *Change direction*—Line 1 passes to line 2 and takes three steps directly toward 2. On the third step he plants his right foot and quickly and sharply changes direction and cuts sharply to the basket for a return pass and lay-up. (Diagram 17-14)

supplementary drills for improving offensive technique 221

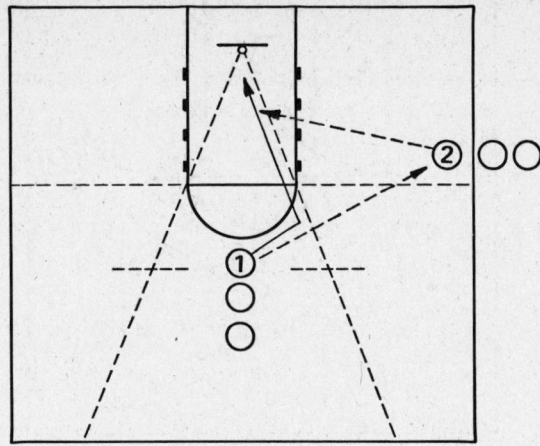

Diagram 17-14
Pass and Change Direction

3. *Fake down*—Line 1 fakes a pass to line 2. Line 2, upon seeing the ball is not released, honors the fake and cuts quickly and sharply to the basket, receives a pass from 1, and shoots a lay-up. (Diagram 17-15)

4. *Pass-screen-roll*—Line 1 passes to line 2 and quickly follows the pass and sets a screen for 2. Line 2 drives off the

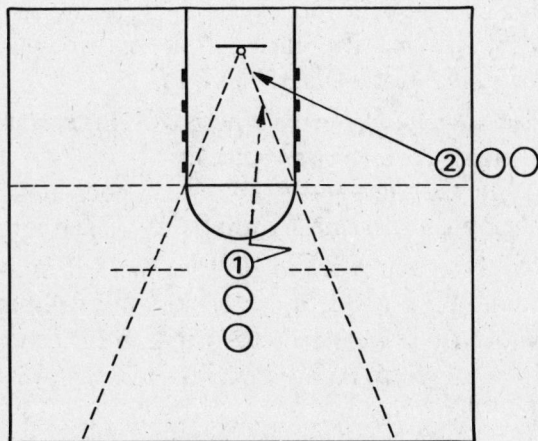

Diagram 17-15
Fake Down

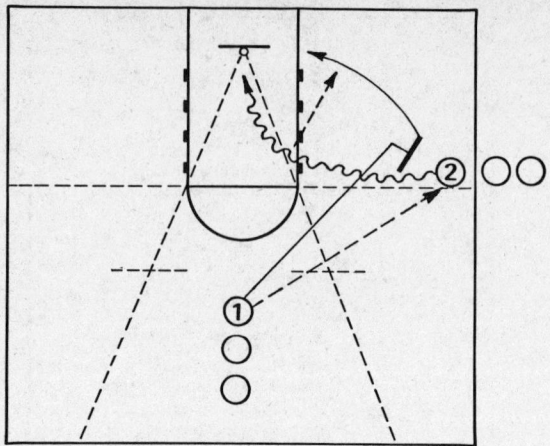

Diagram 17-16
Pass, Screen, Drive, Roll, and Check Pass

screen for the basket. Line 1 rolls out to the basket. (Diagram 17-16)

5. *Pass-screen-roll and check pass*—This procedure is exactly the same as the previous move except line 2, instead of driving all the way to the basket, check passes to line 1 rolling out of the screen. (Diagram 17-16)

6. *Pass-screen-drive-jump shot* — Same as two previous moves except line 2 comes off the screen set by line 1 and shoots a jump shot. (Diagram 17-17)

7. *Pass-screen-drive-check pass off jump shot*—Line 1 and line 2 start their moves exactly as in the three previous moves. Line 2, coming off the screen, goes up for a jump shot and check passes to line 1 rolling out. (Diagram 17-17)

8. *Dribble hand off and drive*—Line 1 dribbles toward and inside line 2. Line 2, upon seeing the dribble action, cuts closely off of line 1, receives the handoff and drives to the basket for a lay-up. (Diagram 17-18)

9. *Dribble hand off, drive and check pass*—This move is exactly the same as described in the previous move and in Diagram 17-18 except line 2 check passes to line 1 as he rolls to basket.

10. *Dribble to hand off jump shot*—The same move as the

supplementary drills for improving offensive technique   223

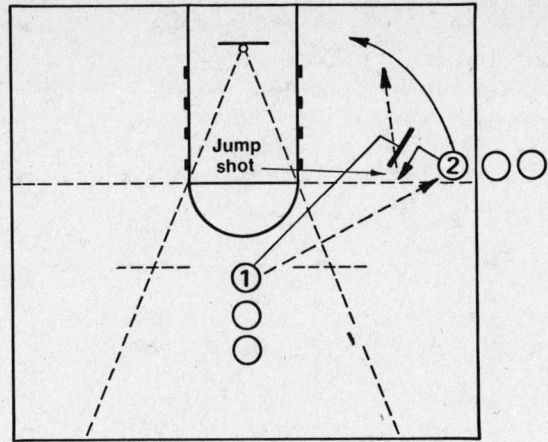

Diagram 17-17
Pass, Screen, Jump Shot or Check Pass

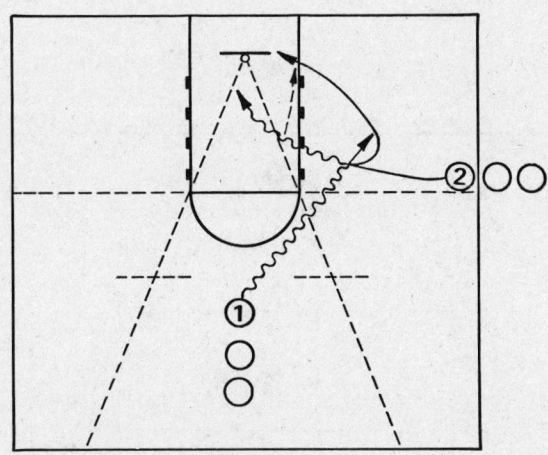

Diagram 17-18
*Dribble Over, Hand Off,
Drive, Rollout and Check Pass*

two previous moves except line 2 shoots a jump shot as he receives the handoff from line 1. (Diagram 17-19)

11. *Dribble to hand off check pass off jump shot*—Absolutely the same moves as Diagram 17-19 and previous description except as line 2 goes up for a jump shot he check passes to line 1 rolling to the basket.

12. *Pass and cut behind*—Line 1 passes to line 2 meeting the pass and cut behind line 2, receiving a handoff from line 2, driving closely and quickly to the basket for a lay-up. (Diagram 17-20)

13. *Pass cut behind check pass*—Exact move as Diagram 17-20, adding check pass to line 2.

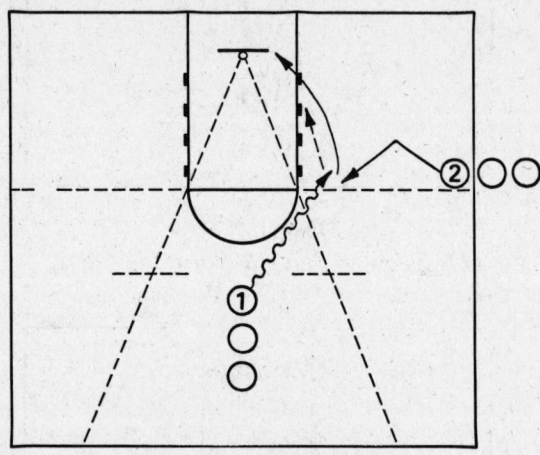

Diagram 17-19
*Dribble Over, Hand Off
Check Pass Off Jump Shot*

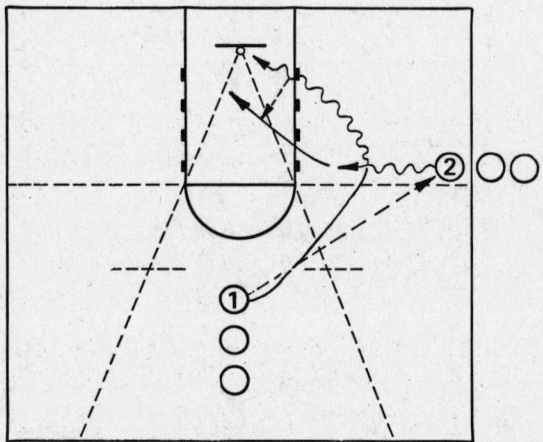

Diagram 17-20
*Pass Cut Behind, Drive
or Check Pass to Rollout*

14. *Pass cut behind jump shot*—This is the same action as the two previous moves and Diagram 17-20 with the added jump shot factor. Line 1 takes a jump shot immediately as he receives the hand off from line 2. (Diagram 17-21)

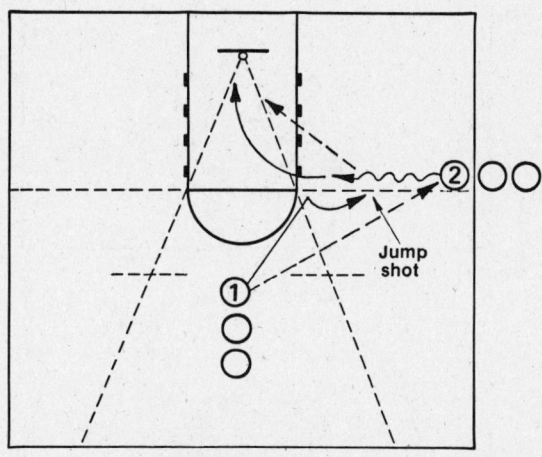

Diagram 17-21
*Pass Cut Behind for
Jump Shot on Check Pass*

15. *Pass-go behind jump shot-check pass*—Line 1 checks back to line 2 rolling out off of line 1's jump shot. (Diagram 17-21)

16. *Dribble all the way*—Line 1 dribbles all the way around 2. Line 2 moves forward on seeing 1 dribble toward him, turns and rolls as 1 drives hard and fast around him for the basket. (Diagram 17-22)

17. *Dribble all the way and check back*—Exactly the same as previous move and Diagram 17-22, but add the check pass from line 1 back inside to line 2.

18. *Guard around*—Line 1 passes to line 2 and fakes away. He now drives off line 2, who has faked away, received the pass, and dribbled to the corner of the free throw lane. Line 2 gives 1 a two-hand back flip pass as 1 drives around him to the basket. (Diagram 17-23)

19. *Forward to guard screen and roll*—Here we change the alignment to a normal forward-guard alignment and execute

226 supplementary drills for improving offensive technique

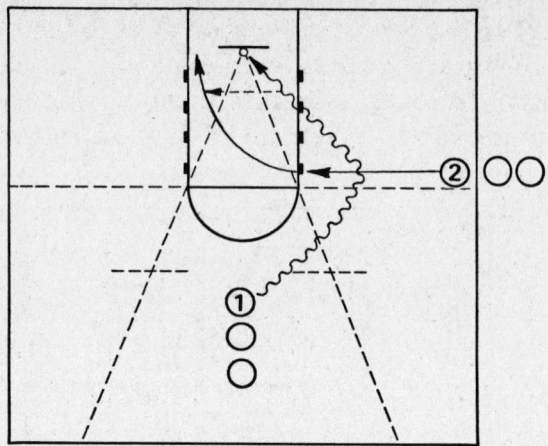

Diagram 17-22
Dribble All the Way Around

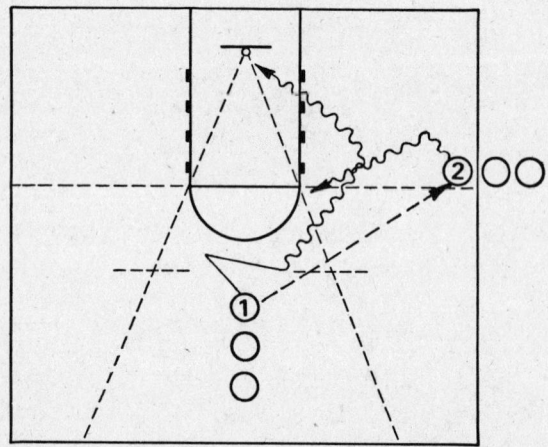

Diagram 17-23
Guard Around

the old forward to guard screen. The guard line 1 drives off the forward screen for a drive or jump shot as forward 2 rolls to the basket. (Diagram 17-24)

The next four moves are with three line alignments.

20. *Backdoor forward*—Line 1 passes to line 2 as he flashes to the high post. The moment the ball hits 3's hands,

supplementary drills for improving offensive technique 227

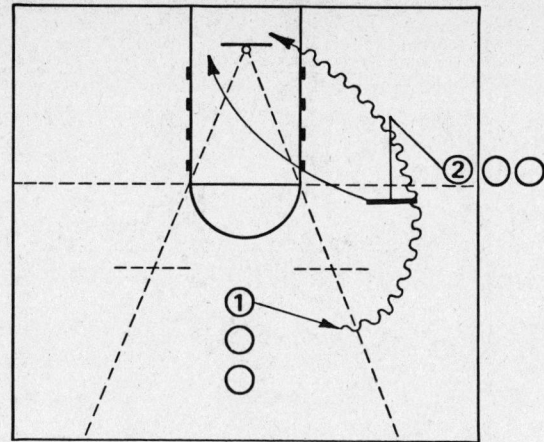

Diagram 17-24
Forward Screen for Guard

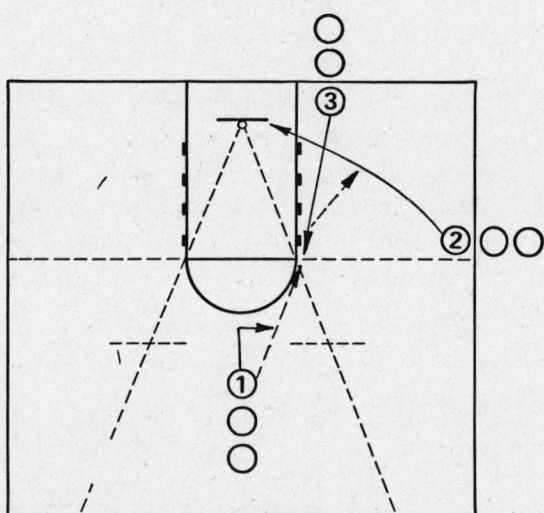

Diagram 17-25
Backdoor Wing

line 2 cuts backdoor and receives a quick pass from 3 for a lay-up. (Diagram 17-25)

21. *Backdoor follow*—This move is the same as Diagram 17-25 with emphasis on the fact that after line 1 passes to line 3, he moves straight forward, setting up the follow in the event 3 cannot pass to 1 cutting backdoor. Line 1 cuts over

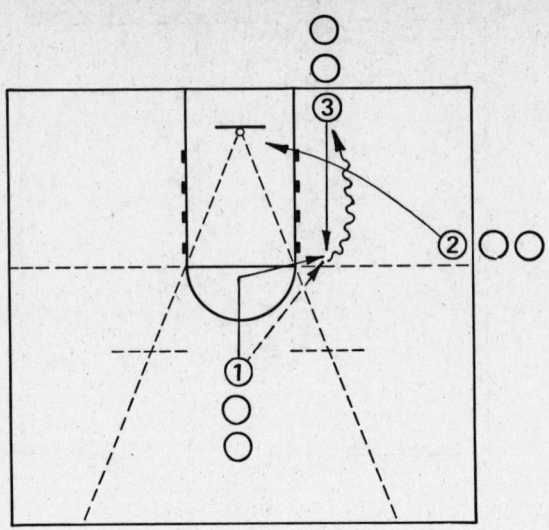

Diagram 17-26
Backdoor Follow Cut

line 3, receives the ball, and drives, jump shoots, or check passes. (Diagram 17-26)

22. *Backdoor guard*—Line 1 passes to line 2. Line 3 cuts directly toward and halfway to the basket, quickly changes direction to corner of the foul line, and receives pass from line 2. Line 1 cuts backdoor as the pass touches 3's hands. (Diagram 17-27)

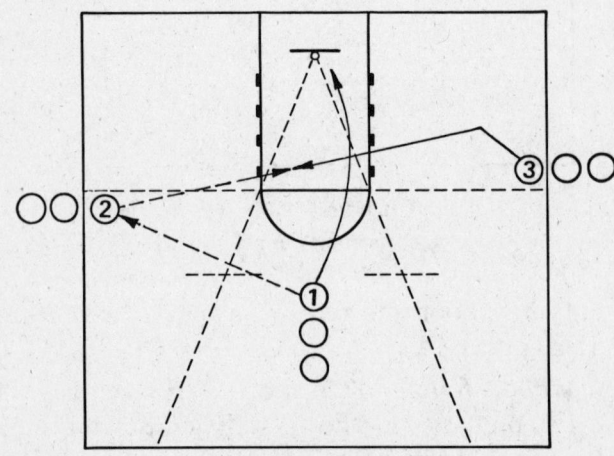

Diagram 17-27
Backdoor Point

After a few sessions where the techniques of each move are taught, we use two balls, which makes the action fast, snappy, and interesting.

As simple as the elements of these sets of moves appear to be, so are they unquestionably basic. Daily attention and proper supervision will emphatically improve basics, techniques, increase ball handling effectiveness, and improve an individual's overall basketball ability.

index

A

Advantages, 18-21
Aggressiveness,
　rebounding, 155, 159, 161
Alignment:
　after first cut, 27
　after swing, 27
　basic working conditions, 25
　center, 25-26
　crouched body position, 24
　flexed body position, 24
　following first pass, 27
　forward, 24-25
　freeing yourself to receive pass, 23
　guard, 25
　passing lanes, 26
　post, 25-26
　post cuts, 28
　spacing, 26, 27
　swing, 27
Allen, Phog, 61
Association concept, 207

B

Backdoor:
　post series, 105
　relief moves, 56, 57
Backdoor cut:
　long overthrow, 67
　relieving pressure, 65-67
　two categories, 35
Back screen by post, 176
Ball possession, 174
Benefits:
　advantageous placement, 18-19
　defense occupied, 19

Benefits (*cont'd*)
　drills, 21
　fits any personnel, 18
　initiative, 19
　players involved, 19
　returnees as teachers, 20
　tempo control, 19-20
Blocking out, rebounding, 157-159
Box-and-one, 20

C

Center, rebounding, 163
Center alignment, 25
Center cuts, 40
Changing point of attack, 69-70
Choke post:
　post series, 107-108
　swing-and-cut, 18
Clear, 52-54
Clear outs, 23
Coach, opposing, 170
Coaching, game, 172
Combination post:
　post series, 109-114 (*see also* Post series)
　swing-and cut into, 120-121
　vs. zone, 153
Contact, evading, 34-35
Control, rebounding, 155, 159
Control and tempo change:
　adjustments, 173
　back screen by post, 176
　ball possession, 174
　basic cuts, 173
　basic fundamentals, 173
　basic relief moves, 173
　control phase, 173
　cut off of post to top, 177

Control and Tempo Change (*cont'd*)
    cuts quick and precise, 175
    delay game, 172
    delay phase, 174
    fast break, 173
    flexibility, 173
    freeze, 174
    game coaching, 172
    game plan, 171
    high and *wide*, 174, 175
    high and wide stationary post, 176
    high stationary post, 175
    key moves, 172
    location of game, 170
    normal phase, 173
    opponents' defense, 170
    opposing coach, 170
    rebounding potential, 173
    score of game, 171
    semi-freeze, 174
    situations considered, 169-172
    specific cuts, 173
    specific shooters, 173
    strength of opponent, 169-170
    substitutions, 170-171
    teams of equal strengths, 174
    time outs, 171
    time remaining, 171
    type of officiating, 170
Control phase, 173
Counteraction:
    defense plays honest, 91
    design, 91
    easy adjustment, 91
    execution of play, 91
    guard counter, 91-92, 93
    if it fails, 91
    lob counter, 97-98
    must, 91
    need for, 91
    post counter, 96-97
    swing-pass counter, 94-96
    three-cut counter, 92-94
    use, 91
Crab, 49, 50
Crouched position, 24
Cutaway, 104
Cut off of post to top, 177
Cuts:
    alternate moves, 46-50

Cuts (*cont'd*)
    center, 40
    crabbing, 49, 50
    five, 45
    forward, 40
    four, 44-45
    guard, 39-40
    intelligence, 39
    one, 40-41
    One-J, 46-48
    properly taught, 39
    quick, sharp, 39
    rehearsed, 39
    screen to same side, 48
    swing and choke, 49-50
    swing and pinch, 50
    switch, 45-46
    three, 43
    timing, 39
    turnover, 45-46
    two, 42
Cutting:
    auxiliary, 32
    backdoor, 35
    basic, 32-33
    counter, 32
    evading contact, 34-35
    influence, 35
    initial, 33-34
    interchanging, 35-38
    post, 32
    quickscore, 35
    tight, 33
    to the top, 32
    wing, 32
Cutting drill, 184-186
Cutting to daylight, 100

D

Daily Dozen, 207-219
Defense, opponent's, 170
Delay game, 172
Delay phase, 174
Double flash post:
    into swing-and-cut, 129-134
        advantages, 130
        backdoor cut, 131
        basic set, 130

Double flash post (cont'd)
    flash post, 131
        pass to wing, 132-134
    post series, 114-115
    swing-and-cut into, 119-120
Double post cuts, 115
Double split:
    post series, 104
    relief moves, 55
Dribble over, 59-60
Drills:
    backdoor follow, 227-228
    backdoor forward, 226-227
    backdoor guard, 228
    basic shooting, 186-188
    change direction, 220-221
    cutting, 184-186
    daily dozen, 207-219
    dribble all the way, 225
    dribble hand off, 222
    dribble to hand off, 222-223
    drives, 217
    fake down, 221
    five-cut shooting, 185-186
    flip-flop, 210-212
    forward to guard screen and roll, 225-226
    four-cut shooting, 183-184
    four man swing-and-cut, 180-182
    guard around, 225
    hook shot, 210
    pass and cut, 220
    pass and cut behind, 224
    pass cut behind check pass, 224
    pass cut behind jump shot, 225
    pass-go behind jump shot-check pass, 225
    pass-screen-drive-check pass off jump shot, 223
    pass-screen-drive-jump shot, 222
    pass-screen-roll, 221-222
    pass-screen-roll and check pass, 222
    pick-up, 215
    provided, 21
    quickie-touch, 217-218
    rim touchers, 207-209
    saddle, 212
    screen-and-roll, 188-189
    short turn and jump shots, 219
    shuttle, 216-217

Drills (cont'd)
    situation, 219-229
    tapping, 209-210
    ten-from-a-spot, 186
    three-cut shooting, 182-183
    two-ball dribble, 213
    wiggle-waggle, 213-215
Drive through:
    relieving pressure, 63-64
    teach, 23

F

Fake screen, 32
Fastbreak:
    after made field goal, 201-203
    after made free throw, 203-204
    complete pattern, 199-200
    first moves after capturing rebound, 196-197
    forward rebounding, 198-199
    normal phase, 173
    opportunities, 193
    philosophy and principle, 191-192
    post rebound, 197-198
    primary ignition point, 194-195
    rebound positions, 195-196
    secondary ignition points, 195
    situations, 193-194
    teaching phases, 194
    3-on-1, 200
    3-on-2, 200
First pass, 27
Five cut:
    most challenging, 45
    post series, 100
Five-cut shooting drill, 185
Flexed position, 24
Flexibility, 173
Flight of ball, 158
Flip-flop drill, 210-212
Floor balance, 18
Form, rebounding, 156
Forward alignment, 24-25
Forward cuts, 40
Four cut, 44-45
Four-cut shooting drill, 183-184
Four man swing-and-cut, 180-182
Freeze, 174

Full-court attack against pressure, 70-75

G

Game:
  coaching, 172
  location, 170
  score, 171
Game plan, 171
Guard, rebounding, 163, 164
Guard alignment, 25
Guard counter:
  after time-out, 92
  diagram, 93
  drive through, 92
  effective called play, 91
  guard selected, 92
  initiated, 92
  normal set, 92
  not too many techniques, 92
  use, 91
Guard cuts, 39-40
Guard-forward interchange, 88-89
Gut play, 100, 101

H

High and *wide*, 174, 175
High and wide stationary post, 176
High stack, 84-85
High stationary post, 175

I

Influence cut, 35
Initial cut, 32, 33-34
Initiative, 19
Inside phase, 16
Interchanging, 35-38

J

J, 46
Judgment, rebounding, 155, 161
Jumping, rebounding, 155

L

Lob counter, 97-98
Learning, association, 207
Location of game, 170
Low double stack, 86-87
Low post, 18
Low stack, 85-86
Low stack and cross, 86

M

Man-for-man, 20
Move back into continuity, 54, 55
Movement:
  abundance, 17
  rebounding, 159, 160, 161, 168
Moving screen, 32
Multiple sets:
  another dimension, 77
  basketball coaches, 77
  different entry, 77
  different look, 77
  football coaches, 77
  guard-forward interchange, 88-89
  high stack, 84-85
  low double stack, 86-87
  low stack, 85-86
  low stack and cross, 86
  one-man front, 80-82
  1-3-1, 80
  1-3-1 initial pass to post, 82
  pressing teams, 77
  quick, individual moves, 77
  return to swing-and-cut, 81
  screening same side, 78-79
  strongside set, 79-80
  three-man front, 82-83

N

Normal phase, 173

O

Offensive entries, 77-89 (*see also* Multiple sets)

Offensive rebounding (*see* Rebounding)
Officiating, type, 170
One cut, 40-41
One-half man, rebounding, 163, 164
One-J, 46-48
One-man front:
  multiple sets, 80-82
  relieving pressure, 67-68
1-3-1:
  into swing-and-cut, 135-141
    high post screen low, 140-141
    pass to high post, 135-137
    pass to wing, 137-140
  one-man front, 80, 82
Opponent:
  defense, 170
  strength, 169-170
Opposing coach, 170
Outside phase, 16-17
Overthrows, 56-58

P

Pass, alignment after first, 27
Passing lanes, 26
Pass to post, 102-103
Penetrating dribble:
  post series, 106, 107
  relief moves, 58-59
Penetration, 17-18
Perimeter screens, 31, 32
Personnel:
  advantageous placement, 18-19
  fits any, 18
Phases, 173-174
Philosophy, 15
Pick-up drill, 215
Pinch post:
  personnel, 18
  post series, 105-106
Plan, game, 171
Point of attack, changing, 69-70
Position, rebounding, 156, 160, 161
Possession, ball, 174
Post, rebounding, 163, 164
Post alignment, 25
Post counter:
  counteraction, 96-97
  post series, 108-109

Post cuts, 28, 32
Post screens, 29-31
Post series:
  alternating posts, 99, 100
  backdoor, 105
  choke post, 107-108
  combination, 109-114
    against zone defenses, 114
    high screen and roll, 113
    post fronted, 112
    reversing ball to top and looking inside, 113
    screen down, 111
    screen high, 112
    strongside alignment, 110
  counteraction, 99
  cutaway, 104
  cutting to daylight, 100
  defensive fouls, 100
  defensive man, 99
  double flash post, 114-115
  double post cuts, 115
  double split, 104
  gut play, 100, 101
  movement, 99
  pass to post, 102-103
  penetrating dribble, 106, 107
  personnel available, 99
  pinch post, 105-106
  players determine success, 99
  post action off pattern, 100-101
  post counter, 108-109
  roll back, 100
  screen down and cut away, 103
  single post, 101-107 (*see also* Single post action)
  single split, 103
  small forward or guard, 99
  sneak post, 116
  two cut, 100, 101
Power move, 162
Preparedness, 144
Pressing tactics, 62
Pressure, constant, 51
Pressure defense, 61

Q

Quickscore cut, 35

index

R

Rebounding:
  aggressiveness, 155, 159, 161
  area, 160
  basic fundamentals, 162
  blocking out, 157, 159
  cardinal sin, 168
  center, 163
  control, 155, 159
  courage, 155
  determined scramble, 161
  fakes, 160
  flight of ball, 158
  form, 156
  from swing-and-cut, 163-164
  guard, 163, 164
  judgment, 155, 161
  jumping ability, 155
  low man in double screen, 163
  meeting ball, 158
  movement, 159, 160, 161, 168
  moving to board, 160
  offensive, 159-163
  one-half man, 163, 164
  point or foul-line area, 167
  position, 156, 160, 161
  post, 163, 164
  potential, 173
  power move, 162
  quickness, 155
  reverse power move, 162-163
  smaller players, 156
  smother man with ball, 161
  snatch, 159
  stagger steps, 160
  strongside wing, 164-167
  techniques, 161
  three and one-half men, 163
  timing, 155
  tipping, 162
  top of key, 166
  turn and jump, 163
  weakside wing, 167, 168
  wing guard, 164
Relief moves:
  backdoor, 56, 57
  back into continuity, 54, 55
  clear, 52-54
  confidence builder, 51

Relief moves (*cont'd*)
  constant pressure, 51
  double split, 55
  dribble over, 59-60
  overthrow, 56-58
  penetrating dribble, 58-59
  rehearse, 51, 60
  split, 54-55
  strong set—ball on wing, 52
Relieving pressure:
  backdoor, 65-67
  changing point of attack, 69-70
  drive through, 63-64
  effect on opposition, 61
  full-court attack versus pressure, 70-75
  mastery of basics, 61
  one-man front, 67-68
  poise and confidence, 61
  pressing tactics, 62
  rehearsed as team, 61
  return to swing-and-cut, 65
  split, 64-65
  team concept, 61
  team that can move, 61
  three-man front, 68-69
  25 or 30 years, 61
Returnees as teachers, 20
Reverse, 17
Reverse power move, 162-163
Rim touchers, 207-209

S

Saddle drill, 212
Score of game, 171
Screen-and-roll drill, 188-189
Screen down and cut away, 103
Screening same side, 78-79
Screening the zone, 150-152
Screens:
  away from ball, 29
  ball handler, 32
  basic screen and roll, 30
  double, high post, 30
  fake, 32
  45-degree angle, 31, 32
  forward and guard, 31
  legal vision, 31

index 237

Screens (*cont'd*)
  moving, unnecessary, 32
  perimeter, 31, 32
  post, 29-31
  rollout, 33
  teaching, 32
  tight move, 32
  to same side, 48
Seams, attacking:
  continuity, 149
  diagram, 148
  movement, 149
  penetrating, 149-150
Semi-freeze, 174
Shoot drill, basic, 186-188
Shuttle drill, 216-217
Single post action:
  backdoor, 105
  cutaway, 104
  double split, 104
  evaluate defense, 102
  into swing-and-cut, 123-129
    alignment, 124, 125
    automatics, 126
    backdoor, 126
    fronted overthrow, 128
    fronted pass to backdoor area, 129
    line of deployment, 126
    operating rules, 124
    overthrow, 126
    penetrating dribble, 127
    side high, 128
    side low, 127
    spacing, 125
    transition, 129
  line of deployment, 102
  old method, 101
  operating rules, 102
  pass to post, 102-103
  penetrating dribble, 106, 107
  personnel, 101, 102
Single post action:
  pinch post, 105-106
  rehearse team, 102
  screen down and cut away, 103
  single split, 103
  swing-and-cut into, 118-119
Single split, 103
Snatch and control, 159
Sneak post, 116

Spacing, 26, 27
Split:
  relief moves, 54-55
  relieving pressure, 64
Stacks, 23
Stagger steps, 160
Strength:
  opponent's 169-170
  teams of equal, 174
Strong set—ball on wing, 52
Strongside set, 79-80
Strongside wing, 164-167
Substitutions, 170-171
Swing, 45-46
Swing action, 17
Swing and choke, 49-50
Swing-and-cut offense:
  advantageous placement, 18
  all players involved, 19
  benefits, 18-21
  defense occupied, 19
  double flash post into, 129-134
    advantages, 130
    backdoor cut, 131
    basic set, 130
    flash post, 131
    pass to wing, 132
  fits any personnel, 18
  floor balance, 18
  individual initiative, 19
  inside phase, 16
  into combination post, 120-121
  into double flash post, 119-120
  into single post, 118-119
  movement, 17
  1-3-1 into, 135-141
    basic set, 136
    high post screen low, 140-141
    low post fronted, 141
    pass to high post, 135-137
    pass to wing, 137-140
    transition, 137, 140
  other patterns into, 123-141
  outside phase, 16-17
  overthrow, 16
  penetration, 17-18
  philosophy, 15
  rebounding (*see* Rebounding)
  returnees teach, 20
  single post into, 123-129
    alignment, 125

Swing-and-cut offense (cont'd)
   automatics, 126
   backdoor, 126
   fronted overthrow, 128
   fronted pass to backdoor, 129
   line of deployment, 126
   operating rules, 124-126
   overthrow, 126
   penetrating dribble, 127
   side high, 128
   side low, 127
   spacing, 125
   transition, 129
 swing action, 17
 teaching drills, 21
 tempo control, 19-20
 vs. zone, 145-148
   bringing in back-side, 147
   movement and swing, 146-147
   points of emphasis, 148
Swing and pinch, 50
Swing-pass counter:
 diagram, 95
 faking counteraction, 95
 low man, 96
 spontaneously executed, 94
 unsuccessful counter attempt, 95

T

Tapping drill, 209-210
Teachers, returnees, as, 20
Teams of equal strengths, 174
Tempo change, control and, 169-177
  (see also Control and tempo change)
Tempo control, 19-20
Ten-from-a-spot, 186
Three cut, 43
Three-cut counter:
 diagrams, 93, 94
 initial pass made, 93
 jump shot, 94
 pass to point, 92
 pass to three spot, 92
 strong side, 93
 swing-and-cut continuity, 94
 zoning or switching problem, 93-94
Three-cut shooting drill, 182-183

Three-man front:
 multiple sets, 82-83
 relieving pressure, 68-69
Tight cut, 33
Time outs, 171
Time remaining, 171
Timing, rebounding, 155
Tipping, 162
Triangle-and-two, 20
Turn and jump, 163
Turnover, 45-46
Two-ball dribble, 213
Two cut:
 center or post cut, 42
 post series, 100, 101

V

V-in-V-out, 23

W

Weakside wing, 167-168
Wide, high and, 174, 175
Wiggle-waggle drill, 213-215
Wing cut, 32
Wing guard, 164
Working position, 23-28 (*see also* Alignment)

Z

Zone:
 attacking seams, 148-150
   movement and continuity, 149
   penetrating seam, 149-150
 ball in your area, 143
 combination post vs., 153
 confidence and poise, 144
 ignore, 144
 many ideas on defeating, 144
 playing ball and area, 143
 preparedness, 144
 screening, 150-152
 stick to philosophy, 144
 surprise, 144
 swing-and-cut into combination

Zone (cont'd)
    post vs., 152-153
  swing-and-cut vs., 145-148
    bringing in back-side, 147
    corner, 148
    cut sharp and fast, 148
    long pass across zone, 148
    movement and swing, 146-147
    patience, 148
    points of emphasis, 148
    post man, 148